D0460879

Presented to:

Mom ♡

I love you!

From:

Jim

365 Daily Devotional

Jesus Calling®

Enjoying Peace in His Presence

Sarah Young

THOMAS NELSON
Since 1798

Jesus Calling®

Published in Nashville, Tennessee, by Thomas Nelson. Thomas Nelson is a registered trademark of HarperCollins Christian Publishing.

Thomas Nelson titles may be purchased in bulk for educational, business, fund-raising, or sales promotional use. For information, please e-mail SpecialMarkets@ThomasNelson.com.

ISBN 978-1-4003-1813-1 (large edition)
ISBN 978-0-7180-9240-5 (custom)

The Library of Congress has cataloged the earlier edition as follows:

Young, Sarah, 1946–
Jesus Calling / by Sarah Young.
p. cm.
ISBN 978-1-59145-188-4 (hardcover)
1. Devotional calendars. 2. Devotional literature, English. I. Title.
BV4811.Y675 2004
242'.2—dc22 2044005474

Printed in China

16 17 18 19 20 DSC 5 4 3 2 1

I dedicate *Jesus Calling* to my mother, whose encouragement inspired me to persevere in writing this book. She demonstrated her appreciation of my writing in poignant ways. She kept my manuscript beside her bed, so she could read it every morning. Once, while away from her home, she even asked me to fax her the readings day by day. After she died from cancer, I found portions of my writings that she had hand-copied into a journal. This mother who had prayed me through thick and thin, including years of rebellion, opened her heart fully to my devotional writing. Her oft-expressed desire to write children's books never came to fruition. But there is a sense in which she has written—through me—this book.

Thank you, Nani! Your legacy lives on.

Introduction

Jesus Calling

I first experienced the Presence of God in a setting of exquisite beauty. I was studying at a Christian community in a tiny Alpine village in France. This was a branch of L'Abri, an international ministry that began in Switzerland through Francis and Edith Schaeffer's work. During my stay at L'Abri, I often explored the fairyland-like environment all around me. It was late winter, and the noonday sun was warm enough for sunbathing, but the depth of the snow kept it from melting. Brilliant sunlight reflecting from pure white snow was cleansing my mind of the darkness that had held it captive for years.

Every day I climbed up a steep hill to attain a view that delighted my soul. As I stood at the top, I would lose myself in a panorama of unbroken beauty. Below me was the village that had become my home. Viewed from this height, the village was dominated by a high-steepled church. Turning 180 degrees, I could see Lake Geneva far below me, shouting greetings in refracted sunbeams. When I looked up, I saw icy tips of Alpine mountains encircling me. I would turn round and round, absorbing as much as I could with two eyes and a finite mind.

The daughter of a college professor, I had been encouraged to read widely and think for myself. I had majored in philosophy at Wellesley College and had almost completed my master's degree in child

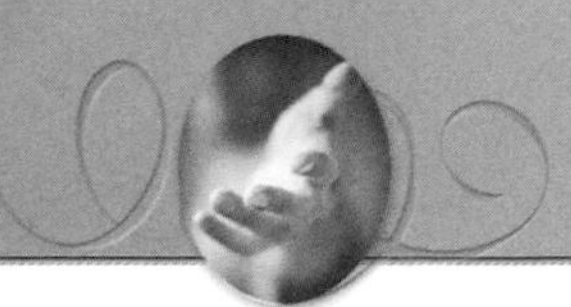

development at Tufts University. A few months earlier, my brother had asked me to read Francis Schaeffer's *Escape from Reason*. To my great surprise and delight, that small book had answered questions I'd long before dismissed as unanswerable. It was the intellectual integrity of Schaeffer's books that had drawn me to this pristine place. I was searching for absolute, unchanging truth—a foundation on which to build my life.

Shortly after I settled into the home I shared with other students, I met a gifted counselor who had come from the Swiss branch of L'Abri to talk with some of us. I went into the room where she was waiting, and she told me to close the door. Before I even had time to sit down, she asked her first question: "Are you a Christian?" I answered that I wasn't sure; I wanted to be a Christian, but I didn't really understand why I needed Jesus. I thought that knowing God might be enough. Her second question was: "What can you *not* forgive yourself for?" This question brought me face to face with my sinfulness, and immediately I understood my need for Jesus—to save me from my many sins. Later, when I was alone, I asked Him to forgive all my sins and to be my Savior-God.

One night I found myself leaving the warmth of our cozy chalet to walk alone in the snowy mountains. I went into a deeply wooded area, feeling vulnerable and awed by cold, moonlit beauty. The air was crisp and dry, piercing to inhale. After a while, I came into an open area and I stopped walking. Time seemed to stand still as I gazed around me in wonder—soaking in the beauty of this place. Suddenly I became aware of a lovely Presence with me, and my involuntary response was

to whisper, "Sweet Jesus." This experience of Jesus' Presence was far more personal than the intellectual answers for which I'd been searching. This was a relationship with the Creator of the universe—the One who is *the way, the truth, and the life* (John 14:6).

The following year, back in the United States, I had another encounter with the Presence of Jesus. I was grieving the loss of a serious dating relationship and wondering whether being a Christian made much difference in the quality of my life.

At that time I was working as a technical writer in Virginia. My boss sent me to Atlanta to attend a conference. I accepted this assignment dutifully and checked into the hotel without enthusiasm. Alone in my room, I felt waves of desolation wash over me. So I began walking the streets of Atlanta aimlessly, trying to escape my solitude. I glanced at some books in an outdoor stall and was drawn to *Beyond Ourselves* by Catherine Marshall. That night, as I read the book, I no longer felt alone. I knelt beside the bed in that sterile room and felt an overwhelming Presence of peace and love come over me. I knew that Jesus was with me and that He sympathized with my heartache. This was unquestionably the same "Sweet Jesus" I had encountered in the snowy splendor of the Alps.

During the next sixteen years, I lived what many people might consider an exemplary Christian life. I went to Covenant Theological Seminary in St. Louis, where I earned a master's degree in counseling and biblical studies. While there, I met my husband, Steve, a third-generation missionary to Japan. After graduation, we spent two four-year terms in Japan doing church-planting ministry. We had a

baby girl during our first term and a baby boy during our furlough in the United States. After our second term, we returned to the US for three years. We lived in Atlanta, where Steve worked with a local Japanese church and I earned a further degree in counseling at Georgia State University.

As part of my training, I worked at a Christian counseling center in the Atlanta area. I cherished my experiences of helping deeply wounded women find healing in Christ. I was also thankful for my kind, loving husband and our two delightful children, who were the main joys of my life. However, not once during those sixteen years did I vividly experience the Presence of Jesus.

So I was ready to begin a new spiritual quest. It started with delving into a devotional book, *The Secret of the Abiding Presence* by Andrew Murray. The theme of this book is that God's Presence is meant to be the continual experience of Christians. Murray emphasizes the importance of spending time alone with God in quiet, uninterrupted communion.

I began reading the book at a very unstructured time in my life. We were waiting for our Australian visas to be approved so that we could begin a church among Japanese people living in Melbourne. I had quit my counseling job to prepare for the move overseas, so I was adjusting to the loss of this fulfilling work. In the midst of those momentous changes, I began seeking God's Presence in earnest. My days started alone with God, equipped with Bible, devotional book, prayer journal, pen, and coffee. An hour or two alone with Him seemed too brief.

The uncertainties I faced at that time deepened my increasing closeness to God. My husband and I had no idea how long it would take

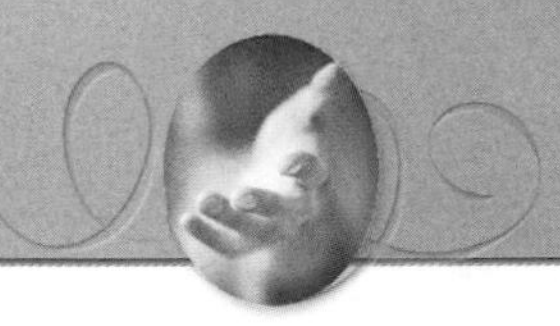

to receive permanent residency visas, so the waiting period seemed to stretch indefinitely into the future. During that period, I had four surgeries, including two for melanoma. A Bible verse that comforted me during this difficult time of waiting also accompanied me on the seemingly endless flight to Australia: "You will go out in joy and be led forth in peace" (Isaiah 55:12).

We settled in Australia and began our dual ministries. I supported Steve in planting the first-ever Japanese church in Melbourne, but my main ministry focus was counseling Australian women, some of whom were coming out of terrible abuse and spiritual bondage.

Our combined ministries subjected our family to intense spiritual warfare, and I prayed for protection every morning. One morning as I prayed, I visualized God protecting each of us. I pictured first our daughter, then our son, and then Steve encircled by God's protective Presence. When I prayed for myself, I was suddenly enveloped in brilliant light and profound peace. I had not sought this powerful experience of God's Presence, but I received it gratefully and was strengthened by it.

Only two or three days later, a counseling client who was an incest survivor began remembering experiences of satanic ritual abuse. This form of Satan worship involves subjecting victims (who are often young children) to incredibly evil, degrading tortures. My courageous client and I walked together into the darkness of her memories. But God had prepared me for stepping into deep darkness by first bathing me in His glorious light. I realized that experiences of God's Presence were not only for my benefit but were also preparation for helping others.

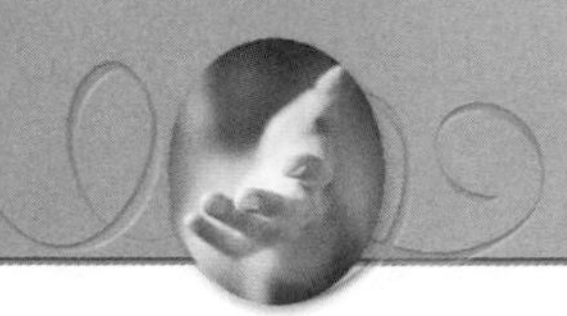

The following year, I began to wonder if I could change my prayer times from monologue to dialogue. I had been writing in prayer journals for many years, but this was one-way communication: I did all the talking. Increasingly, I wanted to hear what God might want to communicate to me on a given day. I decided to "listen" with pen in hand, writing down whatever I "heard" in my mind. As J. I. Packer wrote in his book *Your Father Loves You*: "God . . . guides our minds as we think things out in his presence." This is how I was listening to Him—by focusing on Jesus and His Word, while asking Him to guide my thoughts. I was *not* listening for an audible voice; I was spending time *seeking God's Face* (Psalm 27:8 NKJV).

My journaling thus changed from monologue to dialogue. This new way of communicating with God became the high point of my day. Of course, I knew my writings were not inspired—as only Scripture is—but they were helping me grow closer to God. This became a delightful way to *encourage myself in the Lord* (1 Samuel 30:6 NKJV).

As I was learning to seek God's Face, "Be still, and know that I am God" (Psalm 46:10) became a life-changing verse. Alternate readings for "Be still" are "Relax," "Let go," and "Cease striving" (NASB). This is an enticing invitation from God to lay down our cares and seek His Presence.

Among other resources, *Praying: Finding Our Way Through Duty to Delight* has been helpful. This book, written by J. I. Packer and Carolyn Nystrom, contains a wonderful quote from Martin Luther—"If the Holy Spirit should come and begin to preach to your heart, giving you rich and enlightened thoughts, . . . be quiet and listen to him who can

talk better than you; and note what he proclaims and *write it down*; so will you experience miracles as David says: 'Open my eyes that I may behold wondrous things out of thy law' (Psalm 119:18)."

During the years that I've been waiting in God's Presence and listening with pen in hand, I have found themes of His Peace becoming more prominent in my writing. I'm sure this tendency reflects, in part, my personal need. However, when people open up to me, I find that most of them also desire the balm of Jesus' Peace.

This practice of being still in God's Presence has increased my intimacy with Him more than any other spiritual discipline, so I want to share some of the writings I have gleaned from these quiet moments. In many parts of the world, Christians seem to be searching for a deeper experience of Jesus' Presence and Peace. The devotions that follow address that felt need.

The Bible is the only infallible, inerrant Word of God, and I endeavor to keep my writings consistent with that unchanging standard. I have written from the perspective of Jesus speaking, to help readers feel more personally connected with Him. So the first person singular ("I," "Me," "My," "Mine") always refers to Christ; "you" refers to you, the reader.

I have included Scripture references after each daily reading. As I waited in God's Presence, Bible verses or fragments of verses often came to mind. So I interwove these into the devotions. Words from the Scriptures (some paraphrased, some quoted) are indicated in italics. Certain Bible verses figure rather heavily in my writing. That is because God often uses these passages to strengthen and encourage me, raising

my sights from my "light and momentary troubles" (2 Corinthians 4:17) to His eternal perspective.

Themes of thankfulness and trust recurred often during my listening times. These themes are quite prevalent in the Bible, and they are essential for a close relationship with the Lord.

The devotions in this book are meant to be read slowly, preferably in a quiet place—with your Bible open. Remember that Jesus is Immanuel, *God with us*. May you enjoy His Presence and His Peace in ever-increasing measure.

— *Sarah Young*

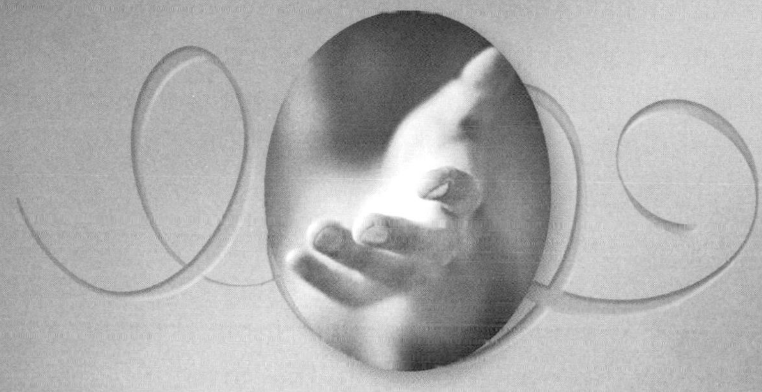

January

"For I know the plans I have for you," declares the LORD*, "plans to prosper you and not to harm you, plans to give you hope and a future."*

JEREMIAH 29:11

January 1

Come to Me with a teachable spirit, eager to be changed. A close walk with Me is a life of continual newness. Do not cling to old ways as you step into a new year. Instead, seek My Face with an open mind, knowing that your journey with Me involves being *transformed by the renewing of your mind.* As you focus your thoughts on Me, be aware that I am fully attentive to you. I see you with a steady eye, because My attention span is infinite. I know and understand you completely; My thoughts embrace you in everlasting Love. *I also know the plans I have for you: plans to prosper you and not to harm you, plans to give you hope and a future.* Give yourself fully to this adventure of increasing attentiveness to My Presence.

Do not conform any longer to the pattern of this world, but be transformed by the renewing of your mind. Then you will be able to test and approve what God's will is—his good, pleasing and perfect will. —Romans 12:2

"For I know the plans I have for you," declares the Lord, "plans to prosper you and not to harm you, plans to give you hope and a future." —Jeremiah 29:11

January 2

Relax in My healing Presence. As you spend time with Me, your thoughts tend to jump ahead to today's plans and problems. Bring your mind back to Me for refreshment and renewal. Let the Light of My Presence soak into you, as you focus your thoughts on Me. Thus I equip you to face whatever the day brings. This sacrifice of time pleases Me and strengthens you. Do not skimp on our time together. Resist the clamor of tasks waiting to be done. *You have chosen what is better, and it will not be taken away from you.*

Look to the Lord and his strength; seek his face always. —Psalm 105:4

She had a sister called Mary, who sat at the Lord's feet listening to what he said. But Martha was distracted by all the preparations that had to be made. She came to him and asked, "Lord, don't you care that my sister has left me to do the work by myself? Tell her to help me!" "Martha, Martha," the Lord answered, "you are worried and upset about many things, but only one thing is needed. Mary has chosen what is better, and it will not be taken away from her." —Luke 10:39–42

January 3

Refresh yourself in the Peace of My Presence. This Peace can be your portion at all times and in all circumstances. Learn to *hide in the secret of My Presence*, even as you carry out your duties in the world. I am both with you and within you. I go before you to open up the way, and I also walk alongside you. There could never be another companion as devoted as I am.

Because I am your constant Companion, there should be a lightness to your step that is observable to others. Do not be weighed down with problems and unresolved issues, for I am your burden-bearer. In the world you have trials and distress, but don't let them get you down. *I have conquered the world and deprived it of power to harm you.* In Me you may have confident Peace.

How great is Your goodness, which You have stored up for those who fear You, which You have wrought for those who take refuge in You, before the sons of men! You hide them in the secret place of Your presence from the conspiracies of man; You keep them secretly in a shelter from the strife of tongues. —Psalm 31:19–20 NASB

"I have told you these things, so that in Me you may have [perfect] peace and confidence. In the world you have tribulation and trials and distress and frustration; but be of good cheer [take courage; be confident, certain, undaunted]! For I have overcome the world. [I have deprived it of power to harm you and have conquered it for you.]" —John 16:33 AMP

January 4

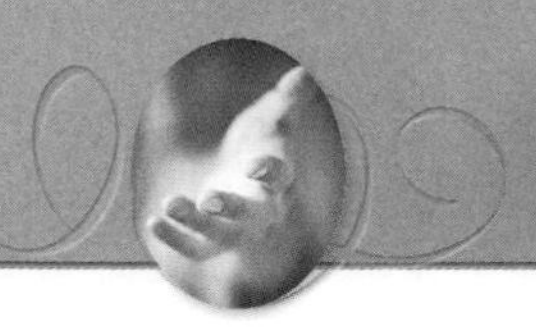

I WANT YOU TO LEARN A NEW HABIT. Try saying, "I trust You, Jesus," in response to whatever happens to you. If there is time, think about who I AM in all My Power and Glory; ponder also the depth and breadth of My Love for you.

This simple practice will help you see Me in every situation, acknowledging My sovereign control over the universe. When you view events from this perspective—through the Light of My universal Presence—fear loses its grip on you. Adverse circumstances become growth opportunities when you affirm your trust in Me no matter what. You receive blessings gratefully, realizing they flow directly from My hand of grace. Your continual assertion of trusting Me will strengthen our relationship and keep you close to Me.

I have seen you in the sanctuary and beheld your power and your glory. —PSALM 63:2

See, the Sovereign LORD comes with power, and his arm rules for him. See, his reward is with him, and his recompense accompanies him. He tends his flock like a shepherd: he gathers the lambs in his arms and carries them close to his heart; he gently leads those that have young. —ISAIAH 40:10–11

Where can I go from your Spirit? Where can I flee from your presence? If I go up to the heavens, you are there; if I make my bed in the depths, you are there. If I rise on the wings of the dawn, if I settle on the far side of the sea, even there your hand will guide me, your right hand will hold me fast. —PSALM 139:7–10

January 5

You can achieve the victorious life through living in deep dependence on Me. People usually associate victory with success: not falling or stumbling, not making mistakes. But those who are successful in their own strength tend to go their own way, forgetting about Me. It is through problems and failure, weakness and neediness that you learn to rely on Me.

True dependence is not simply asking Me to bless what you have decided to do. It is coming to Me with an open mind and heart, inviting Me to plant My desires within you. I may infuse within you a dream that seems far beyond your reach. You know that in yourself you cannot achieve such a goal. Thus begins your journey of profound reliance on Me. It is a faith-walk, taken one step at a time, leaning on Me as much as you need. This is not a path of continual success but of multiple failures. However, each failure is followed by a growth spurt, nourished by increased reliance on Me. Enjoy the blessedness of a victorious life, through deepening your dependence on Me.

The righteous cry out, and the Lord hears them; he delivers them from all their troubles. The Lord is close to the brokenhearted and saves those who are crushed in spirit. —Psalm 34:17–18

For we walk by faith, not by sight. —2 Corinthians 5:7 NKJV

I am able to do far beyond all that you ask or imagine. Come to Me with positive expectations, knowing that there is no limit to what I can accomplish. Ask My Spirit to control your mind, so that you can think great thoughts of Me. Do not be discouraged by the fact that many of your prayers are yet unanswered. Time is a trainer, teaching you to wait upon Me, to trust Me in the dark. The more extreme your circumstances, the more likely you are to see *My Power and Glory* at work in the situation. Instead of letting difficulties draw you into worrying, try to view them as setting the scene for My glorious intervention. Keep your eyes and your mind wide open to all that I am doing in your life.

Now to him who is able to do immeasurably more than all we ask or imagine, according to his power that is at work within us, to him be glory in the church and in Christ Jesus throughout all generations, forever and ever! Amen. —Ephesians 3:20–21

The mind of sinful man is death, but the mind controlled by the Spirit is life and peace. —Romans 8:6

Even the youths shall faint and be weary, and the young men shall utterly fall, but those who wait on the Lord shall renew their strength; they shall mount up with wings like eagles, they shall run and not be weary, they shall walk and not faint. —Isaiah 40:30–31 NKJV

Then I heard every creature in heaven and on earth and under the earth and on the sea, and all that is in them, singing: "To him who sits on the throne and to the Lamb be praise and honor and glory and power, for ever and ever!" —Revelation 5:13

January 7

It is impossible to praise or thank Me too much. As it is written, *I inhabit the praises of My people.* Sometimes your adoration is a spontaneous overflow of Joy, in response to radiant beauty or rich blessings. At other times your praise is more disciplined and measured—an act of your will. I dwell equally in both types of praise. Thankfulness, also, is a royal road to draw near Me. A thankful heart has plenty of room for Me.

When you thank Me for the many pleasures I provide, you affirm that I am God, from whom all blessings flow. When adversity strikes and you thank Me anyway, your trust in My sovereignty is a showpiece in invisible realms. Fill up the spare moments of your life with praise and thanksgiving. This joyous discipline will help you live in the intimacy of My Presence.

But thou art holy, O thou that inhabitest the praises of Israel. —Psalm 22:3 KJV

Praise the Lord. Praise the Lord, O my soul. I will praise the Lord all my life; I will sing praise to my God as long as I live. —Psalm 146:1–2

Give thanks in all circumstances, for this is God's will for you in Christ Jesus. —1 Thessalonians 5:18

SOFTLY I ANNOUNCE MY PRESENCE. Shimmering hues of radiance tap gently at your consciousness, seeking entrance. Though I have all Power in heaven and on earth, I am infinitely tender with you. The weaker you are, the more gently I approach you. Let your weakness be a door to My Presence. Whenever you feel inadequate, remember that I am your *ever-present Help*.

Hope in Me, and you will be protected from depression and self-pity. Hope is like a golden cord connecting you to heaven. The more you cling to this cord, the more I bear the weight of your burdens; thus, you are lightened. Heaviness is not of My kingdom. Cling to hope, and My rays of Light will reach you through the darkness.

God is our refuge and strength, an ever-present help in trouble. —PSALM 46:1

Be joyful in hope, patient in affliction, faithful in prayer. —ROMANS 12:12

May the God of hope fill you with all joy and peace as you trust in him, so that you may overflow with hope by the power of the Holy Spirit. —ROMANS 15:13

January 9

I AM WITH YOU AND FOR YOU. When you decide on a course of action that is in line with My will, nothing in heaven or on earth can stop you. You may encounter many obstacles as you move toward your goal, but don't be discouraged—never give up! With My help, you can overcome any obstacle. Do not expect an easy path as you journey hand in hand with Me, but do remember that I, your *very-present Helper*, am omnipotent.

Much, much stress results from your wanting to make things happen before their times have come. One of the main ways I assert My sovereignty is in the timing of events. If you want to stay close to Me and do things My way, ask Me to show you the path forward moment by moment. Instead of dashing headlong toward your goal, let Me set the pace. Slow down, and enjoy the journey in My Presence.

What, then, shall we say in response to this? If God is for us, who can be against us? —ROMANS 8:31

God is our refuge and strength, a very present help in trouble. Therefore we will not fear, even though the earth be removed, and though the mountains be carried into the midst of the sea; though its waters roar and be troubled, though the mountains shake with its swelling. —PSALM 46:1–3 NKJV

"For nothing is impossible with God." —LUKE 1:37

January 10

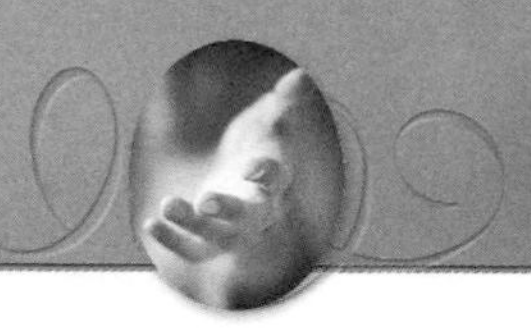

Every time you affirm your trust in Me, you put a coin into My treasury. Thus you build up equity in preparation for days of trouble. I keep safely in My heart all trust invested in Me, with interest compounded continuously. The more you trust Me, the more I empower you to do so.

Practice trusting Me during quiet days, when nothing much seems to be happening. Then when storms come, your trust balance will be sufficient to see you through. *Store up for yourself treasure in heaven,* through placing your trust in Me. This practice will keep you in My Peace.

When I am afraid, I will trust in you. In God, whose word I praise, in God I trust; I will not be afraid. What can mortal man do to me? —Psalm 56:3–4

"But store up for yourselves treasures in heaven, where moth and rust do not destroy, and where thieves do not break in and steal. For where your treasure is, there your heart will be also." —Matthew 6:20–21

JANUARY 11

TRUST ME by relinquishing control into My hands. *Let go, and recognize that I am God.* This is My world: I made it and I control it. Yours is a responsive part in the litany of Love. I search among My children for receptivity to Me. Guard well this gift that I have planted in your heart. Nurture it with the Light of My Presence.

When you bring Me prayer requests, lay out your concerns before Me. Speak to Me candidly; pour out your heart. Then thank Me for the answers that I have set into motion long before you can discern results. When your requests come to mind again, continue to thank Me for the answers that are on the way. If you keep on stating your concerns to Me, you will live in a state of tension. When you thank Me for how I am answering your prayers, your mind-set becomes much more positive. Thankful prayers keep your focus on My Presence and My promises.

Let be and be still, and know (recognize and understand) that I am God. I will be exalted among the nations! I will be exalted in the earth! —PSALM 46:10 AMP

Devote yourselves to prayer, being watchful and thankful. —COLOSSIANS 4:2

His divine power has given us everything we need for life and godliness through our knowledge of him who called us by his own glory and goodness. Through these he has given us his very great and precious promises, so that through them you may participate in the divine nature and escape the corruption in the world caused by evil desires. —2 PETER 1:3–4

Let Me prepare you for the day that stretches out before you. I know exactly what this day will contain, whereas you have only vague ideas about it. You would like to see a map, showing all the twists and turns of your journey. You'd feel more prepared if you could somehow visualize what is on the road ahead. However, there is a better way to be prepared for *whatever* you will encounter today: Spend quality time with Me.

I will not show you what is on the road ahead, but I will thoroughly equip you for the journey. My living Presence is your Companion each step of the way. Stay in continual communication with Me, whispering My Name whenever you need to redirect your thoughts. Thus, you can walk through this day with your focus on Me. My abiding Presence is the best road map available.

The Lord replied, "My Presence will go with you, and I will give you rest." —Exodus 33:14

"Remain in me, and I will remain in you. No branch can bear fruit by itself; it must remain in the vine. Neither can you bear fruit unless you remain in me. I am the vine; you are the branches. If a man remains in me and I in him, he will bear much fruit; apart from me you can do nothing. If anyone does not remain in me, he is like a branch that is thrown away and withers; such branches are picked up, thrown into the fire and burned. If you remain in me and my words remain in you, ask whatever you wish, and it will be given you." —John 15:4–7

January 13

Try to view each day as an adventure, carefully planned out by your Guide. Instead of staring into the day that is ahead of you, attempting to program it according to your will, be attentive to Me and to all I have prepared for you. Thank Me for this day of life, recognizing that it is a precious, unrepeatable gift. Trust that I am with you each moment, whether you sense My Presence or not. A thankful, trusting attitude helps you to see events in your life from My perspective.

A life lived close to Me will never be dull or predictable. Expect each day to contain surprises! Resist your tendency to search for the easiest route through the day. Be willing to follow wherever I lead. No matter how steep or treacherous the path before you, the safest place to be is by My side.

This is the day the Lord has made; let us rejoice and be glad in it. —Psalm 118:24

To this you were called, because Christ suffered for you, leaving you an example, that you should follow in his steps. —1 Peter 2:21

Let Me bless you with My grace and Peace. Open your heart and mind to receive all that I have for you. Do not be ashamed of your emptiness. Instead, view it as the optimal condition for being filled with My Peace.

It is easy to touch up your outward appearance, to look as if you have it all together. Your attempts to look good can fool most people. But I see straight through you, into the depths of your being. There is no place for pretense in your relationship with Me. Rejoice in the relief of being fully understood. Talk with Me about your struggles and feelings of inadequacy. Little by little, I will transform your weaknesses into strengths. Remember that your relationship with Me is saturated in grace. Therefore, *nothing that you do or don't do can separate you from My Presence.*

But the Lord said to Samuel, "Do not consider his appearance or his height, for I have rejected him. The Lord does not look at the things man looks at. Man looks at the outward appearance, but the Lord looks at the heart." —1 Samuel 16:7

For I am convinced that neither death nor life, neither angels nor demons, neither the present nor the future, nor any powers, neither height nor depth, nor anything else in all creation, will be able to separate us from the love of God that is in Christ Jesus our Lord. —Romans 8:38–39

January 15

My Face is shining upon you, beaming out *Peace that transcends understanding.* You are surrounded by a sea of problems, but you are face to Face with Me, your Peace. As long as you focus on Me, you are safe. If you gaze too long at the myriad problems around you, you will sink under the weight of your burdens. When you start to sink, simply call out, "Help me, Jesus!" and I will lift you up.

The closer you live to Me, the safer you are. Circumstances around you are undulating, and there are treacherous-looking waves in the distance. *Fix your eyes on Me*, the One who never changes. By the time those waves reach you, they will have shrunk to proportions of My design. I am always beside you, helping you face *today's* waves. The future is a phantom, seeking to spook you. Laugh at the future! Stay close to Me.

And the peace of God, which transcends all understanding, will guard your hearts and your minds in Christ Jesus. —Philippians 4:7

Then Peter got down out of the boat, walked on the water and came toward Jesus. But when he saw the wind, he was afraid and, beginning to sink, cried out, "Lord, save me!" —Matthew 14:29–30

Let us fix our eyes on Jesus, the author and perfecter of our faith, who for the joy set before him endured the cross, scorning its shame, and sat down at the right hand of the throne of God. —Hebrews 12:2

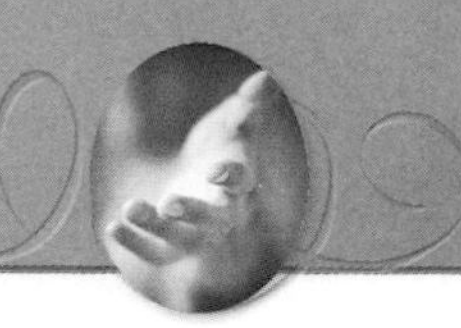

COME TO ME, and rest in My loving Presence. You know that this day will bring difficulties, and you are trying to think your way through those trials. As you anticipate what is ahead of you, you forget that *I am with you*—now and always. Rehearsing your troubles results in experiencing them many times, whereas you are meant to go through them only when they actually occur. Do not multiply your suffering in this way! Instead, come to Me, and relax in My Peace. I will strengthen you and prepare you for this day, transforming your fear into confident trust.

"Come to me, all you who are weary and burdened, and I will give you rest. Take my yoke upon you and learn from me, for I am gentle and humble in heart, and you will find rest for your souls. For my yoke is easy and my burden is light." —MATTHEW 11:28–30

"No one will be able to stand up against you all the days of your life. As I was with Moses, so I will be with you; I will never leave you nor forsake you. . . . Have I not commanded you? Be strong and courageous. Do not be terrified; do not be discouraged, for the LORD your God will be with you wherever you go." —JOSHUA 1:5, 9

January 17

Come to Me with a thankful heart, so that you can enjoy My Presence. This is the day that I have made. I want you to rejoice *today,* refusing to worry about tomorrow. Search for all that I have prepared for you, anticipating abundant blessings and accepting difficulties as they come. I can weave miracles into the most mundane day if you keep your focus on Me.

Come to Me with all your needs, knowing that *My glorious riches* are a more-than-adequate supply. Stay in continual communication with Me, so that you can live above your circumstances even while you are in the midst of them. *Present your requests to Me with thanksgiving, and My Peace, which surpasses all comprehension, will guard your heart and mind.*

This is the day the Lord *has made; let us rejoice and be glad in it.* —Psalm 118:24

And my God shall supply all your need according to His riches in glory by Christ Jesus. . . . Be anxious for nothing, but in everything by prayer and supplication, with thanksgiving, let your requests be made known to God; and the peace of God, which surpasses all understanding, will guard your hearts and minds through Christ Jesus. —Philippians 4:19, 6–7 NKJV

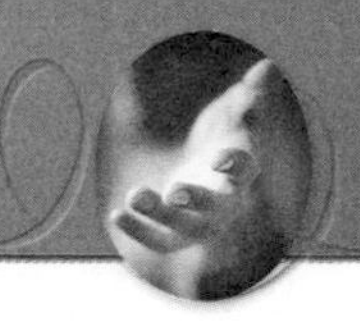

I AM LEADING YOU ALONG THE HIGH ROAD, but there are descents as well as ascents. In the distance you see snow-covered peaks glistening in brilliant sunlight. Your longing to reach those peaks is good, but you must not take shortcuts. Your assignment is to follow Me, allowing Me to direct your path. Let the heights beckon you onward, but stay close to Me.

Learn to trust Me when things go "wrong." Disruptions to your routine highlight your dependence on Me. Trusting acceptance of trials brings blessings that *far outweigh them all*. Walk hand in hand with Me through this day. I have lovingly planned every inch of the way. Trust does not falter when the path becomes rocky and steep. Breathe deep draughts of My Presence, and hold tightly to My hand. Together we can make it!

Jesus said this to indicate the kind of death by which Peter would glorify God. Then he said to him, "Follow me!" —JOHN 21:19

For our light and momentary troubles are achieving for us an eternal glory that far outweighs them all. —2 CORINTHIANS 4:17

The Sovereign LORD is my strength; he makes my feet like the feet of a deer, he enables me to go on the heights. —HABAKKUK 3:19

Seek My Face, and you will find more than you ever dreamed possible. *Let Me displace worry at the center of your being.* I am like a supersaturated cloud, showering Peace into the pool of your mind. My Nature is to bless. Your nature is to receive with thanksgiving. This is a true fit, designed before the foundation of the world. Glorify Me by receiving My blessings gratefully.

I am the goal of all your searching. *When you seek Me, you find Me* and are satisfied. When lesser goals capture your attention, I fade into the background of your life. I am still there, watching and waiting; but you function as if you were alone. Actually, My Light shines on every situation you will ever face. Live radiantly by expanding your focus to include Me in all your moments. Let nothing dampen your search for Me.

When You said, "Seek My face," my heart said to You,
"Your face, Lord, I will seek." —Psalm 27:8 NKJV

Before you know it, a sense of God's wholeness, everything coming together for good, will come and settle you down. It's wonderful what happens when Christ displaces worry at the center of your life. —Philippians 4:7 MSG

"You will seek me and find me when you seek me
with all your heart." —Jeremiah 29:13

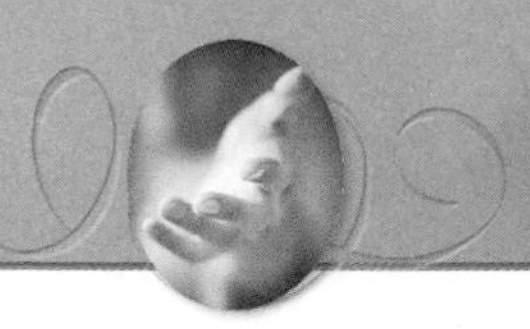

APPROACH THIS DAY WITH AWARENESS OF WHO IS BOSS. As you make plans for the day, remember that it is I who orchestrate the events of your life. On days when things go smoothly, according to your plans, you may be unaware of My sovereign Presence. On days when your plans are thwarted, be on the lookout for Me! I may be doing something important in your life, something quite different from what you expected. It is essential at such times to stay in communication with Me, accepting My way as better than yours. Don't try to figure out what is happening. Simply trust Me and thank Me in advance for the good that will come out of it all. *I know the plans I have for you, and they are good.*

"As the heavens are higher than the earth, so are my ways higher than your ways and my thoughts than your thoughts. As the rain and the snow come down from heaven, and do not return to it without watering the earth and making it bud and flourish, so that it yields seed for the sower and bread for the eater, so is my word that goes out from my mouth: It will not return to me empty, but will accomplish what I desire and achieve the purpose for which I sent it." —ISAIAH 55:9–11

"For I know the plans I have for you," declares the LORD, *"plans to prosper you and not to harm you, plans to give you hope and a future."* —JEREMIAH 29:11

January 21

I WANT YOU TO BE ALL MINE. I am weaning you from other dependencies. Your security rests in Me alone—not in other people, not in circumstances. Depending only on Me may feel like walking on a tightrope, but there is a safety net underneath: *the everlasting arms.* So don't be afraid of falling. Instead, look ahead to Me. I am always before you, beckoning you on—one step at a time. *Neither height nor depth, nor anything else in all creation, can separate you from My loving Presence.*

The eternal God is your refuge, and underneath are the everlasting arms. He will drive out your enemy before you, saying, "Destroy him!" —DEUTERONOMY 33:27

Neither height nor depth, nor anything else in all creation, will be able to separate us from the love of God that is in Christ Jesus our Lord. —ROMANS 8:39

Strive to trust Me in more and more areas of your life. Anything that tends to make you anxious is a growth opportunity. Instead of running away from these challenges, embrace them, eager to gain all the blessings I have hidden in the difficulties. If you believe that I am sovereign over every aspect of your life, it is possible to trust Me in all situations. Don't waste energy regretting the way things are or thinking about what might have been. Start at the present moment—accepting things exactly as they are—and search for My way in the midst of those circumstances.

Trust is like a staff you can lean on, as you journey uphill with Me. If you are trusting in Me consistently, the staff will bear as much of your weight as needed. *Lean on, trust, and be confident in Me with all your heart and mind.*

But I am like an olive tree flourishing in the house of God; I trust in God's unfailing love for ever and ever. —Psalm 52:8

Lean on, trust in, and be confident in the Lord with all your heart and mind and do not rely on your own insight or understanding. In all your ways know, recognize, and acknowledge Him, and He will direct and make straight and plain your paths. —Proverbs 3:5–6 AMP

JANUARY 23

IT'S ALL RIGHT TO BE HUMAN. When your mind wanders while you are praying, don't be surprised or upset. Simply return your attention to Me. Share a secret smile with Me, knowing that I understand. Rejoice in My Love for you, which has no limits or conditions. Whisper My Name in loving contentment, assured that *I will never leave you or forsake you*. Intersperse these peaceful interludes abundantly throughout your day. This practice will enable you to attain *a quiet and gentle spirit*, which is pleasing to Me.

As you live in close contact with Me, the Light of My Presence filters through you to bless others. Your weakness and woundedness are the openings through which *the Light of the knowledge of My Glory* shines forth. *My strength and power show themselves most effective in your weakness.*

Be strong and courageous. Do not be afraid or terrified because of them, for the LORD your God goes with you; he will never leave you nor forsake you. —DEUTERONOMY 31:6

Instead, it should be that of your inner self, the unfading beauty of a gentle and quiet spirit, which is of great worth in God's sight. —1 PETER 3:4

For God, who said, "Let light shine out of darkness," made his light shine in our hearts to give us the light of the knowledge of the glory of God in the face of Christ. But we have this treasure in jars of clay to show that this all-surpassing power is from God and not from us. —2 CORINTHIANS 4:6–7

But He said to me . . . My strength and power are made perfect (fulfilled and completed) and show themselves most effective in [your] weakness. —2 CORINTHIANS 12:9 AMP

MY PEACE is the treasure of treasures: *the pearl of great price*. It is an exquisitely costly gift, both for the Giver and the receiver. I purchased this Peace for you with My blood. You receive this gift by trusting Me in the midst of life's storms. If you have the world's peace—everything going your way—you don't seek My unfathomable Peace. Thank Me when things do not go your way, because spiritual blessings come wrapped in trials. Adverse circumstances are normal in a fallen world. Expect them each day. Rejoice in the face of hardship, *for I have overcome the world*.

Who, when he had found one pearl of great price, went and sold all that he had and bought it. —MATTHEW 13:46 NKJV

Consider it pure joy, my brothers, whenever you face trials of many kinds. —JAMES 1:2

"I have told you these things, so that in me you may have peace. In this world you will have trouble. But take heart! I have overcome the world." —JOHN 16:33

January 25

Let My Love enfold you in the radiance of My Glory. Sit still in the Light of My Presence, and receive My Peace. These quiet moments with Me transcend time, accomplishing far more than you can imagine. Bring Me the sacrifice of your time, and watch to see how abundantly I bless you and your loved ones.

Through the intimacy of our relationship, you are *being transformed* from the inside out. As you keep your focus on Me, I form you into the one I desire you to be. Your part is to yield to My creative work in you, neither resisting it nor trying to speed it up. Enjoy the tempo of a God-breathed life by letting Me set the pace. Hold My hand in childlike trust, and the way before you will open up step by step.

Through Jesus, therefore, let us continually offer to God a sacrifice of praise—the fruit of lips that confess his name. —Hebrews 13:15

And we, who with unveiled faces all reflect the Lord's glory, are being transformed into his likeness with ever-increasing glory, which comes from the Lord, who is the Spirit. —2 Corinthians 3:18

Yet I am always with you; you hold me by my right hand. You guide me with your counsel, and afterward you will take me into glory. —Psalm 73:23–24

JANUARY 26

GIVE UP THE ILLUSION that you deserve a problem-free life. Part of you is still hungering for the resolution of all difficulties. This is a false hope! As I told My disciples, *in the world you will have trouble.* Link your hope not to problem solving in this life but to the promise of an eternity of problem-free life in heaven. Instead of seeking perfection in this fallen world, pour your energy into seeking Me: the Perfect One.

It is possible to enjoy Me and glorify Me in the midst of adverse circumstances. In fact, My Light shines most brightly through believers who trust Me in the dark. That kind of trust is supernatural: a production of My indwelling Spirit. When things seem all wrong, trust Me anyway. I am much less interested in right circumstances than in right responses to whatever comes your way.

"I have told you these things, so that in me you may have peace. In this world you will have trouble. But take heart! I have overcome the world." —JOHN 16:33

Even in darkness light dawns for the upright, for the gracious and compassionate and righteous man. . . . He will have no fear of bad news; his heart is steadfast, trusting in the LORD. —PSALM 112:4, 7

January 27

TRUST IS A GOLDEN PATHWAY TO HEAVEN. When you walk on this path, you live above your circumstances. My glorious Light shines more brightly on those who follow this path of Life. Dare to walk on the high road with Me, for it is the most direct route to heaven. The low road is circuitous: twisting and turning in agonizing knots. There the air hangs heavy—and dark, ominous clouds predominate. *Relying on your own understanding* will weigh you down. *Trust in Me absolutely, and I will make your path straight.*

"Do not let your hearts be troubled. Trust in God; trust also in me. In my Father's house are many rooms; if it were not so, I would have told you. I am going there to prepare a place for you." —JOHN 14:1–2

Trust in the LORD with all your heart and lean not on your own understanding; in all your ways acknowledge him, and he will make your paths straight. —PROVERBS 3:5–6

January 28

I am with you always. I spoke these words to My disciples after My resurrection. I continue to proclaim this promise to all who will listen. People respond to My continual Presence in various ways. Most Christians accept this teaching as truth but ignore it in their daily living. Some ill-taught or wounded believers fear (and may even resent) My awareness of all they do, say, and think. A few people center their lives around this glorious promise and find themselves blessed beyond all expectations.

When My Presence is the focal point of your consciousness, all the pieces of your life fall into place. As you gaze at Me through the eyes of your heart, you can see the world around you from My perspective. The fact that *I am with you* makes every moment of your life meaningful.

"And teaching them to obey everything I have commanded you. And surely I am with you always, to the very end of the age." —Matthew 28:20

O Lord, you have searched me and you know me. You know when I sit and when I rise; you perceive my thoughts from afar. You discern my going out and my lying down; you are familiar with all my ways. Before a word is on my tongue you know it completely, O Lord. —Psalm 139:1–4

JANUARY 29

KEEP YOUR FOCUS ON ME. I have gifted you with amazing freedom, including the ability to choose the focal point of your mind. Only the crown of My creation has such remarkable capability; this is a sign of being *made in My image*.

Let the goal of this day be to *bring every thought captive to Me*. Whenever your mind wanders, lasso those thoughts and bring them into My Presence. In My radiant Light, anxious thoughts shrink and shrivel away. Judgmental thoughts are unmasked as you bask in My unconditional Love. Confused ideas are untangled while you rest in the simplicity of My Peace. *I will guard you and keep you in constant Peace, as you focus your mind on Me.*

You made him a little lower than the heavenly beings and crowned him with glory and honor. —PSALM 8:5

Then God said, "Let us make man in our image, in our likeness, and let them rule over the fish of the sea and the birds of the air, over the livestock, over all the earth, and over all the creatures that move along the ground." So God created man in his own image, in the image of God he created him; male and female he created them. —GENESIS 1:26–27

We demolish arguments and every pretension that sets itself up against the knowledge of God, and we take captive every thought to make it obedient to Christ. —2 CORINTHIANS 10:5

You will guard him and keep him in perfect and constant peace whose mind [both its inclination and its character] is stayed on You, because he commits himself to You, leans on You, and hopes confidently in You. —ISAIAH 26:3 AMP

Worship Me only. Whatever occupies your mind the most becomes your god. Worries, if indulged, develop into idols. Anxiety gains a life of its own, parasitically infesting your mind. Break free from this bondage by affirming your trust in Me and refreshing yourself in My Presence. What goes on in your mind is invisible, undetectable to other people. But I read your thoughts continually, searching for evidence of trust in Me. I rejoice when your mind turns toward Me. Guard your thoughts diligently; good thought-choices will keep you close to Me.

He will have no fear of bad news; his heart is steadfast, trusting in the Lord. —Psalm 112:7

When I was a child, I talked like a child, I thought like a child, I reasoned like a child. When I became a man, I put childish ways behind me. —1 Corinthians 13:11

January 31

I am your Strength and Shield. I plan out each day and have it ready for you, long before you arise from bed. I also provide the strength you need each step of the way. Instead of assessing your energy level and wondering about what's on the road ahead, concentrate on staying in touch with Me. My Power flows freely into you through our open communication. Refuse to waste energy worrying, and you will have strength to spare.

Whenever you start to feel afraid, remember that I am your Shield. But unlike inanimate armor, I am always alert and active. My Presence watches over you continually, protecting you from both known and unknown dangers. Entrust yourself to My watchcare, which is the best security system available. *I am with you and will watch over you wherever you go.*

The Lord is my strength and my shield; my heart trusts in him, and I am helped. My heart leaps for joy and I will give thanks to him in song. —Psalm 28:7

"Therefore do not worry about tomorrow, for tomorrow will worry about itself. Each day has enough trouble of its own." —Matthew 6:34

When I am afraid, I will trust in you. In God, whose word I praise, in God I trust; I will not be afraid. What can mortal man do to me?—Psalm 56:3–4

"I am with you and will watch over you wherever you go, and I will bring you back to this land. I will not leave you until I have done what I have promised you." —Genesis 28:15

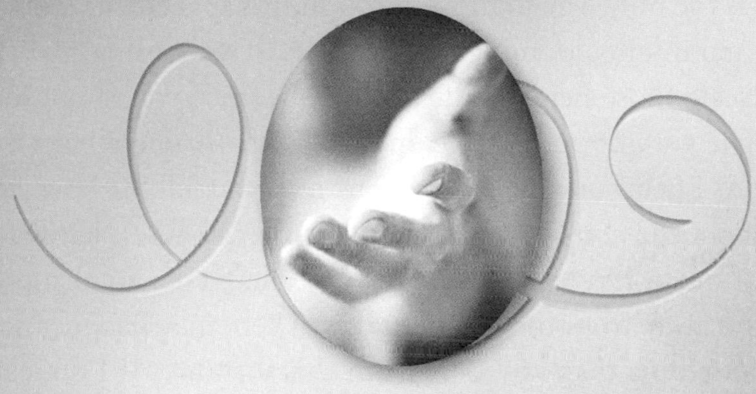

February

Look to the Lord and his strength;
seek his face always.

Psalm 105:4

February 1

Follow Me one step at a time. That is all I require of you. In fact, that is the only way to move through this space/time world. You see huge mountains looming, and you start wondering how you're going to scale those heights. Meanwhile, because you're not looking where you're going, you stumble on the easy path where I am leading you now. As I help you get back on your feet, you tell Me how worried you are about the cliffs up ahead. But you don't know what will happen today, much less tomorrow. Our path may take an abrupt turn, leading you away from those mountains. There may be an easier way up the mountains than is visible from this distance. If I do lead you up the cliffs, I will equip you thoroughly for that strenuous climb. *I will even give My angels charge over you, to preserve you in all your ways.*

Keep your mind on the present journey, enjoying My Presence. *Walk by faith, not by sight,* trusting Me to open up the way before you.

With your help I can advance against a troop; with my God I can scale a wall. —Psalm 18:29

For He will give His angels [especial] charge over you to accompany and defend and preserve you in all your ways [of obedience and service]. They shall bear you up on their hands, lest you dash your foot against a stone. —Psalm 91:11–12 AMP

For we walk by faith, not by sight. —2 Corinthians 5:7 NKJV

I AM RENEWING YOUR MIND. When your thoughts flow freely, they tend to move toward problems. Your focus gets snagged on a given problem, circling round and round it in attempts to gain mastery. Your energy is drained away from other matters through this negative focus. Worst of all, you lose sight of Me.

A renewed mind is Presence-focused. Train your mind to seek Me in every moment, every situation. Sometimes you can find Me in your surroundings: a lilting birdsong, a loved one's smile, golden sunlight. At other times, you must draw inward to find Me. I am always present in your spirit. Seek My Face, speak to Me, and I will light up your mind.

Do not conform any longer to the pattern of this world, but be transformed by the renewing of your mind. Then you will be able to test and approve what God's will is—his good, pleasing and perfect will. —ROMANS 12:2

Look to the LORD and his strength; seek his face always. —PSALM 105:4

February 3

I am with you and for you. You face nothing alone—*nothing*! When you feel anxious, know that you are focusing on the visible world and leaving Me out of the picture. The remedy is simple: *Fix your eyes not on what is seen but on what is unseen.* Verbalize your trust in Me, *the Living One who sees you always.* I will get you safely through this day and all your days. But you can find Me only in the present. Each day is a precious gift from My Father. How ridiculous to grasp for future gifts when today's is set before you! Receive today's gift gratefully, unwrapping it tenderly and delving into its depths. As you savor this gift, you find Me.

What, then, shall we say in response to this? If God is for us, who can be against us? —Romans 8:31

So we fix our eyes not on what is seen, but on what is unseen. For what is seen is temporary, but what is unseen is eternal. —2 Corinthians 4:18

So she called the name of the Lord Who spoke to her, You are a God of seeing, for she said, Have I [not] even here [in the wilderness] looked upon Him Who sees me [and lived]? Or have I here also seen [the future purposes or designs of] Him Who sees me? Therefore the well was called Beer-lahai-roi [A well to the Living One Who sees me]. —Genesis 16:13–14 amp

BRING ME YOUR WEAKNESS, and receive My Peace. Accept yourself and your circumstances just as they are, remembering that I am sovereign over everything. Do not wear yourself out with analyzing and planning. Instead, let thankfulness and trust be your guides through this day; they will keep you close to Me. As you live in the radiance of My Presence, My Peace shines upon you. You will cease to notice how weak or strong you feel, because you will be focusing on Me. The best way to get through this day is step by step with Me. Continue this intimate journey, trusting that the path you are following is headed for heaven.

The LORD gives strength to his people; the LORD blesses his people with peace. —PSALM 29:11

"The LORD bless you and keep you; the LORD make his face shine upon you and be gracious to you; the LORD turn his face toward you and give you peace." —NUMBERS 6:24–26

But I trust in your unfailing love; my heart rejoices in your salvation. —PSALM 13:5

February 5

Seek My Face, and you will find not only My Presence but also My Peace. To receive My Peace, you must change your grasping, controlling stance to one of openness and trust. The only thing you can grasp without damaging your soul is My hand. Ask My Spirit within you to order your day and control your thoughts, for *the mind controlled by the Spirit is Life and Peace.*

You can have as much of Me and My Peace as you want, through thousands of correct choices each day. The most persistent choice you face is whether to trust Me or to worry. You will never run out of things to worry about, but you can choose to trust Me no matter what. I am *an ever-present help in trouble.* Trust Me, *though the earth give way and the mountains fall into the heart of the sea.*

The mind of sinful man is death, but the mind controlled by the Spirit is life and peace. —Romans 8:6

God is our refuge and strength, an ever-present help in trouble. Therefore we will not fear, though the earth give way and the mountains fall into the heart of the sea. —Psalm 46:1–2

COME TO ME AND REST. I am all around you, to bless and restore. Breathe Me in with each breath. The way just ahead of you is very steep. Slow down and cling tightly to My hand. I am teaching you a difficult lesson, learned only by hardship.

Lift up empty hands of faith to receive My precious Presence. Light, Life, Joy, and Peace flow freely through this gift. When your focus turns away from Me, you grasp for other things. You drop the glowing gift of My Presence as you reach for lifeless ashes. Return to Me; regain My Presence.

"Come to me, all you who are weary and burdened, and I will give you rest. Take my yoke upon you and learn from me, for I am gentle and humble in heart, and you will find rest for your souls." —MATTHEW 11:28–29

I want men everywhere to lift up holy hands in prayer, without anger or disputing. —1 TIMOTHY 2:8

February 7

Come to Me for rest and refreshment. The journey has been too much for you, and you are bone-weary. Do not be ashamed of your exhaustion. Instead, see it as an opportunity for Me to take charge of your life.

Remember that *I can fit everything into a pattern for good*, including the things you wish were different. Start with where you are at this point in time and space, accepting that this is where I intend you to be. You will get through today one step, one moment at a time. Your main responsibility is to remain attentive to Me, letting Me guide you through the many choices along your pathway.

This sounds like an easy assignment, but it is not. Your desire to live in My Presence goes against the grain of "the world, the flesh, and the devil." Much of your weariness results from your constant battle against these opponents. However, you are on the path of My choosing, so do not give up! *Hope in Me, for you will again praise Me for the help of My Presence.*

We are assured and know that [God being a partner in their labor] all things work together and are [fitting into a plan] for good to and for those who love God and are called according to [His] design and purpose. —Romans 8:28 AMP

Why are you in despair, O my soul? And why *have you become disturbed within me? Hope in God, for I shall again praise Him for the help of His presence.* —Psalm 42:5 NASB

I am above all things: your problems, your pain, and the swirling events in this ever-changing world. When you behold My Face, you rise above circumstances and rest with Me in *heavenly realms*. This is the way of Peace, living in the Light of My Presence. I guarantee that you will always have problems in this life, but they must not become your focus. When you feel yourself sinking in the sea of circumstances, say "*Help me, Jesus*!" and I will draw you back to Me. If you have to say that thousands of times daily, don't be discouraged. I know your weakness, and I meet you in that very place.

And God raised us up with Christ and seated us with him in the heavenly realms in Christ Jesus. —Ephesians 2:6

"Lord, if it's you," Peter replied, "tell me to come to you on the water." "Come," he said. Then Peter got down out of the boat, walked on the water and came toward Jesus. But when he saw the wind, he was afraid and, beginning to sink, cried out, "Lord, save me!" Immediately Jesus reached out his hand and caught him. "You of little faith," he said, "why did you doubt?" And when they climbed into the boat, the wind died down. —Matthew 14:28–32

February 9

Seek My Face more and more. You are really just beginning your journey of intimacy with Me. It is not an easy road, but it is a delightful and privileged way: a treasure hunt. I am the Treasure, and the Glory of My Presence glistens and shimmers along the way. Hardships are part of the journey too. I mete them out ever so carefully, in just the right dosage, with a tenderness you can hardly imagine. Do not recoil from afflictions, since they are among My most favored gifts. *Trust Me and don't be afraid, for I am your Strength and Song.*

When You said, "Seek My face," my heart said to You,
"Your face, Lord, I will seek." —Psalm 27:8 NKJV

But we have this treasure in jars of clay to show that this all-surpassing power is from God and not from us. —2 Corinthians 4:7

Surely God is my salvation; I will trust and not be afraid.
The Lord, the Lord, is my strength and my song; he
has become my salvation. —Isaiah 12:2

TRUST ME ENOUGH to spend ample time with Me, pushing back the demands of the day. Refuse to feel guilty about something that is so pleasing to Me, the King of the universe. Because I am omnipotent, I am able to bend time and events in your favor. You will find that you can accomplish *more* in less time, after you have given yourself to Me in rich communion. Also, as you align yourself with My perspective, you can sort out what is important and what is not.

Don't fall into the trap of being constantly on the go. Many, many things people do in My Name have no value in My kingdom. To avoid doing meaningless works, stay in continual communication with Me. *I will instruct you and teach you in the way you should go; I will counsel you with My eye upon you.*

"Martha, Martha," the Lord answered, "you are worried and upset about many things, but only one thing is needed. Mary has chosen what is better, and it will not be taken away from her." —LUKE 10:41–42

I will instruct you and teach you in the way which you should go; I will counsel you with My eye upon you. —PSALM 32:8 NASB

February 11

My Peace is like a shaft of golden Light shining on you continuously. During days of bright sunshine, it may blend in with your surroundings. On darker days, My Peace stands out in sharp contrast to your circumstances. See times of darkness as opportunities for My Light to shine in transcendent splendor. I am training you to practice Peace that overpowers darkness. Collaborate with Me in this training. *Do not grow weary and lose heart.*

In Him was Life, and the Life was the Light of men. And the Light shines on in the darkness, for the darkness has never overpowered it [put it out or absorbed it or appropriated it, and is unreceptive to it]. —John 1:4–5 AMP

Consider him who endured such opposition from sinful men, so that you will not grow weary and lose heart. —Hebrews 12:3

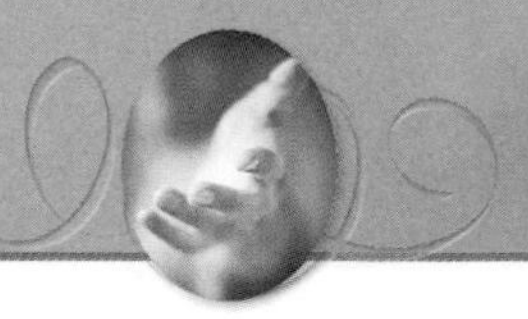

I AM EVER SO NEAR YOU, hovering over your shoulder, reading every thought. People think that thoughts are fleeting and worthless, but yours are precious to Me. I smile when you think lovingly of Me. My Spirit, who lives within you, helps you to think My thoughts. As your thinking goes, so goes your entire being.

Let Me be your positive Focus. When you look to Me, knowing Me as *God with you*, you experience Joy. This is according to My ancient design, when I first crafted man. Modern man seeks his positive focus elsewhere: in sports, sensations, acquiring new possessions. Advertising capitalizes on the longing of people for a positive focus in their lives. I planted that longing in human souls, knowing that only I could fully satisfy it. *Delight yourself in Me; let Me become the Desire of your heart.*

"The virgin will be with child and will give birth to a son, and they will call him Immanuel"—which means, "God with us." —MATTHEW 1:23

Delight yourself in the LORD and he will give you the desires of your heart. —PSALM 37:4

February 13

Peace be with you! Ever since the resurrection, this has been My watchword to those who yearn for Me. As you sit quietly, let My Peace settle over you and enfold you in My loving Presence. To provide this radiant Peace for you, I died a criminal's death. Receive *My Peace* abundantly and thankfully. It is a rare treasure, dazzling in delicate beauty yet strong enough to withstand all onslaughts. Wear My Peace with regal dignity. It will keep your heart and mind close to Mine.

On the evening of that first day of the week, when the disciples were together, with the doors locked for fear of the Jews, Jesus came and stood among them and said, "Peace be with you!" . . . Again Jesus said, "Peace be with you! As the Father has sent me, I am sending you." —John 20:19, 21

"Peace I leave with you; my peace I give you. I do not give to you as the world gives. Do not let your hearts be troubled and do not be afraid." —John 14:27

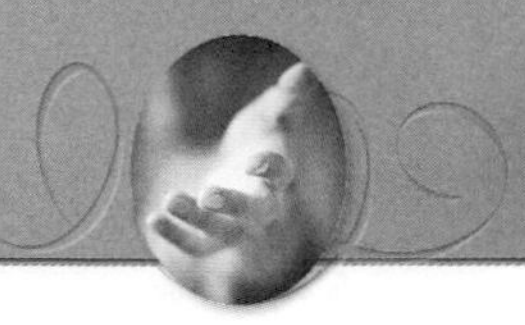

Give yourself fully to the adventure of today. Walk boldly along the path of Life, relying on your ever-present Companion. You have every reason to be confident, because My Presence accompanies you all the days of your life—and onward into eternity.

Do not give in to fear or worry, those robbers of abundant living. Trust Me enough to face problems as they come, rather than trying to anticipate them. *Fix your eyes on Me, the Author and Perfecter of your faith*, and many difficulties on the road ahead will vanish before you reach them. Whenever you start to feel afraid, remember that *I am holding you by your right hand*. Nothing can separate you from My Presence!

Let us fix our eyes on Jesus, the author and perfecter of our faith, who for the joy set before him endured the cross, scorning its shame, and sat down at the right hand of the throne of God. —Hebrews 12:2

"For I am the Lord, your God, who takes hold of your right hand and says to you, Do not fear; I will help you." —Isaiah 41:13

February 15

Come to Me with all your weaknesses: physical, emotional, and spiritual. Rest in the comfort of My Presence, remembering that *nothing is impossible with Me.*

Pry your mind away from your problems so you can focus your attention on Me. Recall that I am *able to do immeasurably more than all you ask or imagine.* Instead of trying to direct Me to do this and that, seek to attune yourself to what I am *already* doing.

When anxiety attempts to wedge its way into your thoughts, remind yourself that *I am your Shepherd.* The bottom line is that I am taking care of you; therefore, you needn't be afraid of anything. Rather than trying to maintain control over your life, abandon yourself to My will. Though this may feel frightening—even dangerous, the safest place to be is in My will.

"For nothing is impossible with God." —Luke 1:37

Now to him who is able to do immeasurably more than all we ask or imagine, according to his power that is at work within us, to him be glory in the church and in Christ Jesus throughout all generations, forever and ever! Amen. —Ephesians 3:20–21

The Lord is my shepherd, I shall not be in want. He makes me lie down in green pastures, he leads me beside quiet waters, he restores my soul. He guides me in paths of righteousness for his name's sake. Even though I walk through the valley of the shadow of death, I will fear no evil, for you are with me; your rod and your staff, they comfort me. —Psalm 23:1–4

THANK ME for the conditions that are requiring you to *be still.* Do not spoil these quiet hours by wishing them away, waiting impatiently to be active again. Some of the greatest works in My kingdom have been done from sickbeds and prison cells. Instead of resenting the limitations of a weakened body, search for My way in the midst of these very circumstances. Limitations can be liberating when your strongest desire is living close to Me.

Quietness and trust enhance your awareness of My Presence with you. Do not despise these simple ways of serving Me. Although you feel cut off from the activity of the world, your quiet trust makes a powerful statement in spiritual realms. *My Strength and Power show themselves most effective in weakness.*

"Be still before the LORD, all mankind, because he has roused himself from his holy dwelling." —ZECHARIAH 2:13

This is what the Sovereign LORD, the Holy One of Israel, says: "In repentance and rest is your salvation, in quietness and trust is your strength, but you would have none of it." —ISAIAH 30:15

But He said to me, My grace (My favor and loving-kindness and mercy) is enough for you [sufficient against any danger and enables you to bear the trouble manfully]; for My strength and power are made perfect (fulfilled and completed) and show themselves most effective in [your] weakness. Therefore, I will all the more gladly glory in my weaknesses and infirmities, that the strength and power of Christ (the Messiah) may rest (yes, may pitch a tent over and dwell) upon me! —2 CORINTHIANS 12:9 AMP

I AM THE RISEN ONE who shines upon you always. You worship a living Deity, not some idolatrous, man-made image. Your relationship with Me is meant to be vibrant and challenging, as I invade more and more areas of your life. Do not fear change, for I am making you a *new creation, with old things passing away and new things continually on the horizon.* When you cling to old ways and sameness, you resist My work within you. I want you to embrace all that I am doing in your life, finding your security in Me alone.

It is easy to make an idol of routine, finding security within the boundaries you build around your life. Although each day contains twenty-four hours, every single one presents a unique set of circumstances. Don't try to force-fit today into yesterday's mold. Instead, ask Me to open your eyes, so you can find all I have prepared for you in this precious day of Life.

The angel said to the women, "Do not be afraid, for I know that you are looking for Jesus, who was crucified. He is not here; he has risen, just as he said. Come and see the place where he lay. Then go quickly and tell his disciples: 'He has risen from the dead and is going ahead of you into Galilee. There you will see him.' Now I have told you." —MATTHEW 28:5–7

Therefore, if anyone is in Christ, he is a new creation; the old has gone, the new has come! —2 CORINTHIANS 5:17

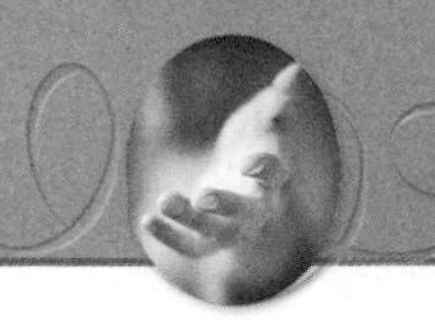

I AM WITH YOU. These four words are like a safety net, protecting you from falling into despair. Because you are human, you will always have ups and downs in your life experience. But the promise of My Presence limits how far down you can go. Sometimes you may feel as if you are in a free fall, when people or things you had counted on let you down. Yet as soon as you remember that *I am with you*, your perspective changes radically. Instead of bemoaning your circumstances, you can look to Me for help. You recall that not only am I with you, *I am holding you by your right hand. I guide you with My counsel, and afterward I will take you into Glory.* This is exactly the perspective you need: the reassurance of My Presence, and the glorious hope of heaven.

The LORD your God is with you, he is mighty to save. He will take great delight in you, he will quiet you with his love, he will rejoice over you with singing. —ZEPHANIAH 3:17

Yet I am always with you; you hold me by my right hand. You guide me with your counsel, and afterward you will take me into glory. Whom have I in heaven but you? And earth has nothing I desire besides you. My flesh and my heart may fail, but God is the strength of my heart and my portion forever. —PSALM 73:23–26

FEBRUARY 19

YOU ARE FEELING WEIGHED DOWN by a plethora of problems, both big and small. They seem to require more and more of your attention, but you must not give in to those demands. When the difficulties in your life feel as if they're closing in on you, break free by spending quality time with Me. You need to remember who I AM in all My Power and Glory. Then, humbly bring Me your prayers and petitions. Your problems will pale when you view them in the Light of My Presence. You can learn to *be joyful in Me, your Savior*, even in the midst of adverse circumstances. Rely on Me, *your Strength*; *I make your feet like the feet of a deer, enabling you to go on the heights.*

God said to Moses, "I AM WHO I AM. This is what you are to say to the Israelites: 'I AM has sent me to you.'" —EXODUS 3:14

Though the fig tree does not bud and there are no grapes on the vines, though the olive crop fails and the fields produce no food, though there are no sheep in the pen and no cattle in the stalls, yet I will rejoice in the LORD, I will be joyful in God my Savior. The Sovereign LORD is my strength; he makes my feet like the feet of a deer, he enables me to go on the heights. —HABAKKUK 3:17–19

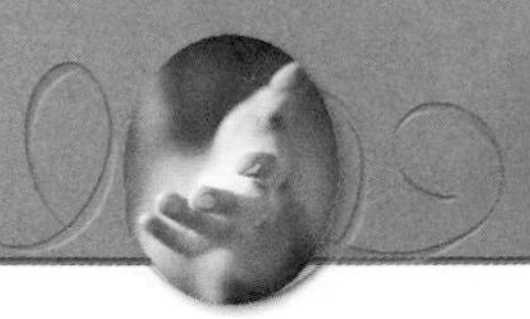

LEARN TO LIVE from your true Center in Me. I reside in the deepest depths of your being, in eternal union with your spirit. It is at this deep level that My Peace reigns continually. You will not find lasting peace in the world around you, in circumstances, or in human relationships. The external world is always in flux—under the curse of death and decay. But there is a gold mine of Peace deep within you, waiting to be tapped. Take time to delve into the riches of My residing Presence. I want you to live increasingly from your real Center, where My Love has an eternal grip on you. *I am Christ in you, the hope of Glory.*

Let the peace of Christ rule in your hearts, since as members of one body you were called to peace. And be thankful. —COLOSSIANS 3:15

To them God has chosen to make known among the Gentiles the glorious riches of this mystery, which is Christ in you, the hope of glory. —COLOSSIANS 1:27

FEBRUARY 21

TRUST AND THANKFULNESS WILL get you safely through this day. Trust protects you from worrying and obsessing. Thankfulness keeps you from criticizing and complaining: those "sister sins" that so easily entangle you.

Keeping your eyes on Me is the same thing as trusting Me. It is a free choice that you must make thousands of times daily. The more you choose to trust Me, the easier it becomes. Thought patterns of trust become etched into your brain. Relegate troubles to the periphery of your mind, so that I can be central in your thoughts. Thus you focus on Me, entrusting your concerns into My care.

So then, just as you received Christ Jesus as Lord, continue to live in him, rooted and built up in him, strengthened in the faith as you were taught, and overflowing with thankfulness. —COLOSSIANS 2:6–7

But my eyes are fixed on you, O Sovereign LORD; in you I take refuge—do not give me over to death. —PSALM 141:8

Cast all your anxiety on him because he cares for you. —1 PETER 5:7

YOU NEED ME EVERY MOMENT. Your awareness of your constant need for Me is your greatest strength. Your neediness, properly handled, is a link to My Presence. However, there are pitfalls that you must be on guard against: self-pity, self-preoccupation, giving up. Your inadequacy presents you with a continual choice—deep dependence on Me, or despair. The emptiness you feel within will be filled either with problems or with My Presence. Make Me central in your consciousness by *praying continually*: simple, short prayers flowing out of the present moment. Use My Name liberally, to remind you of My Presence. *Keep on asking and you will receive, so that your gladness may be full and complete.*

Pray continually. —1 THESSALONIANS 5:17

Up to this time you have not asked a [single] thing in My Name [as presenting all that I AM]; but now ask and keep on asking and you will receive, so that your joy (gladness, delight) may be full and complete. —JOHN 16:24 AMP

February 23

Be on guard against the pit of self-pity. When you are weary or unwell, this demonic trap is the greatest danger you face. Don't even go near the edge of the pit. Its edges crumble easily, and before you know it, you are on the way down. It is ever so much harder to get out of the pit than to keep a safe distance from it. That is why I tell you to be on guard.

There are several ways to protect yourself from self-pity. When you are occupied with praising and thanking Me, it is impossible to feel sorry for yourself. Also, the closer you live to Me, the more distance there is between you and the pit. Live in the Light of My Presence by *fixing your eyes on Me.* Then you will be able *to run with endurance the race that is set before you*, without stumbling or falling.

Blessed are those who have learned to acclaim you, who walk in the light of your presence, O Lord. —Psalm 89:15

Therefore, since we have so great a cloud of witnesses surrounding us, let us also lay aside every encumbrance and the sin which so easily entangles us, and let us run with endurance the race that is set before us, fixing our eyes on Jesus, the author and perfecter of faith, who for the joy set before Him endured the cross, despising the shame, and has sat down at the right hand of the throne of God. —Hebrews 12:1–2 NASB

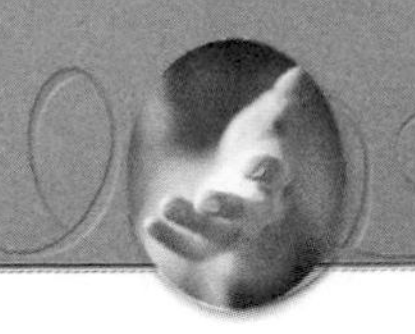

BE STILL IN THE LIGHT of My Presence, while I communicate Love to you. There is no force in the universe as powerful as My Love. You are constantly aware of limitations: your own and others'. But there is no limit to My Love; it fills all of space, time, and eternity.

Now you see through a glass, darkly, but someday you will see Me face to Face. Then you will be able to experience fully *how wide and long and high and deep is My Love for you.* If you were to experience that now, you would be overwhelmed to the point of feeling crushed. But you have an eternity ahead of you, absolutely guaranteed, during which you can enjoy My Presence in unrestricted ecstasy. For now, the knowledge of My loving Presence is sufficient to carry you through each day.

For now we see through a glass, darkly; but then face to face: now I know in part; but then shall I know even as also I am known. —1 CORINTHIANS 13:12 KJV

I pray that out of his glorious riches he may strengthen you with power through his Spirit in your inner being, so that Christ may dwell in your hearts through faith. And I pray that you, being rooted and established in love, may have power, together with all the saints, to grasp how wide and long and high and deep is the love of Christ, and to know this love that surpasses knowledge—that you may be filled to the measure of all the fullness of God. —EPHESIANS 3:16–19

February 25

Rest in My Presence, allowing Me to take charge of this day. Do not bolt into the day like a racehorse suddenly released. Instead, walk purposefully with Me, letting Me direct your course one step at a time. Thank Me for each blessing along the way; this brings Joy to both you and Me. A grateful heart protects you from negative thinking. Thankfulness enables you to see the abundance I shower upon you daily. Your prayers and petitions are winged into heaven's throne room when they are permeated with thanksgiving. *In everything give thanks, for this is My will for you.*

Devote yourselves to prayer, being watchful and thankful. —Colossians 4:2

In everything give thanks; for this is God's will for you in Christ Jesus. —1 Thessalonians 5:18 NASB

I AM LEADING YOU, STEP BY STEP, through your life. Hold My hand in trusting dependence, letting Me guide you through this day. Your future looks uncertain and feels flimsy—even precarious. That is how it should be. *Secret things belong to the Lord*, and future things are secret things. When you try to figure out the future, you are grasping at things that are Mine. This, like all forms of worry, is an act of rebellion: doubting My promises to care for you.

Whenever you find yourself worrying about the future, repent and return to Me. I will show you the next step forward, and the one after that, and the one after that. Relax and enjoy the journey in My Presence, trusting Me to open up the way before you as you go.

The secret things belong to the LORD our God, but the things revealed belong to us and to our children forever, that we may follow all the words of this law. —DEUTERONOMY 29:29

I will instruct you and teach you in the way you should go; I will counsel you and watch over you. —PSALM 32:8

February 27

Keep your eyes on Me! Waves of adversity are washing over you, and you feel tempted to give up. As your circumstances consume more and more of your attention, you are losing sight of Me. Yet *I am with you always, holding you by your right hand.* I am fully aware of your situation, *and I will not allow you to be tempted beyond what you are able to bear.*

Your gravest danger is worrying about tomorrow. If you try to carry tomorrow's burdens today, you will stagger under the load and eventually fall flat. You must discipline yourself to live within the boundaries of today. It is in the present moment that I walk close to you, helping you carry your burdens. Keep your focus on My Presence in the present.

Yet I am always with you; you hold me by my right hand. —Psalm 73:23

No temptation has seized you except what is common to man. And God is faithful; he will not let you be tempted beyond what you can bear. But when you are tempted, he will also provide a way out so that you can stand up under it. —1 Corinthians 10:13

STOP JUDGING AND EVALUATING YOURSELF, for this is not your role. Above all, stop comparing yourself with other people. This produces feelings of pride or inferiority; sometimes, a mixture of both. I lead each of My children along a path that is uniquely tailor-made for him or her. Comparing is not only wrong; it is also meaningless.

Don't look for affirmation in the wrong places: your own evaluations, or those of other people. The only source of real affirmation is My unconditional Love. Many believers perceive Me as an unpleasable Judge, angrily searching out their faults and failures. Nothing could be farther from the truth! I died for your sins, so that I might *clothe you in My garments of salvation*. This is how I see you: *radiant in My robe of righteousness*. When I discipline you, it is never in anger or disgust; it is to prepare you for face-to-Face fellowship with Me throughout all eternity. Immerse yourself in My loving Presence. Be receptive to My affirmation, which flows continually from the throne of grace.

"Do not judge, and you will not be judged. Do not condemn, and you will not be condemned. Forgive, and you will be forgiven." LUKE 6:37

I will rejoice greatly in the LORD, my soul will exult in my God; for He has clothed me with garments of salvation, He has wrapped me with the robe of righteousness, as a bridegroom decks himself with a garland, and as a bride adorns herself with her jewels. —ISAIAH 61:10 NASB

My son, do not despise the LORD's discipline and do not resent his rebuke, because the LORD disciplines those he loves, as a father the son he delights in. —PROVERBS 3:11–12

February 29

You are on the right path. Listen more to Me, and less to your doubts. I am leading you along the way I designed just for you. Therefore, it is a lonely way, humanly speaking. But I go before you as well as alongside you, so you are never alone. Do not expect anyone to understand fully My ways with you, any more than you can comprehend My dealings with others. I am revealing to you the path of Life day by day, and moment by moment. As I said to My disciple Peter, so I repeat to you: *Follow Me.*

Your word is a lamp to my feet and a light for my path. —Psalm 119:105

Jesus answered, "If I want him to remain alive until I return, what is that to you? You must follow me." —John 21:22

March

"When he has brought out all his own, he goes on ahead of them, and his sheep follow him because they know his voice."

John 10:4

When something in your life or thoughts makes you anxious, come to Me and talk about it. Bring Me your *prayer and petition with thanksgiving*, saying: "Thank You, Jesus, for this opportunity to trust You more." Though the lessons of trust that I send to you come wrapped in difficulties, the benefits far outweigh the cost.

Well-developed trust will bring you many blessings, not the least of which is My Peace. I have promised to *keep you in perfect Peace* to the extent that you trust in Me. The world has it backwards, teaching that peace is the result of having enough money, possessions, insurance, and security systems. *My* Peace, however, is such an all-encompassing gift that it is independent of all circumstances. Though you lose everything else, if you gain My Peace you are rich indeed.

Do not be anxious about anything, but in everything, by prayer and petition, with thanksgiving, present your requests to God. —Philippians 4:6

You will keep in perfect peace him whose mind is steadfast, because he trusts in you. —Isaiah 26:3

Now may the Lord of peace Himself give you peace always in every way. The Lord be with you all.—2 Thessalonians 3:16 NKJV

I am the resurrection and the Life; all lasting Life emanates from Me. People search for life in many wrong ways: chasing after fleeting pleasures, accumulating possessions and wealth, trying to deny the inevitable effects of aging. Meanwhile, I freely offer abundant Life to everyone who turns toward Me. As you *come to Me and take My yoke upon you*, I fill you with My very Life. This is how I choose to live in the world and accomplish My purposes. This is also how I bless you with *Joy unspeakable and full of Glory*. The Joy is Mine, and the Glory is Mine; but I bestow them on you as you live in My Presence, inviting Me to live fully in you.

Jesus said to her, "I am the resurrection and the life. He who believes in me will live, even though he dies." —John 11:25

"Come to me, all you who are weary and burdened, and I will give you rest. Take my yoke upon you and learn from me, for I am gentle and humble in heart, and you will find rest for your souls." —Matthew 11:28–29

Whom having not seen, ye love; in whom, though now ye see him not, yet believing, ye rejoice with joy unspeakable and full of glory: Receiving the end of your faith, even the salvation of your souls. —1 Peter 1:8–9 KJV

March 3

I LOVE YOU FOR WHO YOU ARE, not for what you do. Many voices vie for control of your mind, especially when you sit in silence. You must learn to discern what is My voice and what is not. Ask My Spirit to give you this discernment. Many of My children run around in circles, trying to obey the various voices directing their lives. This results in fragmented, frustrating patterns of living. Do not fall into this trap. Walk closely with Me each moment, listening for My directives and enjoying My Companionship. Refuse to let other voices tie you up in knots. *My sheep know My voice and follow Me wherever I lead.*

As a prisoner for the Lord, then, I urge you to live a life worthy of the calling you have received. Be completely humble and gentle; be patient, bearing with one another in love. Make every effort to keep the unity of the Spirit through the bond of peace. There is one body and one Spirit—just as you were called to one hope when you were called—one Lord, one faith, one baptism; one God and Father of all, who is over all and through all and in all. —EPHESIANS 4:1–6

"When he has brought out all his own, he goes on ahead of them, and his sheep follow him because they know his voice." —JOHN 10:4

REFUSE TO WORRY! In this world there will always be something enticing you to worry. That is the nature of a fallen, fractured planet: Things are not as they should be. So the temptation to be anxious is constantly with you, trying to worm its way into your mind. The best defense is *continual communication with Me, richly seasoned with thanksgiving.* Awareness of My Presence fills your mind with Light and Peace, leaving no room for fear. This awareness lifts you up above your circumstances, enabling you to see problems from My perspective. Live close to Me! Together we can keep the wolves of worry at bay.

"Who of you by worrying can add a single hour to his life? Since you cannot do this very little thing, why do you worry about the rest?" —LUKE 12:25–26

Be joyful always; pray continually; give thanks in all circumstances, for this is God's will for you in Christ Jesus. —1 THESSALONIANS 5:16–18

March 5

Make friends with the problems in your life. Though many things feel random and wrong, remember that I am sovereign over everything. *I can fit everything into a pattern for good*, but only to the extent that you trust Me. Every problem can teach you something, transforming you little by little into the masterpiece I created you to be. The very same problem can become a stumbling block over which you fall, if you react with distrust and defiance. The choice is up to you, and you will have to choose many times each day whether to trust Me or defy Me.

The best way to befriend your problems is to thank Me for them. This simple act opens your mind to the possibility of benefits flowing from your difficulties. You can even give persistent problems nicknames, helping you to approach them with familiarity rather than with dread. The next step is to introduce them to Me, enabling Me to embrace them in My loving Presence. I will not necessarily remove your problems, but My wisdom is sufficient to bring good out of every one of them.

We are assured and know that [God being a partner in their labor] all things work together and are [fitting into a plan] for good to and for those who love God and are called according to [His] design and purpose. —Romans 8:28 AMP

But we preach Christ crucified: a stumbling block to Jews and foolishness to Gentiles, but to those whom God has called, both Jews and Greeks, Christ the power of God and the wisdom of God. —1 Corinthians 1:23–24

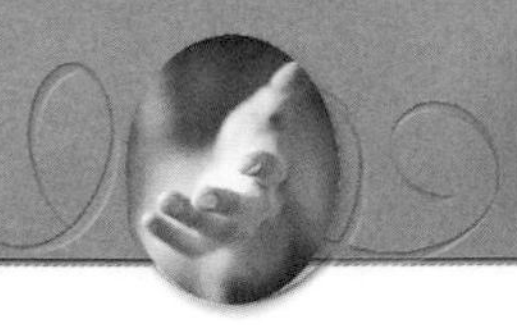

CONTINUE ON THIS PATH WITH ME, enjoying My Presence even in adversity. I am always before you, as well as alongside you. See Me beckoning to you: Come! Follow Me. The One who goes ahead of you, opening up the way, is the same One who stays close and never lets go of your hand. I am not subject to limitations of time or space. I am everywhere at every time, ceaselessly working on your behalf. That is why your best efforts are trusting Me and living close to Me.

Therefore he is able to save completely those who come to God through him, because he always lives to intercede for them. —HEBREWS 7:25

Trust in the LORD and do good; dwell in the land and enjoy safe pasture. Delight yourself in the LORD and he will give you the desires of your heart. —PSALM 37:3–4

March 7

Let Me help you through this day. The challenges you face are far too great for you to handle alone. You are keenly aware of your helplessness in the scheme of events you face. This awareness opens up a choice: to doggedly go it alone or to walk with Me in humble steps of dependence. Actually, this choice is continually before you, but difficulties highlight the decision-making process. So, *consider it all joy whenever you are enveloped in various trials*. These are gifts from Me, reminding you to rely on Me alone.

God is our refuge and strength,
an ever-present help in trouble. —Psalm 46:1

Because you are my help, I sing in the shadow of your wings. My soul clings to you; your right hand upholds me. —Psalm 63:7–8

Consider it wholly joyful, my brethren, whenever you are enveloped in or encounter trials of any sort or fall into various temptations. Be assured and understand that the trial and proving of your faith bring out endurance and steadfastness and patience. —James 1:2–3 AMP

SAVE YOUR BEST STRIVING FOR SEEKING MY FACE. I am constantly communicating with you. To find Me and hear My voice, you must seek Me above all else. Anything that you desire more than Me becomes an idol. When you are determined to get your own way, you blot Me out of your consciousness. Instead of single-mindedly pursuing some goal, talk with Me about it. Let the Light of My Presence shine on this pursuit, so that you can see it from My perspective. If the goal fits into My plans for you, I will help you reach it. If it is contrary to My will for you, I will gradually change the desire of your heart. *Seek Me first* and foremost; then the rest of your life will fall into place, piece by piece.

Look to the LORD and his strength; seek his face always. —1 CHRONICLES 16:11

There are many plans in a man's heart, nevertheless the LORD's counsel—that will stand. —PROVERBS 19:21 NKJV

"But seek first his kingdom and his righteousness, and all these things will be given to you as well." —MATTHEW 6:33

March 9

Rest in My radiant Presence. The world around you seems to spin faster and faster, till everything is a blur. Yet there is a cushion of calm at the center of your life, where you live in union with Me. Return to this soothing Center as often as you can, for this is where you are energized: filled with My Love, Joy, and Peace.

The world is a needy place; do not go there for sustenance. Instead, come to Me. Learn to depend on Me alone, and your weakness will become saturated with My Power. When you find your completeness in Me, you can help other people without using them to meet your own needs. Live in the Light of My Presence, and your light will shine brightly into the lives of others.

But the fruit of the Spirit is love, joy, peace, patience, kindness, goodness, faithfulness. —Galatians 5:22

He said to me, "My grace is sufficient for you, for my power is made perfect in weakness." Therefore I will boast all the more gladly about my weaknesses, so that Christ's power may rest on me. —2 Corinthians 12:9

No one has ever seen God; but if we love one another, God lives in us and his love is made complete in us. —1 John 4:12

YOU ARE MINE FOR ALL TIME—and beyond time, into eternity. No power can deny you your inheritance in heaven. I want you to realize how utterly secure you are! Even if you falter as you journey through life, I will never let go of your hand.

Knowing that your future is absolutely assured can free you to live abundantly today. I have prepared this day for you with the most tender concern and attention to detail. Instead of approaching the day as a blank page that you need to fill up, try living it in a responsive mode: being on the lookout for all that I am doing. This sounds easy, but it requires a deep level of trust, based on the knowledge that *My way is perfect.*

Praise be to the God and Father of our Lord Jesus Christ! In his great mercy he has given us new birth into a living hope through the resurrection of Jesus Christ from the dead, and into an inheritance that can never perish, spoil or fade—kept in heaven for you. —1 PETER 1:3–4

If the LORD delights in a man's way, he makes his steps firm; though he stumble, he will not fall, for the LORD upholds him with his hand. —PSALM 37:23–24

As for God, his way is perfect; the word of the LORD is flawless. He is a shield for all who take refuge in him. —PSALM 18:30

March 11

Walk by faith, not by sight. As you take steps of faith, depending on Me, I will show you how much I can do for you. If you live your life too safely, you will never know the thrill of seeing Me work through you. When I gave you My Spirit, I empowered you to live beyond your natural ability and strength. That's why it is so wrong to measure your energy level against the challenges ahead of you. The issue is not your strength but Mine, which is limitless. By walking close to Me, you can accomplish My purposes in My strength.

For we walk by faith, not by sight. —2 Corinthians 5:7 NKJV

Since we live by the Spirit, let us keep in step with the Spirit. —Galatians 5:25

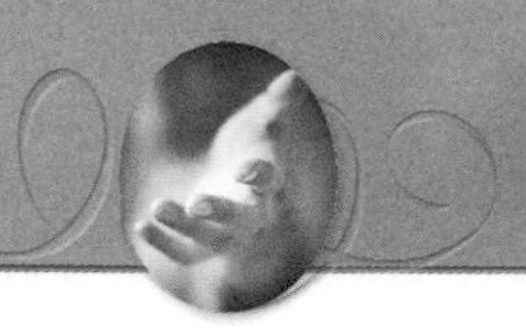

WAITING, TRUSTING, AND HOPING are intricately connected, like golden strands interwoven to form a strong chain. Trusting is the central strand, because it is the response from My children that I desire the most. Waiting and hoping embellish the central strand and strengthen the chain that connects you to Me. Waiting for Me to work, with your eyes on Me, is evidence that you really do trust Me. If you mouth the words "I trust You" while anxiously trying to make things go your way, your words ring hollow. Hoping is future-directed, connecting you to your inheritance in heaven. However, the benefits of hope fall fully on you in the present.

Because you are Mine, you don't just pass time in your waiting. You can wait expectantly, in hopeful trust. Keep your "antennae" out to pick up even the faintest glimmer of My Presence.

"Do not let your hearts be troubled. Trust in God; trust also in me." —JOHN 14:1

Wait for the LORD; be strong and take heart and wait for the LORD. —PSALM 27:14

God did this so that, by two unchangeable things in which it is impossible for God to lie, we who have fled to take hold of the hope offered to us may be greatly encouraged. We have this hope as an anchor for the soul, firm and secure. It enters the inner sanctuary behind the curtain, where Jesus, who went before us, has entered on our behalf. He has become a high priest forever, in the order of Melchizedek. —HEBREWS 6:18–20

LEARN TO LIVE above your circumstances. This requires focused time with Me, the *One who overcame the world*. Trouble and distress are woven into the very fabric of this perishing world. Only My Life in you can empower you to face this endless flow of problems with *good chee*r.

As you sit quietly in My Presence, I shine Peace into your troubled mind and heart. Little by little, you are freed from earthly shackles and lifted up above your circumstances. You gain My perspective on your life, enabling you to distinguish between what is important and what is not. Rest in My Presence, *receiving Joy that no one can take away from you*.

"These things I have spoken to you, that in Me you may have peace. In the world you will have tribulation; but be of good cheer, I have overcome the world." —JOHN 16:33 NKJV

"So with you: Now is your time of grief, but I will see you again and you will rejoice, and no one will take away your joy." —JOHN 16:22

Do not hesitate to receive Joy from Me, for I bestow it on you abundantly. The more you rest in My Presence, the more freely My blessings flow into you. In the Light of My Love, you are gradually *transformed from glory to glory.* It is through spending time with Me that you realize *how wide and long and high and deep is My Love for you.*

Sometimes the relationship I offer you seems too good to be true. I pour My very Life into you, and all you have to do is receive Me. In a world characterized by working and taking, the admonition to rest and receive seems too easy. There is a close connection between receiving and believing: As you trust Me more and more, you are able to receive Me and My blessings abundantly. *Be still, and know that I am God.*

But we all, with unveiled face, beholding as in a mirror the glory of the Lord, are being transformed into the same image from glory to glory, just as from the Lord, the Spirit. —2 Corinthians 3:18 NASB

So that Christ may dwell in your hearts through faith. And I pray that you, being rooted and established in love, may have power, together with all the saints, to grasp how wide and long and high and deep is the love of Christ, and to know this love that surpasses knowledge—that you may be filled to the measure of all the fullness of God. —Ephesians 3:17–19

"Be still, and know that I am God; I will be exalted among the nations, I will be exalted in the earth." —Psalm 46:10

March 15

LISTEN TO THE LOVE SONG that I am continually singing to you. *I take great delight in you. I rejoice over you with singing.* The voices of the world are a cacophony of chaos, pulling you this way and that. Don't listen to those voices; challenge them with My Word. Learn to take minibreaks from the world, finding a place to be still in My Presence and listen to My voice.

There is immense hidden treasure to be found through listening to Me. Though I pour out blessings upon you always, some of My richest blessings have to be actively sought. I love to reveal Myself to you, and your seeking heart opens you up to receive more of My disclosure. *Ask and it will be given to you; seek and you will find; knock and the door will be opened to you.*

The LORD your God is with you, he is mighty to save. He will take great delight in you, he will quiet you with his love, he will rejoice over you with singing. —ZEPHANIAH 3:17

"Ask and it will be given to you; seek and you will find; knock and the door will be opened to you." —MATTHEW 7:7

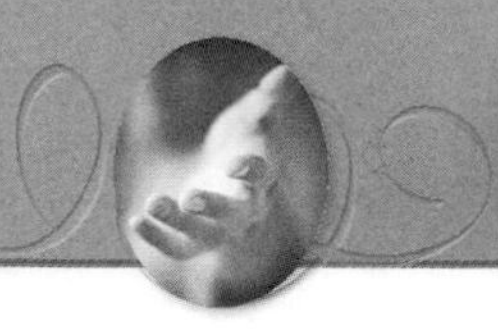

It is good that you recognize your weakness. That keeps you looking to Me, your Strength. Abundant life is not necessarily health and wealth; it is living in continual dependence on Me. Instead of trying to fit this day into a preconceived mold, relax and be on the lookout for what I am doing. This mind-set will free you to enjoy Me and to find what I have planned for you to do. This is far better than trying to make things go according to your own plan.

Don't take yourself so seriously. Lighten up and laugh with Me. You have Me on your side, so what are you worried about? I can equip you to do absolutely anything, as long as it is My will. The more difficult your day, the more I yearn to help you. Anxiety wraps you up in yourself, trapping you in your own thoughts. When you look to Me and whisper My Name, you break free and receive My help. Focus on Me, and you will find Peace in My Presence.

I have strength for all things in Christ Who empowers me [I am ready for anything and equal to anything through Him Who infuses inner strength into me; I am self-sufficient in Christ's sufficiency]. —Philippians 4:13 AMP

A cheerful heart is good medicine, but a crushed spirit dries up the bones. —Proverbs 17:22

March 17

Come to Me for understanding, since I know you far better than you know yourself. I comprehend you in all your complexity; *no detail of your life is hidden from Me.* I view you through eyes of grace, so don't be afraid of My intimate awareness. Allow the Light of My healing Presence to shine into the deepest recesses of your being—cleansing, healing, refreshing, and renewing you. Trust Me enough to accept the full forgiveness that I offer you continually. This great gift, which cost Me My Life, is yours for all eternity. Forgiveness is at the very core of My abiding Presence. *I will never leave you or forsake you.*

When no one else seems to understand you, simply draw closer to Me. Rejoice in the One who understands you completely and loves you perfectly. As I fill you with My Love, you become a reservoir of love, overflowing into the lives of other people.

O Lord, you have searched me and you know me. You know when I sit and when I rise; you perceive my thoughts from afar. You discern my going out and my lying down; you are familiar with all my ways. Before a word is on my tongue you know it completely, O Lord. —Psalm 139:1–4

Now it is God who makes both us and you stand firm in Christ. He anointed us, set his seal of ownership on us, and put his Spirit in our hearts as a deposit, guaranteeing what is to come. —2 Corinthians 1:21–22

"No one will be able to stand up against you all the days of your life. As I was with Moses, so I will be with you; I will never leave you nor forsake you." —Joshua 1:5

March 18

Trust Me one day at a time. This keeps you close to Me, responsive to My will. Trust is not a natural response, especially for those who have been deeply wounded. My Spirit within you is your resident Tutor, helping you in this supernatural endeavor. Yield to His gentle touch; be sensitive to His prompting.

Exert your will to trust Me in all circumstances. Don't let your need to understand distract you from My Presence. I will equip you to get through this day victoriously, as you live in deep dependence on Me. *Tomorrow is busy worrying about itself*; *don't get tangled up in its worry-webs*. Trust Me one day at a time.

O Lord Almighty, blessed is the man who trusts in you. —Psalm 84:12

Do you not know that your body is a temple of the Holy Spirit, who is in you, whom you have received from God? You are not your own. —1 Corinthians 6:19

Blessed is the man who trusts in the Lord, and whose hope is the Lord. —Jeremiah 17:7 NKJV

"Therefore do not worry about tomorrow, for tomorrow will worry about itself. Each day has enough trouble of its own." —Matthew 6:34

March 19

I speak to you from the depths of your being. Hear Me saying soothing words of Peace, assuring you of My Love. Do not listen to voices of accusation, for they are not from Me. I speak to you in love-tones, lifting you up. My Spirit convicts cleanly, without crushing words of shame. Let the Spirit take charge of your mind, combing out tangles of deception. Be transformed by the truth that I live within you.

The Light of My Presence is shining upon you, in benedictions of Peace. Let My Light shine in you; don't dim it with worries or fears. Holiness is letting Me live through you. Since I dwell in you, you are fully equipped to be holy. Pause before responding to people or situations, giving My Spirit space to act through you. Hasty words and actions leave no room for Me; this is atheistic living. I want to inhabit all your moments—gracing your thoughts, words, and behavior.

Therefore, there is now no condemnation for those who are in Christ Jesus, because through Christ Jesus the law of the Spirit of life set me free from the law of sin and death. —Romans 8:1–2

To them God has chosen to make known among the Gentiles the glorious riches of this mystery, which is Christ in you, the hope of glory. —Colossians 1:27

Do you not know that your body is a temple of the Holy Spirit, who is in you, whom you have received from God? You are not your own. —1 Corinthians 6:19

THANK ME FOR THE GLORIOUS GIFT OF MY SPIRIT. This is like priming the pump of a well. As you bring Me the sacrifice of thanksgiving, regardless of your feelings, My Spirit is able to work more freely within you. This produces more thankfulness and more freedom, until you are overflowing with gratitude.

I shower blessings on you daily, but sometimes you don't perceive them. When your mind is stuck on a negative focus, you see neither Me nor My gifts. In faith, thank Me for whatever is preoccupying your mind. This will clear the blockage so that you can find Me.

Now it is God who has made us for this very purpose and has given us the Spirit as a deposit, guaranteeing what is to come. —2 CORINTHIANS 5:5

Now the Lord is the Spirit, and where the Spirit of the Lord is, there is freedom. —2 CORINTHIANS 3:17

Sacrifice thank offerings to God, fulfill your vows to the Most High. —PSALM 50:14

March 21

Trust Me and don't be afraid, for I am your Strength and Song. Think what it means to have Me as your Strength. I spoke the universe into existence; My Power is absolutely unlimited! Human weakness, consecrated to Me, is like a magnet, drawing My Power into your neediness. However, fear can block the flow of My Strength into you. Instead of trying to fight your fears, concentrate on trusting Me. When you relate to Me in confident trust, there is no limit to how much I can strengthen you.

Remember that I am also your Song. I want you to share My Joy, living in conscious awareness of My Presence. Rejoice as we journey together toward heaven; join Me in singing My Song.

"Surely God is my salvation; I will trust and not be afraid. The Lord, the Lord, is my strength and my song; he has become my salvation." With joy you will draw water from the wells of salvation. —Isaiah 12:2–3

Surely you have granted him eternal blessings and made him glad with the joy of your presence. —Psalm 21:6

March 22

REJOICE AND BE THANKFUL! As you walk with Me through this day, practice trusting and thanking Me all along the way. Trust is the channel through which My Peace flows into you. Thankfulness lifts you up above your circumstances.

I do My greatest works through people with grateful, trusting hearts. Rather than planning and evaluating, practice trusting and thanking Me continually. This is a paradigm shift that will revolutionize your life.

Rejoice in the Lord always. I will say it again: Rejoice!—PHILIPPIANS 4:4

Come, let us sing for joy to the LORD; let us shout aloud to the Rock of our salvation. Let us come before him with thanksgiving and extol him with music and song. —PSALM 95:1–2

Those who know your name will trust in you, for you, LORD, have never forsaken those who seek you. —PSALM 9:10

March 23

I am a God of both intricate detail and overflowing abundance. When you entrust the details of your life to Me, you are surprised by how thoroughly I answer your petitions. I take pleasure in hearing your prayers, so feel free to bring Me all your requests. The more you pray, the more answers you can receive. Best of all, your faith is strengthened as you see how precisely I respond to your specific prayers.

Because I am infinite in all My ways, you need not fear that I will run out of resources. *Abundance* is at the very heart of who I am. Come to Me in joyful expectation of receiving all you need—and sometimes much more! I delight in showering blessings on My beloved children. Come to Me with open hands and heart, ready to receive all I have for you.

How priceless is your unfailing love! Both high and low among men find refuge in the shadow of your wings. They feast on the abundance of your house; you give them drink from your river of delights. For with you is the fountain of life; in your light we see light. —Psalm 36:7–9

"I will bless her with abundant provisions; her poor will I satisfy with food." —Psalm 132:15

When they had all had enough to eat, he said to his disciples, "Gather the pieces that are left over. Let nothing be wasted." So they gathered them and filled twelve baskets with the pieces of the five barley loaves left over by those who had eaten. —John 6:12–13

THIS IS A TIME in your life when you must learn to let go: of loved ones, of possessions, of control. In order to let go of something that is precious to you, you need to rest in My Presence, where you are complete. Take time to bask in the Light of My Love. As you relax more and more, your grasping hand gradually opens up, releasing your prized possession into My care.

You can feel secure, even in the midst of cataclysmic changes, through awareness of My continual Presence. The One who never leaves you is the same One who never changes: *I am the same yesterday, today, and forever.* As you release more and more things into My care, remember that I never let go of your hand. Herein lies your security, which no one and no circumstance can take from you.

Blessed are those who have learned to acclaim you, who walk in the light of your presence, O Lord. —Psalm 89:15

Jesus Christ is the same yesterday and today and forever. —Hebrews 13:8

"For I am the Lord, your God, who takes hold of your right hand and says to you, Do not fear; I will help you." —Isaiah 41:13

MARCH 25

LET THANKFULNESS TEMPER ALL YOUR THOUGHTS. A thankful mind-set keeps you in touch with Me. I hate it when My children grumble, casually despising My sovereignty. Thankfulness is a safeguard against this deadly sin. Furthermore, a grateful attitude becomes a grid through which you perceive life. Gratitude enables you to see the Light of My Presence shining on all your circumstances. Cultivate a thankful heart, for this glorifies Me and fills you with Joy.

And do not grumble, as some of them did—and were killed by the destroying angel. —1 CORINTHIANS 10:10

Therefore, since we are receiving a kingdom that cannot be shaken, let us be thankful, and so worship God acceptably with reverence and awe, for our "God is a consuming fire." —HEBREWS 12:28–29

March 26

Waiting on Me means directing your attention to Me in hopeful anticipation of what I will do. It entails trusting Me with every fiber of your being, instead of trying to figure things out yourself. Waiting on Me is the way I designed you to live: all day, every day. I created you to stay conscious of Me as you go about your daily duties.

I have promised many blessings to those who wait on Me: *renewed strength*, living above one's circumstances, resurgence of hope, awareness of My continual Presence. Waiting on Me enables you to glorify Me by living in deep dependence on Me, ready to do My will. It also helps you to enjoy Me; *in My Presence is fullness of Joy.*

I say to myself, "The Lord is my portion; therefore I will wait for him." The Lord is good to those whose hope is in him, to the one who seeks him; it is good to wait quietly for the salvation of the Lord. —Lamentations 3:24–26

But those who hope in the Lord will renew their strength. They will soar on wings like eagles; they will run and not grow weary, they will walk and not be faint. —Isaiah 40:31

You will show me the path of life; in Your presence is fullness of joy; at Your right hand are pleasures forevermore. —Psalm 16:11 NKJV

March 27

Be still in My Presence, even though countless tasks clamor for your attention. Nothing is as important as spending time with Me. While you wait in My Presence, I do My best work within you: *transforming you by the renewing of your mind.* If you skimp on this time with Me, you may plunge headlong into the wrong activities, missing the richness of what I have planned for you.

Do not seek Me primarily for what I can give you. Remember that I, the Giver, am infinitely greater than any gift I might impart to you. Though I delight in blessing My children, I am deeply grieved when My blessings become idols in their hearts. Anything can be an idol if it distracts you from Me as your *First Love.* When I am the ultimate Desire of your heart, you are safe from the danger of idolatry. As you wait in My Presence, enjoy the greatest gift of all: *Christ in you, the hope of Glory*!

Do not conform any longer to the pattern of this world, but be transformed by the renewing of your mind. Then you will be able to test and approve what God's will is—his good, pleasing and perfect will. —Romans 12:2

"Yet I hold this against you: You have forsaken your first love." —Revelation 2:4

To them God has chosen to make known among the Gentiles the glorious riches of this mystery, which is Christ in you, the hope of glory. —Colossians 1:27

I AM A GOD WHO GIVES and gives and gives. When I died for you on the cross, I held back nothing; I poured out My Life *like a drink offering*. Because giving is inherent in My nature, I search for people who are able to receive in full measure. To increase your intimacy with Me, the two traits you need the most are receptivity and attentiveness. Receptivity is opening up your innermost being to be filled with My abundant riches. Attentiveness is directing your gaze to Me: searching for Me in all your moments. It is possible to *stay your mind on Me*, as the prophet Isaiah wrote. Through such attentiveness you receive a glorious gift: My perfect Peace.

But even if I am being poured out like a drink offering on the sacrifice and service coming from your faith, I am glad and rejoice with all of you. —PHILIPPIANS 2:17

"I tell you the truth, anyone who will not receive the kingdom of God like a little child will never enter it." —MARK 10:15

You will keep him in perfect peace, whose mind is stayed on You, because he trusts in You. —ISAIAH 26:3 NKJV

March 29

Stop trying to work things out before their times have come. Accept the limitations of living one day at a time. When something comes to your attention, ask Me whether or not it is part of today's agenda. If it isn't, release it into My care and go on about today's duties. When you follow this practice, there will be a beautiful simplicity about your life: *a time for everything, and everything in its time.*

A life lived close to Me is not complicated or cluttered. When your focus is on My Presence, many things that once troubled you lose their power over you. Though the world around you is messy and confusing, remember that *I have overcome the world. I have told you these things, so that in Me you may have Peace.*

There is a time for everything, and a season for every activity under heaven. —Ecclesiastes 3:1

"I have told you these things, so that in me you may have peace. In this world you will have trouble. But take heart! I have overcome the world." —John 16:33

I AM TAKING CARE OF YOU. Trust Me at all times. Trust Me in all circumstances. *Trust Me with all your heart.* When you are weary and everything seems to be going wrong, you can still utter these four words: "I trust You, Jesus." By doing so, you release matters into My control, and you fall back into the security of *My everlasting arms.*

Before you arise from your bed in the morning, I have already arranged the events of your day. Every day provides many opportunities for you to learn My ways and grow closer to Me. Signs of My Presence brighten even the dullest day when you have eyes that really see. Search for Me as for hidden treasure. *I will be found by you.*

Trust in the LORD with all your heart and lean not on your own understanding. —PROVERBS 3:5

The eternal God is your refuge, and underneath are the everlasting arms. He will drive out your enemy before you, saying, "Destroy him!" —DEUTERONOMY 33:27

"You will seek me and find me when you seek me with all your heart. I will be found by you," declares the LORD, "and will bring you back from captivity. I will gather you from all the nations and places where I have banished you," declares the LORD, "and will bring you back to the place from which I carried you into exile." —JEREMIAH 29:13–14

March 31

Taste and see that I am good. The more intimately you experience Me, the more convinced you become of My goodness. I am *the Living One who sees you* and longs to participate in your life. I am training you to find Me in each moment and to be a channel of My loving Presence. Sometimes My blessings come to you in mysterious ways: through pain and trouble. At such times you can know My goodness only through your trust in Me. Understanding will fail you, but trust will keep you close to Me.

Thank Me for the gift of My Peace, a gift of such immense proportions that you cannot fathom its depth or breadth. When I appeared to My disciples after the resurrection, it was Peace that I communicated first of all. I knew this was their deepest need: to calm their fears and clear their minds. I also speak Peace to you, for I know your anxious thoughts. Listen to Me! Tune out other voices, so that you can hear Me more clearly. I designed you to dwell in Peace all day, every day. Draw near to Me; receive My Peace.

Taste and see that the Lord is good; blessed is the man who takes refuge in him. —Psalm 34:8

So she called the name of the Lord Who spoke to her . . . [the Living One Who sees me]. —Genesis 16:13–14 AMP

On the evening of that first day of the week, when the disciples were together, with the doors locked for fear of the Jews, Jesus came and stood among them and said, "Peace be with you!" —John 20:19

Let the peace of Christ rule in your hearts, since as members of one body you were called to peace. And be thankful. —Colossians 3:15

April

In all your ways acknowledge him,
and he will make your paths straight.

PROVERBS 3:6

April 1

I AM CALLING YOU to a life of constant communion with Me. Basic training includes learning to live above your circumstances, even while interacting on that cluttered plane of life. You yearn for a simplified lifestyle, so that your communication with Me can be uninterrupted. But I challenge you to relinquish the fantasy of an uncluttered world. Accept each day just as it comes, and find Me in the midst of it all.

Talk with Me about every aspect of your day, including your feelings. Remember that your ultimate goal is not to control or fix everything around you; it is to keep communing with Me. A successful day is one in which you have stayed in touch with Me, even if many things remain undone at the end of the day. Do not let your to-do list (written or mental) become an idol directing your life. Instead, ask My Spirit to guide you moment by moment. He will keep you close to Me.

Pray continually. —1 THESSALONIANS 5:17

In all your ways acknowledge him, and he will make your paths straight. —PROVERBS 3:6

April 2

I HAVE PROMISED *to meet all your needs according to My glorious riches.* Your deepest, most constant need is for My Peace. I have planted Peace in the garden of your heart, where I live; but there are weeds growing there too: pride, worry, selfishness, unbelief. I am the Gardener, and I am working to rid your heart of those weeds. I do My work in various ways. When you sit quietly with Me, I shine the Light of My Presence directly into your heart. In this heavenly Light, Peace grows abundantly and weeds shrivel up. I also send trials into your life. When you trust Me in the midst of trouble, Peace flourishes and weeds die away. Thank Me for troublesome situations; the Peace they can produce *far outweighs* the trials you endure.

And my God will meet all your needs according to his glorious riches in Christ Jesus. —PHILIPPIANS 4:19

For our light and momentary troubles are achieving for us an eternal glory that far outweighs them all. —2 CORINTHIANS 4:17

April 3

IN ME YOU HAVE EVERYTHING. In Me you are complete. Your capacity to experience Me is increasing, through My removal of debris and clutter from your heart. As your yearning for Me increases, other desires are gradually lessening. Since I am infinite and abundantly accessible to you, desiring Me above all else is the best way to live.

It is impossible for you to have a need that I cannot meet. After all, I created you and everything that is. The world is still at My beck and call, though it often appears otherwise. Do not be fooled by appearances. *Things that are visible are brief and fleeting, while things that are invisible are everlasting.*

Now to him who is able to do immeasurably more than all we ask or imagine, according to his power that is at work within us. —EPHESIANS 3:20

Since we consider and look not to the things that are seen but to the things that are unseen; for the things that are visible are temporal (brief and fleeting), but the things that are invisible are deathless and everlasting. —2 CORINTHIANS 4:18 AMP

I MEET YOU in the stillness of your soul. It is there that I seek to commune with you. A person who is open to My Presence is exceedingly precious to Me. My eyes *search to and fro throughout the earth*, looking for one whose heart is seeking Me. I see you trying to find Me; our mutual search results in joyful fulfillment.

Stillness of soul is increasingly rare in this world addicted to noise and speed. I am pleased with your desire to create a quiet space where you and I can meet. Don't be discouraged by the difficulty of achieving this goal. I monitor all your efforts and am blessed by each of your attempts to seek My Face.

"Be still before the LORD, all mankind, because he has roused himself from his holy dwelling." —ZECHARIAH 2:13

For the eyes of the LORD run to and fro throughout the whole earth, to show Himself strong on behalf of those whose heart is loyal to Him. In this you have done foolishly; therefore from now on you shall have wars. —2 CHRONICLES 16:9 NKJV

He makes me to lie down in green pastures; He leads me beside the still waters. He restores my soul; He leads me in the paths of righteousness for His name's sake. —PSALM 23:2–3 NKJV

April 5

Let Me fill you with my Love, Joy, and Peace. These are Glory-gifts, flowing from my living Presence. Though you are an *earthen vessel*, I designed you to be filled with heavenly contents. Your weakness is not a deterrent to being filled with My Spirit; on the contrary, it provides an opportunity for My Power to shine forth more brightly.

As you go through this day, trust Me to provide the strength that you need moment by moment. Don't waste energy wondering whether you are adequate for today's journey. My Spirit within you is more than sufficient to handle whatever this day may bring. That is the basis for your confidence! *In quietness* (spending time alone with Me) *and confident trust* (relying on My sufficiency) *is your strength.*

But we have this treasure in earthen vessels, so that the surpassing greatness of the power will be of God and not from ourselves. —2 Corinthians 4:7 NASB

This is what the Sovereign Lord, the Holy One of Israel, says: "In repentance and rest is your salvation, in quietness and trust is your strength, but you would have none of it." —Isaiah 30:15

Bring Me the sacrifice of thanksgiving. Take nothing for granted, not even the rising of the sun. Before Satan tempted Eve in the Garden of Eden, thankfulness was as natural as breathing. Satan's temptation involved pointing Eve to the one thing that was forbidden her. The garden was filled with luscious, desirable fruits, but Eve focused on the one fruit she couldn't have rather than being thankful for the many good things freely available. This negative focus darkened her mind, and she succumbed to temptation.

When you focus on what you don't have or on situations that displease you, your mind also becomes darkened. You take for granted life, salvation, sunshine, flowers, and countless other gifts from Me. You look for what is wrong and refuse to enjoy life until that is "fixed."

When you approach Me with thanksgiving, the Light of My Presence pours into you, transforming you through and through. *Walk in the Light* with Me by practicing the discipline of thanksgiving.

I will offer to You the sacrifice of thanksgiving, and will call upon the name of the Lord. —Psalm 116:17 NKJV

The woman said to the serpent, "We may eat fruit from the trees in the garden, but God did say, 'You must not eat fruit from the tree that is in the middle of the garden, and you must not touch it, or you will die.'" "You will not surely die," the serpent said to the woman. —Genesis 3:2–4

But if we walk in the light, as he is in the light, we have fellowship with one another, and the blood of Jesus, his Son, purifies us from all sin. —1 John 1:7

April 7

I AM THE POTTER; you are My clay. I designed you before the foundation of the world. I arrange the events of each day to form you into this preconceived pattern. My everlasting Love is at work in every event of your life. On some days your will and Mine flow smoothly together. You tend to feel in control of your life when our wills are in harmony. On other days you feel as if you are swimming upstream, against the current of My purposes. When that happens, stop and seek My Face. The opposition you feel may be from Me, or it may be from the evil one.

Talk with Me about what you are experiencing. Let My Spirit guide you through treacherous waters. As you move through the turbulent stream with Me, let circumstances mold you into the one I desire you to be. Say *yes* to your Potter as you go through this day.

Yet, O LORD, you are our Father. We are the clay, you are the potter; we are all the work of your hand. —ISAIAH 64:8

My heart says of you, "Seek his face!" Your face, LORD, I will seek. —PSALM 27:8

April 8

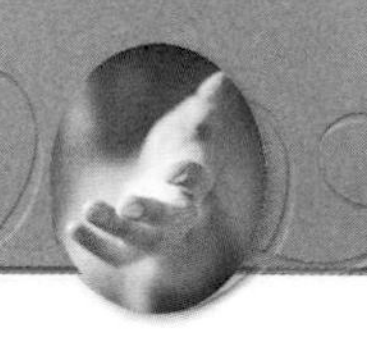

I AM WITH YOU AND FOR YOU, your constant Companion and Provider. The question is whether you are with Me and for Me. Though I never leave you, you can essentially "leave" Me by ignoring Me: thinking or acting as if I am not with you. When you feel distance in our relationship, you know where the problem lies. My Love for you is constant; *I am the same yesterday, today, and forever.* It is you who change like shifting sand, letting circumstances toss you this way and that.

When you feel far from Me, whisper My Name. This simple act, done in childlike faith, opens your heart to My Presence. Speak to Me in love tones; prepare to receive My Love, which flows eternally from the cross. I am delighted when you open yourself to My loving Presence.

"I am with you and will watch over you wherever you go, and I will bring you back to this land. I will not leave you until I have done what I have promised you." —GENESIS 28:15

What, then, shall we say in response to this? If God is for us, who can be against us? —ROMANS 8:31

Jesus Christ is the same yesterday and today and forever. —HEBREWS 13:8

April 9

You are Mine for all time; *nothing can separate you from My Love.* Since I have invested My very Life in you, be well assured that I will also take care of you. When your mind goes into neutral and your thoughts flow freely, you tend to feel anxious and alone. Your focus becomes problem solving. To get your mind back into gear, just turn toward Me, bringing yourself and your problems into My Presence.

Many problems vanish instantly in the Light of My Love, because you realize you are never alone. Other problems may remain, but they become secondary to knowing Me and rejoicing in the relationship I so freely offer you. Each moment you can choose to practice My Presence or to practice the presence of problems.

For I am convinced that neither death nor life, neither angels nor demons, neither the present nor the future, nor any powers, neither height nor depth, nor anything else in all creation, will be able to separate us from the love of God that is in Christ Jesus our Lord. —Romans 8:38–39

The Lord replied, "My Presence will go with you, and I will give you rest." —Exodus 33:14

TRUST ME IN EVERY DETAIL of your life. Nothing is random in My kingdom. *Everything that happens fits into a pattern for good, to those who love Me.* Instead of trying to analyze the intricacies of the pattern, focus your energy on trusting Me and thanking Me at all times. Nothing is wasted when you walk close to Me. Even your mistakes and sins can be recycled into something good, through My transforming grace.

While you were still living in darkness, I began to shine the Light of My Presence into your sin-stained life. Finally, I *lifted you up out of the mire into My marvelous Light.* Having sacrificed My very Life for you, I can be trusted in every facet of your life.

"But blessed is the man who trusts in the LORD, whose confidence is in him." —JEREMIAH 17:7

We are assured and know that [God being a partner in their labor] all things work together and are [fitting into a plan] for good to and for those who love God and are called according to [His] design and purpose. —ROMANS 8:28 AMP

He drew me up out of a horrible pit [a pit of tumult and of destruction], out of the miry clay (froth and slime), and set my feet upon a rock, steadying my steps and establishing my goings. —PSALM 40:2 AMP

But you are a chosen generation, a royal priesthood, a holy nation, His own special people, that you may proclaim the praises of Him who called you out of darkness into His marvelous light. —1 PETER 2:9 NKJV

April 11

This is the day that I have made. Rejoice and be glad in it. Begin the day with open hands of faith, ready to receive all that I am pouring into this brief portion of your life. Be careful not to complain about anything, even the weather, since I am the Author of your circumstances. The best way to handle unwanted situations is to thank Me for them. This act of faith frees you from resentment and frees Me to work My ways into the situation, so that good emerges from it.

To find Joy in this day, you must live within its boundaries. I knew what I was doing when I divided time into twenty-four-hour segments. I understand human frailty, and I know that you can bear the weight of only one day at a time. Do not worry about tomorrow or get stuck in the past. There is abundant Life in My Presence today.

This is the day the Lord has made; let us rejoice and be glad in it. —Psalm 118:24

Brothers, I do not consider myself yet to have taken hold of it. But one thing I do: Forgetting what is behind and straining toward what is ahead, I press on toward the goal to win the prize for which God has called me heavenward in Christ Jesus. —Philippians 3:13–14

Trusting Me is a moment-by-moment choice. My people have not always understood this truth. After I performed miracles in the wilderness, My chosen children trusted Me intensely—but only temporarily. Soon the grumbling began again, testing My patience to the utmost.

Isn't it often the same way with you? You trust Me when things go well, when you see Me working on your behalf. This type of trust flows readily within you, requiring no exertion of your will. When things go wrong, your trust-flow slows down and solidifies. You are forced to choose between trusting Me intentionally or rebelling: resenting My ways with you. This choice constitutes a fork in the road. Stay on the path of Life with Me, enjoying My Presence. Choose to trust Me in all circumstances.

Then Moses led Israel from the Red Sea and they went into the Desert of Shur. For three days they traveled in the desert without finding water. When they came to Marah, they could not drink its water because it was bitter. (That is why the place is called Marah.) So the people grumbled against Moses, saying, "What are we to drink?" Then Moses cried out to the Lord, and the Lord showed him a piece of wood. He threw it into the water, and the water became sweet. There the Lord made a decree and a law for them, and there he tested them. —Exodus 15:22–25

But I trust in you, O Lord; I say, "You are my God." —Psalm 31:14

April 13

When I give you no special guidance, stay where you are. Concentrate on doing your everyday tasks in awareness of My Presence with you. The Joy of My Presence will shine on you, as you do everything for Me. Thus you invite Me into every aspect of your life. Through collaborating with Me in all things, you allow My Life to merge with yours. This is the secret not only of joyful living but also of victorious living. I designed you to depend on Me moment by moment, recognizing that *apart from Me you can do nothing.*

Be thankful for quiet days, when nothing special seems to be happening. Instead of being bored by the lack of action, use times of routine to seek My Face. Although this is an invisible transaction, it speaks volumes in spiritual realms. Moreover, you are richly blessed when you walk trustingly with Me through the routines of your day.

Whatever you do, work at it with all your heart, as working for the Lord, not for men. —Colossians 3:23

"I am the vine; you are the branches. If a man remains in me and I in him, he will bear much fruit; apart from me you can do nothing." —John 15:5

Look to the Lord *and his strength; seek his face always.* —Psalm 105:4

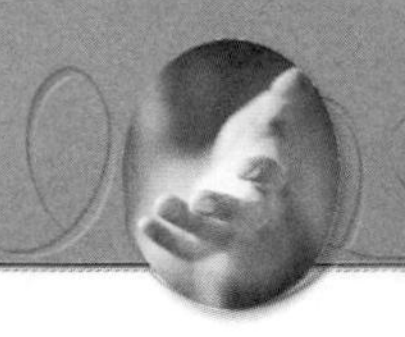

HEAVEN IS both present and future. As you walk along your life-path holding My hand, you are already in touch with the essence of heaven: nearness to Me. You can also find many hints of heaven along your pathway, because the earth is radiantly alive with My Presence. Shimmering sunshine awakens your heart, gently reminding you of My brilliant Light. Birds and flowers, trees and skies evoke praises to My holy Name. Keep your eyes and ears fully open as you journey with Me.

At the end of your life-path is an entrance to heaven. Only I know when you will reach that destination, but I am preparing you for it each step of the way. The absolute certainty of your heavenly home gives you Peace and Joy, to help you along your journey. You know that you will reach your home in My perfect timing: not one moment too soon or too late. Let the hope of heaven encourage you, as you walk along the path of Life with Me.

But Christ has indeed been raised from the dead, the firstfruits of those who have fallen asleep. For since death came through a man, the resurrection of the dead comes also through a man. For as in Adam all die, so in Christ all will be made alive. But each in his own turn: Christ, the firstfruits; then, when he comes, those who belong to him. —1 CORINTHIANS 15:20–23

We have this hope as an anchor for the soul, firm and secure. It enters the inner sanctuary behind the curtain. —HEBREWS 6:19

April 15

TRUST ME, and don't be afraid. Many things feel out of control. Your routines are not running smoothly. You tend to feel more secure when your life is predictable. Let Me lead you to *the rock that is higher than you* and your circumstances. *Take refuge in the shelter of My wings*, where you are absolutely secure.

When you are shaken out of your comfortable routines, grip My hand tightly and look for growth opportunities. Instead of bemoaning the loss of your comfort, accept the challenge of something new. *I lead you on from glory to glory*, making you fit for My kingdom. Say *yes* to the ways I work in your life. Trust Me, and don't be afraid.

Surely God is my salvation; I will trust and not be afraid. The LORD, the LORD, is my strength and my song; he has become my salvation. —ISAIAH 12:2

From the ends of the earth I call to you, I call as my heart grows faint; lead me to the rock that is higher than I. For you have been my refuge, a strong tower against the foe. I long to dwell in your tent forever and take refuge in the shelter of your wings. —PSALM 61:2–4

But we all, with unveiled face, beholding as in a mirror the glory of the Lord, are being transformed into the same image from glory to glory, just as by the Spirit of the Lord. —2 CORINTHIANS 3:18 NKJV

April 16

I AM CALLING YOU to a life of thankfulness. I want all your moments to be punctuated with thanksgiving. The basis for your gratitude is My sovereignty. I am the Creator and Controller of the universe. Heaven and earth are filled with My glorious Presence.

When you criticize or complain, you are acting as if you think *you* could run the world better than I do. From your limited human perspective, it may look as if I'm mismanaging things. But you don't know what I know or see what I see. If I pulled back the curtain to allow you to view heavenly realms, you would understand much more. However, I have designed you to *live by faith, not by sight*. I lovingly shield you from knowing the future or seeing into the spirit world. Acknowledge My sovereignty by *giving thanks in all circumstances.*

And they were calling to one another: "Holy, holy, holy is the LORD Almighty; the whole earth is full of his glory." —ISAIAH 6:3

We live by faith, not by sight. —2 CORINTHIANS 5:7

Give thanks in all circumstances, for this is God's will for you in Christ Jesus. —1 THESSALONIANS 5:18

April 17

I AM TRAINING YOU IN STEADINESS. Too many things interrupt your awareness of Me. I know that you live in a world of sight and sound, but you must not be a slave to those stimuli. Awareness of Me can continue in all circumstances, no matter what happens. This is the steadiness I desire for you.

Don't let unexpected events throw you off course. Rather, respond calmly and confidently, remembering that I am with you. As soon as something grabs your attention, talk with Me about it. Thus I share your joys and your problems; I help you cope with whatever is before you. This is how I live in you and work through you. This is the way of Peace.

He will have no fear of bad news; his heart is steadfast, trusting in the LORD. —PSALM 112:7

"Fear not, for I am with you; be not dismayed, for I am your God. I will strengthen you, Yes, I will help you, I will uphold you with My righteous right hand." —ISAIAH 41:10 NKJV

Peace is My continual gift to you. It flows abundantly from My throne of grace. Just as the Israelites could not store up manna for the future but had to gather it daily, so it is with My Peace. The day-by-day collecting of manna kept My people aware of their dependence on Me. Similarly, I give you sufficient Peace for the present, when you come to me *by prayer and petition with thanksgiving.* If I gave you permanent Peace, independent of My Presence, you might fall into the trap of self-sufficiency. May that never be!

I have designed you to need Me moment by moment. As your awareness of your neediness increases, so does your realization of My abundant sufficiency. *I can meet every one of your needs* without draining My resources at all. *Approach My throne of grace with bold confidence*, receiving My Peace with a thankful heart.

Moses said to them, "It is the bread the Lord has given you to eat. This is what the Lord has commanded: 'Each one is to gather as much as he needs.' . . . No one is to keep any of it until morning." —Exodus 16:15–16, 19

Do not be anxious about anything, but in everything, by prayer and petition, with thanksgiving, present your requests to God. And the peace of God, which transcends all understanding, will guard your hearts and your minds in Christ Jesus. . . . And my God will meet all your needs according to his glorious riches in Christ Jesus. —Philippians 4:6–7, 19

Let us then approach the throne of grace with confidence, so that we may receive mercy and find grace to help us in our time of need. —Hebrews 4:16

April 19

I LOVE YOU regardless of how well you are performing. Sometimes you feel uneasy, wondering if you are doing enough to be worthy of My Love. No matter how exemplary your behavior, the answer to that question will always be no. Your performance and My Love are totally different issues, which you need to sort out. *I love you with an everlasting Love* that flows out from eternity without limits or conditions. *I have clothed you in My robe of righteousness*, and this is an eternal transaction: Nothing and no one can reverse it. Therefore, your accomplishment as a Christian has no bearing on My Love for you. Even your ability to assess how well you are doing on a given day is flawed. Your limited human perspective and the condition of your body, with its mercurial variations, distort your evaluations.

Bring your performance anxiety to Me, and receive in its place *My unfailing Love.* Try to stay conscious of My loving Presence with you in all that you do, and I will direct your steps.

The LORD appeared to us in the past, saying: "I have loved you with an everlasting love; I have drawn you with loving-kindness." —JEREMIAH 31:3

I delight greatly in the LORD; my soul rejoices in my God. For he has clothed me with garments of salvation and arrayed me in a robe of righteousness, as a bridegroom adorns his head like a priest, and as a bride adorns herself with her jewels. —ISAIAH 61:10

Let your face shine on your servant; save me in your unfailing love. —PSALM 31:16

Let them give thanks to the LORD for his unfailing love and his wonderful deeds for men. —PSALM 107:8

DO NOT BE AFRAID, for I am with you. Hear Me saying *Peace, be still* to your restless heart. No matter what happens, *I will never leave you or forsake you*. Let this assurance soak into your mind and heart, until you overflow with Joy. *Though the earth give way and the mountains fall into the heart of the sea*, you need not fear!

The media relentlessly proclaim bad news: for breakfast, lunch, and dinner. A steady diet of their fare will sicken you. Instead of focusing on fickle, ever-changing news broadcasts, tune in to the living Word—the One who is always the same. Let Scripture saturate your mind and heart, and you will walk steadily along the path of Life. Even though you don't know what will happen tomorrow, you can be absolutely sure of your ultimate destination. *I hold you by your right hand, and afterward I will take you into Glory.*

Then He arose and rebuked the wind, and said to the sea, "Peace, be still!" And the wind ceased and there was a great calm. —MARK 4:39 NKJV

Be strong and courageous. Do not be afraid or terrified because of them, for the LORD your God goes with you; he will never leave you nor forsake you. —DEUTERONOMY 31:6

Therefore we will not fear, though the earth give way and the mountains fall into the heart of the sea. —PSALM 46:2

Yet I am always with you; you hold me by my right hand. You guide me with your counsel, and afterward you will take me into glory. —PSALM 73:23–24

Let Me control your mind. The mind is the most restless, unruly part of mankind. Long after you have learned the discipline of holding your tongue, your thoughts defy your will and set themselves up against Me. Man is the pinnacle of My creation, and the human mind is wondrously complex. I risked all by granting you freedom to think for yourself. This is godlike privilege, forever setting you apart from animals and robots. *I made you in My image*, precariously close to deity.

Though My blood has fully redeemed you, your mind is the last bastion of rebellion. Open yourself to My radiant Presence, letting My Light permeate your thinking. *When My Spirit is controlling your mind, you are filled with Life and Peace.*

Then God said, "Let us make man in our image, in our likeness, and let them rule over the fish of the sea and the birds of the air, over the livestock, over all the earth, and over all the creatures that move along the ground." So God created man in his own image, in the image of God he created him; male and female he created them. —Genesis 1:26–27

The mind of sinful man is death, but the mind controlled by the Spirit is life and peace. —Romans 8:6

Listen to Me continually. I have much to communicate to you, so many people and situations in need of prayer. I am training you to set your mind on Me more and more, tuning out distractions through the help of My Spirit.

Walk with Me in holy trust, responding to My initiatives rather than trying to make things fit your plans. I died to set you free, and that includes freedom from compulsive planning. When your mind spins with a multitude of thoughts, you cannot hear My voice. A mind preoccupied with planning pays homage to the idol of control. Turn from this idolatry back to Me. Listen to Me and live abundantly!

"So if the Son sets you free, you will be free indeed." —John 8:36

Many are the plans in a man's heart, but it is the Lord's purpose that prevails. —Proverbs 19:21

"My sheep listen to my voice; I know them, and they follow me." —John 10:27

April 23

Keep your eyes on Me, not only for direction but also for empowerment. I never lead you to do something without equipping you for the task. That is why it's so important to seek My will in everything you do. There are many burned-out Christians who think more is always better, who deem it unspiritual to say no.

In order to know My will, you must spend time with Me—enjoying My Presence. This is not an onerous task but a delightful privilege. I will show you *the path of Life*; *in My Presence is fullness of Joy*; *at My right hand there are pleasures forevermore.*

But my eyes are fixed on you, O Sovereign Lord; in you I take refuge—do not give me over to death. —Psalm 141:8

You will show me the path of life; in Your presence is fullness of joy; at Your right hand are pleasures forevermore. —Psalm 16:11 NKJV

Rest in the stillness of My Presence while I prepare you for this day. Let the radiance of My Glory shine upon you, as you wait on Me in confident trust. *Be still and know that I am God.* There is both a passive and an active side to trusting Me. As you rest in My Presence, focusing on Me, I quietly build bonds of trust between us. When you respond to the circumstances of your life with affirmations of trust, you actively participate in this process.

I am always with you, so you have no reason to be afraid. Your fear often manifests itself in excessive planning. Your mind is so accustomed to this pattern of thinking that you are only now becoming aware of how pervasive it is and how much it hinders your intimacy with Me. Repent of this tendency and resist it, whenever you realize you are wandering down this well-worn path. Return to My Presence, which always awaits you in the present moment. I accept you back with *no condemnation.*

"Be still, and know that I am God; I will be exalted among the nations, I will be exalted in the earth." —Psalm 46:10

Therefore, there is now no condemnation for those who are in Christ Jesus. —Romans 8:1

April 25

Make Me your focal point as you move through this day. Just as a spinning ballerina must keep returning her eyes to a given point to maintain her balance, so you must keep returning your focus to Me. Circumstances are in flux, and the world seems to be whirling around you. The only way to keep your balance is to *fix your eyes on Me*, the One who never changes. If you gaze too long at your circumstances, you will become dizzy and confused. Look to Me, refreshing yourself in My Presence, and your steps will be steady and sure.

Let us fix our eyes on Jesus, the author and perfecter of our faith, who for the joy set before him endured the cross, scorning its shame, and sat down at the right hand of the throne of God. —Hebrews 12:2

But you remain the same, and your years will never end. —Psalm 102:27

April 26

WELCOME PROBLEMS as perspective-lifters. My children tend to sleepwalk through their days until they bump into an obstacle that stymies them.

If you encounter a problem with no immediate solution, your response to that situation will take you either up or down. You can lash out at the difficulty, resenting it and feeling sorry for yourself. This will take you down into a pit of self-pity. Alternatively, the problem can be a ladder, enabling you to climb up and see your life from My perspective. Viewed from above, the obstacle that frustrated you is only *a light and momentary trouble*. Once your perspective has been heightened, you can look away from the problem altogether. Turn toward Me, and see *the Light of My Presence* shining upon you.

Therefore we do not lose heart. Though outwardly we are wasting away, yet inwardly we are being renewed day by day. For our light and momentary troubles are achieving for us an eternal glory that far outweighs them all. So we fix our eyes not on what is seen, but on what is unseen. For what is seen is temporary, but what is unseen is eternal. —2 CORINTHIANS 4:16–18

Blessed are those who have learned to acclaim you, who walk in the light of your presence, O LORD. —PSALM 89:15

April 27

Come to Me with empty hands and an open heart, ready to receive abundant blessings. I know the depth and breadth of your neediness. Your life-path has been difficult, draining you of strength. Come to Me for nurture. Let Me fill you up with My Presence: I in you, and you in Me.

My Power flows most freely into weak ones aware of their need for Me. Faltering steps of dependence are not lack of faith; they are links to My Presence.

"My prayer is not for them alone. I pray also for those who will believe in me through their message, that all of them may be one, Father, just as you are in me and I am in you. May they also be in us so that the world may believe that you have sent me. I have given them the glory that you gave me, that they may be one as we are one: I in them and you in me. May they be brought to complete unity to let the world know that you sent me and have loved them even as you have loved me." —John 17:20–23

He gives strength to the weary and increases the power of the weak. Even youths grow tired and weary, and young men stumble and fall; but those who hope in the Lord will renew their strength. They will soar on wings like eagles; they will run and not grow weary, they will walk and not be faint. —Isaiah 40:29–31

April 28

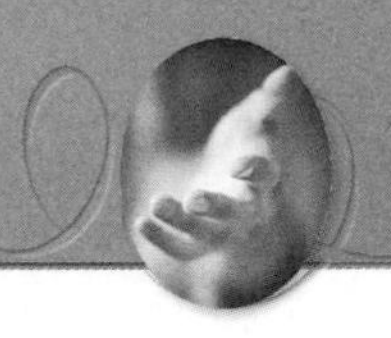

AS YOU LOOK into the day that stretches out before you, you see many choice-points along the way. The myriad possibilities these choices present can confuse you. Draw your mind back to the threshold of this day, where I stand beside you, lovingly preparing you for what is ahead.

You must make your choices one at a time, since each is contingent upon the decision that precedes it. Instead of trying to create a mental map of your path through this day, focus on My loving Presence with you. I will equip you as you go, so that you can handle whatever comes your way. Trust Me to supply what you need when you need it.

Because of the LORD's great love we are not consumed, for his compassions never fail. They are new every morning; great is your faithfulness. I say to myself, "The LORD is my portion; therefore I will wait for him." The LORD is good to those whose hope is in him, to the one who seeks him; it is good to wait quietly for the salvation of the LORD. —LAMENTATIONS 3:22–26

Oh, taste and see that the LORD is good; blessed is the man who trusts in Him! —PSALM 34:8 NKJV

April 29

Let Me teach you thankfulness. Begin by acknowledging that everything—all your possessions and all that you are—belongs to Me. The dawning of each new day is a gift from Me, not to be taken for granted. The earth is vibrantly alive with My blessings, giving vivid testimony to My Presence. If you slow down your pace of life, you can find Me anywhere.

Some of My most precious children have been laid aside in sickbeds or shut away in prisons. Others have voluntarily learned the discipline of spending time alone with Me. The secret of being thankful is learning to see everything from My perspective. My world is your classroom. *My Word is a lamp to your feet and a light for your path.*

Therefore, since we are receiving a kingdom that cannot be shaken, let us be thankful, and so worship God acceptably with reverence and awe, for our "God is a consuming fire." —Hebrews 12:28–29

Your word is a lamp to my feet and a light for my path. —Psalm 119:105

When some basic need is lacking—time, energy, money—consider yourself blessed. Your very lack is an opportunity to latch onto Me in unashamed dependence. When you begin a day with inadequate resources, you must concentrate your efforts on the present moment. This is where you are meant to live—in the present; it is the place where I always await you. Awareness of your inadequacy is a rich blessing, training you to rely wholeheartedly on Me.

The truth is that self-sufficiency is a myth perpetuated by pride and temporary success. Health and wealth can disappear instantly, as can life itself. Rejoice in your insufficiency, knowing that *My Power is made perfect in weakness.*

Consider it pure joy, my brothers, whenever you face trials of many kinds. —James 1:2

And He has said to me, "My grace is sufficient for you, for power is perfected in weakness." Most gladly, therefore, I will rather boast about my weaknesses, so that the power of Christ may dwell in me. —2 Corinthians 12:9 NASB

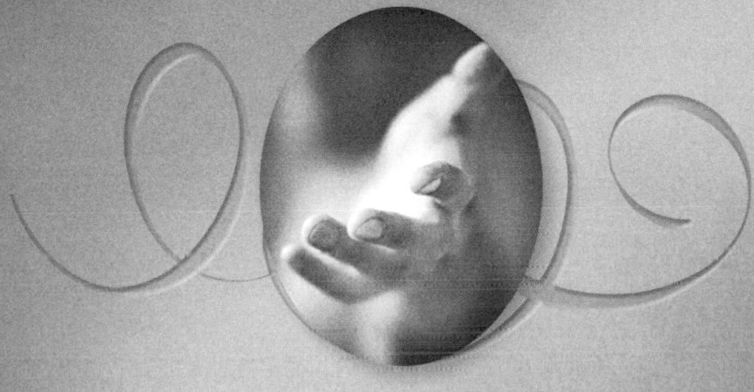

May

Ascribe to the Lord the glory due his name;
worship the Lord in the splendor of his holiness.

Psalm 29:2

May 1

You are on the path of My choosing. There is no randomness about your life. Here and Now comprise the coordinates of your daily life. Most people let their moments slip through their fingers, half-lived. They avoid the present by worrying about the future or longing for a better time and place. They forget that they are creatures who are subject to the limitations of time and space. They forget their Creator, who walks with them only in the present.

Every moment is alive with My glorious Presence, to those whose hearts are intimately connected with Mine. As you give yourself more and more to a life of constant communion with Me, you will find that you simply have no time for worry. Thus, you are freed to let My Spirit direct your steps, enabling you to walk along *the path of Peace.*

"Who of you by worrying can add a single hour to his life? Since you cannot do this very little thing, why do you worry about the rest?" —Luke 12:25–26

To shine on those living in darkness and in the shadow of death, to guide our feet into the path of peace. —Luke 1:79

LIVING IN DEPENDENCE ON ME is the way to enjoy abundant life. You are learning to appreciate tough times, because they amplify your awareness of My Presence. Tasks that you used to dread are becoming rich opportunities to enjoy My closeness. When you feel tired, you remember that I am your Strength; you take pleasure in leaning on Me. I am pleased by your tendency to turn to Me more and more frequently, especially when you are alone.

When you are with other people, you often lose sight of My Presence. Your fear of displeasing people puts you in bondage to them, and they become your primary focus. When you realize this has happened, whisper My Name; this tiny act of trust brings Me to the forefront of your consciousness, where I belong. As you bask in the blessing of My nearness, My life can flow through you to others. This is abundant life!

Fear of man will prove to be a snare, but whoever trusts in the LORD is kept safe. —PROVERBS 29:25

"The thief does not come except to steal, and to kill, and to destroy. I have come that they may have life, and that they may have it more abundantly." —JOHN 10:10 NKJV

May 3

You cannot serve two masters. If I am truly your Master, you will desire to please Me above all others. If pleasing people is your goal, you will be enslaved to them. People can be harsh taskmasters when you give them this power over you.

If I am the Master of your life, I will also be your *First Love.* Your serving Me is rooted and grounded in My vast, unconditional Love for you. The lower you bow down before Me, the higher I lift you up into intimate relationship with Me. *The Joy of living in My Presence* outshines all other pleasures. I want you to reflect My joyous Light by living in increasing intimacy with Me.

"No one can serve two masters. Either he will hate the one and love the other, or he will be devoted to the one and despise the other. You cannot serve both God and Money." —Matthew 6:24

"Yet I hold this against you: You have forsaken your first love." —Revelation 2:4

I pray that out of his glorious riches he may strengthen you with power through his Spirit in your inner being, so that Christ may dwell in your hearts through faith. And I pray that you, being rooted and established in love . . . —Ephesians 3:16–17

You have made known to me the path of life; you will fill me with joy in your presence, with eternal pleasures at your right hand. —Psalm 16:11

Meet Me in morning stillness, while the earth is fresh with the dew of My Presence. *Worship Me in the beauty of holiness.* Sing love songs to My holy Name. As you give yourself to Me, My Spirit swells within you till you are flooded with divine Presence.

The world's way of pursuing riches is grasping and hoarding. You attain *My* riches by letting go and giving. The more you give yourself to Me and My ways, the more I fill you with *inexpressible, heavenly Joy.*

Give unto the Lord the glory due to His name; worship the Lord in the beauty of holiness. —Psalm 29:2 NKJV

Though you have not seen him, you love him; and even though you do not see him now, you believe in him and are filled with an inexpressible and glorious joy. —1 Peter 1:8

May 5

Come to Me for all that you need. Come into My Presence with thanksgiving, for thankfulness opens the door to My treasures. When you are thankful, you affirm the central truth that I am Good. *I am Light, in whom there is no darkness at all.* The assurance that I am entirely Good meets your basic need for security. Your life is not subject to the whims of a sin-stained deity.

Relax in the knowledge that the One who controls your life is totally trustworthy. Come to Me with confident expectation. There is nothing you need that I cannot provide.

Let us come before him with thanksgiving and extol him with music and song. —Psalm 95:2

This is the message we have heard from him and declare to you: God is light; in him there is no darkness at all. —1 John 1:5

Do not search for security in the world you inhabit. You tend to make mental checklists of things you need to do in order to gain control of your life. If only you could check everything off your list, you could relax and be at peace. But the more you work to accomplish that goal, the more things crop up on your list. The harder you try, the more frustrated you become.

There is a better way to find security in this life. Instead of scrutinizing your checklist, focus your attention on My Presence with you. This continual contact with Me will keep you in My Peace. Moreover, I will help you sort out what is important and what is not, what needs to be done now and what does not. *Fix your eyes not on what is seen (your circumstances), but on what is unseen (My Presence).*

You will keep him in perfect peace, whose mind is stayed on You, because he trusts in You. —Isaiah 26:3 NKJV

So we fix our eyes not on what is seen, but on what is unseen. For what is seen is temporary, but what is unseen is eternal. —2 Corinthians 4:18

IF YOU LEARN TO TRUST ME—really trust Me—with your whole being, then nothing can separate you from My Peace. Everything you endure can be put to good use by allowing it to train you in trusting Me. This is how you foil the works of evil, growing in grace through the very adversity that was meant to harm you. Joseph was a prime example of this divine reversal, declaring to his brothers: "*You meant evil against me, but God meant it for good.*"

Do not fear what this day, or any day, may bring your way. Concentrate on trusting Me and on doing what needs to be done. Relax in My sovereignty, remembering that I go before you, as well as with you, into each day. *Fear no evil*, for I can bring good out of every situation you will ever encounter.

As for you, you meant evil against me, but God meant it for good in order to bring about this present result, to preserve many people alive. —GENESIS 50:20 NASB

Even though I walk through the valley of the shadow of death, I will fear no evil, for you are with me; your rod and your staff, they comfort me. —PSALM 23:4

Do not long for the absence of problems in your life. That is an unrealistic goal, since *in this world you will have trouble.* You have an eternity of problem-free living reserved for you in heaven. Rejoice in that inheritance, which no one can take away from you, but do not seek your heaven on earth.

Begin each day anticipating problems, asking Me to equip you for whatever difficulties you will encounter. The best equipping is My living Presence, *My hand that never lets go of yours.* Discuss everything with Me. Take a lighthearted view of trouble, seeing it as a challenge that you and I together can handle. Remember that I am on your side, and *I have overcome the world.*

"I have told you these things, so that in me you may have peace. In this world you will have trouble. But take heart! I have overcome the world." —John 16:33

"For I am the Lord, your God, who takes hold of your right hand and says to you, Do not fear; I will help you." —Isaiah 41:13

I can do everything through him who gives me strength. —Philippians 4:13

May 9

Don't be so hard on yourself. I can bring good even out of your mistakes. Your finite mind tends to look backward, longing to undo decisions you have come to regret. This is a waste of time and energy, leading only to frustration. Instead of floundering in the past, release your mistakes to Me. Look to Me in trust, anticipating that My infinite creativity can weave both good choices and bad into a lovely design.

Because you are human, you will continue to make mistakes. Thinking that you should live an error-free life is symptomatic of pride. Your failures can be a source of blessing, humbling you and giving you empathy for other people in their weaknesses. Best of all, failure highlights your dependence on Me. I am able to bring beauty out of the morass of your mistakes. Trust Me, and watch to see what I will do.

And we know that in all things God works for the good of those who love him, who have been called according to his purpose. —Romans 8:28

But as for me, I watch in hope for the Lord, I wait for God my Savior; my God will hear me. —Micah 7:7

DO NOT RESIST OR RUN from the difficulties in your life. These problems are not random mistakes; they are hand-tailored blessings designed for your benefit and growth. Embrace all the circumstances that I allow in your life, trusting Me to bring good out of them. View problems as opportunities to rely more fully on Me.

When you start to feel stressed, let those feelings alert you to your need for Me. Thus, your needs become doorways to deep dependence on Me and increasing intimacy between us. Although self-sufficiency is acclaimed in the world, reliance on Me produces abundant living in My kingdom. Thank Me for the difficulties in your life, since they provide protection from the idolatry of self-reliance.

"I am the vine; you are the branches. If a man remains in me and I in him, he will bear much fruit; apart from me you can do nothing." —JOHN 15:5

We do not want you to be uninformed, brothers, about the hardships we suffered in the province of Asia. We were under great pressure, far beyond our ability to endure, so that we despaired even of life. Indeed, in our hearts we felt the sentence of death. But this happened that we might not rely on ourselves but on God, who raises the dead. —2 CORINTHIANS 1:8–9

Always giving thanks to God the Father for everything, in the name of our Lord Jesus Christ. —EPHESIANS 5:20

May 11

THANK ME FOR YOUR PROBLEMS. As soon as your mind gets snagged on a difficulty, bring it to Me with thanksgiving. Then ask Me to show you My way to handle the situation. The very act of thanking Me releases your mind from its negative focus. As you turn your attention to Me, the problem fades in significance and loses its power to trip you up. Together we can deal with the situation, either facing it head-on or putting it aside for later consideration.

Most of the situations that entangle your mind are not today's concerns; you have borrowed them from tomorrow. In this case, I lift the problem out of today and deposit it in the future, where it is veiled from your eyes. In its place I give you My Peace, which flows freely from My Presence.

Do not be anxious about anything, but in everything, by prayer and petition, with thanksgiving, present your requests to God. —PHILIPPIANS 4:6

"Peace I leave with you; my peace I give you. I do not give to you as the world gives. Do not let your hearts be troubled and do not be afraid." —JOHN 14:27

LEARN TO RELATE to others through My Love rather than yours. Your human love is ever so limited, full of flaws and manipulation. My loving Presence, which always enfolds you, is available to bless others as well as you. Instead of trying harder to help people through your own paltry supplies, become aware of My unlimited supply, which is accessible to you continually. Let My Love envelop your outreach to other people.

Many of My precious children have fallen prey to burnout. A better description of their condition might be "drainout." Countless interactions with needy people have drained them, without their conscious awareness. You are among these weary ones, who are like wounded soldiers needing R&R. Take time to rest in the Love-Light of My Presence. I will gradually restore to you the energy that you have lost over the years. *Come to Me, all you who are weary and burdened, and you will find rest for your souls.*

The LORD replied, "My Presence will go with you, and I will give you rest." —EXODUS 33:14

"Come to me, all you who are weary and burdened, and I will give you rest. Take my yoke upon you and learn from me, for I am gentle and humble in heart, and you will find rest for your souls." —MATTHEW 11:28–29

THANK ME IN THE MIDST of the crucible. When things seem all wrong, look for growth opportunities. Especially, look for areas where you need to let go, leaving your cares in My able hands. Do you trust Me to orchestrate your life events as I choose, or are you still trying to make things go according to your will? If you keep trying to carry out your intentions while I am leading you in another direction, you deify your desires.

Be on the lookout for what I am doing in your life. Worship Me by living close to Me, *thanking Me in all circumstances.*

Humble yourselves, therefore, under God's mighty hand, that he may lift you up in due time. Cast all your anxiety on him because he cares for you. —1 PETER 5:6–7

Give thanks in all circumstances, for this is God's will for you in Christ Jesus. —1 THESSALONIANS 5:18

I AM A MIGHTY GOD. *Nothing is too difficult for Me.* I have chosen to use weak ones like you to accomplish My purposes. Your weakness is designed to open you up to My Power. Therefore, do not fear your limitations or measure the day's demands against your strength. What I require of you is to stay connected to Me, living in trusting dependence on My limitless resources. When you face unexpected demands, there is no need to panic. Remember that *I am with you.* Talk with Me, and listen while I talk you through each challenging situation.

I am not a careless God. When I allow difficulties to come into your life, I equip you fully to handle them. Relax in My Presence, trusting in My Strength.

"For nothing is impossible with God." —LUKE 1:37

But he said to me, "My grace is sufficient for you, for my power is made perfect in weakness." Therefore I will boast all the more gladly about my weaknesses, so that Christ's power may rest on me. —2 CORINTHIANS 12:9

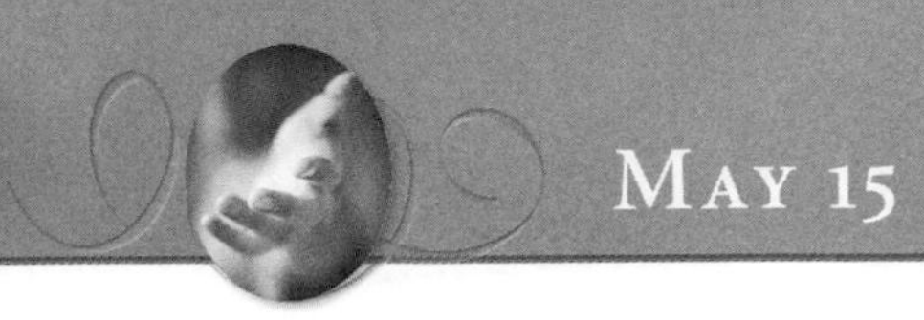

May 15

Spending time alone with Me is essential for your well-being. It is not a luxury or an option; it is a necessity. Therefore, do not feel guilty about taking time to be with Me. Remember that Satan is *the accuser of believers*. He delights in heaping guilt feelings upon you, especially when you are enjoying My Presence. When you feel Satan's arrows of accusation, you are probably on the right track. Use your *shield of faith* to protect yourself from him. Talk with Me about what you are experiencing, and ask Me to show you the way forward. *Resist the devil, and he will flee from you. Come near to Me, and I will come near to you.*

Then I heard a loud voice in heaven say: "Now have come the salvation and the power and the kingdom of our God, and the authority of his Christ. For the accuser of our brothers, who accuses them before our God day and night, has been hurled down." —Revelation 12:10

In addition to all this, take up the shield of faith, with which you can extinguish all the flaming arrows of the evil one. —Ephesians 6:16

Submit yourselves, then, to God. Resist the devil, and he will flee from you. Come near to God and he will come near to you. Wash your hands, you sinners, and purify your hearts, you double-minded. —James 4:7–8

May 16

I AM YOUR LORD! Seek Me as Friend and Lover of your soul, but remember that I am also King of kings—sovereign over all. You can make some plans as you gaze into the day that stretches out before you. But you need to hold those plans tentatively, anticipating that I may have other ideas. The most important thing to determine is what to do right now. Instead of scanning the horizon of your life, looking for things that need to be done, concentrate on the task before you and the One who never leaves your side. Let everything else fade into the background. This will unclutter your mind, allowing Me to occupy more and more of your consciousness.

Trust Me to show you what to do when you have finished what you are doing now. I will guide you step by step, as you bend your will to Mine. Thus you stay close to Me on the *path of Peace.*

Many are the plans in a man's heart, but it is the LORD*'s purpose that prevails.* —PROVERBS 19:21

To shine on those living in darkness and in the shadow of death, to guide our feet into the path of peace. —LUKE 1:79

May 17

As you sit quietly in My Presence, remember that I am a God of abundance. I will never run out of resources; My capacity to bless you is unlimited. You live in a world of supply and demand, where necessary things are often scarce. Even if you personally have enough, you see poverty in the world around you. It is impossible for you to comprehend the lavishness of My provisions: the fullness of My *glorious riches.*

Through spending time in My Presence, you gain glimpses of My overflowing vastness. These glimpses are tiny foretastes of what you will experience eternally in heaven. Even now you have access to as much of Me as you have faith to receive. Rejoice in My abundance—*living by faith, not by sight.*

And my God will meet all your needs according to his glorious riches in Christ Jesus. —Philippians 4:19

We live by faith, not by sight. —2 Corinthians 5:7

Come to Me with your plans held in abeyance. *Worship Me in spirit and in truth*, allowing My Glory to permeate your entire being. Trust Me enough to let Me guide you through this day, accomplishing My purposes in My timing. Subordinate your myriad plans to My Master Plan. I am sovereign over every aspect of your life!

The challenge continually before you is to trust Me and search for My way through each day. Do not blindly follow your habitual route, or you will miss what I have prepared for you. *As the heavens are higher than the earth, so are My ways higher than your ways and My thoughts than your thoughts.*

"God is spirit, and his worshipers must worship in spirit and in truth." —John 4:24

"For My thoughts are not your thoughts, nor are your ways My ways," says the Lord*. "For as the heavens are higher than the earth, so are My ways higher than your ways, and My thoughts than your thoughts."* —Isaiah 55:8–9 NKJV

May 19

I WANT YOU TO KNOW how safe and secure you are in My Presence. That is a fact, totally independent of your feelings. You are on your way to heaven; nothing can prevent you from reaching that destination. There you will see Me face to Face, and your Joy will be off the charts by any earthly standards. Even now, you are never separated from Me, though you must see Me through eyes of faith. I will walk with you till the end of time, and onward into eternity.

Although My Presence is a guaranteed promise, that does not necessarily change your feelings. When you forget I am with you, you may experience loneliness or fear. It is through awareness of My Presence that Peace displaces negative feelings. Practice the discipline of walking consciously with Me through each day.

Now we see but a poor reflection as in a mirror; then we shall see face to face. Now I know in part; then I shall know fully, even as I am fully known. —1 CORINTHIANS 13:12

The LORD gives strength to his people; the LORD blesses his people with peace. —PSALM 29:11

WHEN YOUR SINS WEIGH HEAVILY upon you, come to Me. Confess your wrongdoing, which I know all about before you say a word. Stay in the Light of My Presence, receiving forgiveness, cleansing, and healing. Remember that *I have clothed you in My righteousness*, so nothing can separate you from Me. Whenever you stumble or fall, I am there to help you up.

Man's tendency is to hide from his sin, seeking refuge in the darkness. There he indulges in self-pity, denial, self-righteousness, blaming, and hatred. But *I am the Light of the world*, and My illumination decimates the darkness. Come close to Me and let My Light envelop you, driving out darkness and permeating you with Peace.

But if we walk in the light, as he is in the light, we have fellowship with one another, and the blood of Jesus, his Son, purifies us from all sin. —1 JOHN 1:7

I delight greatly in the LORD; my soul rejoices in my God. For he has clothed me with garments of salvation and arrayed me in a robe of righteousness, as a bridegroom adorns his head like a priest, and as a bride adorns herself with her jewels. —ISAIAH 61:10

When Jesus spoke again to the people, he said, "I am the light of the world. Whoever follows me will never walk in darkness, but will have the light of life." —JOHN 8:12

May 21

I, THE CREATOR OF THE UNIVERSE, am with you and for you. What more could you need? When you feel some lack, it is because you are not connecting with Me at a deep level. I offer abundant Life; your part is to trust Me, refusing to worry about anything.

It is not so much adverse events that make you anxious as it is your thoughts about those events. Your mind engages in efforts to take control of a situation, to bring about the result you desire. Your thoughts close in on the problem like ravenous wolves. Determined to make things go your way, you forget that I am in charge of your life. The only remedy is to switch your focus from the problem to My Presence. Stop all your striving, and watch to see what I will do. *I am the Lord!*

What, then, shall we say in response to this? If God is for us, who can be against us? He who did not spare his own Son, but gave him up for us all—how will he not also, along with him, graciously give us all things? —ROMANS 8:31–32

But as for me, I watch in hope for the LORD, I wait for God my Savior; my God will hear me. —MICAH 7:7

WHEN THINGS DON'T GO AS YOU would like, accept the situation immediately. If you indulge in feelings of regret, they can easily spill over the line into resentment. Remember that I am sovereign over your circumstances, and *humble yourself under My mighty hand.* Rejoice in what I am doing in your life, even though it is beyond your understanding.

I am the Way, the Truth, and the Life. In Me you have everything you need, both for this life and for the life yet to come. Don't let the impact of the world shatter your thinking or draw you away from focusing on Me. The ultimate challenge is to keep fixing your eyes on Me, no matter what is going on around you. When I am central in your thinking, you are able to view circumstances from My perspective.

Humble yourselves, therefore, under God's mighty hand, that he may lift you up in due time. —1 PETER 5:6

Jesus answered, "I am the way and the truth and the life. No one comes to the Father except through me." —JOHN 14:6

May 23

APPROACH EACH NEW DAY with desire to find Me. Before you get out of bed, I have already been working to prepare the path that will get you through this day. There are hidden treasures strategically placed along the way. Some of the treasures are trials, designed to shake you free from earth-shackles. Others are blessings that reveal My Presence: sunshine, flowers, birds, friendships, answered prayer. I have not abandoned this sin-wracked world; I am still richly present in it.

Search for deep treasure as you go through this day. You will find Me all along the way.

My purpose is that they may be encouraged in heart and united in love, so that they may have the full riches of complete understanding, in order that they may know the mystery of God, namely, Christ, in whom are hidden all the treasures of wisdom and knowledge. —COLOSSIANS 2:2–3

He will be the sure foundation for your times, a rich store of salvation and wisdom and knowledge; the fear of the LORD *is the key to this treasure.* —ISAIAH 33:6

BRING ME YOUR MIND for rest and renewal. Let Me infuse My Presence into your thoughts. As your mind stops racing, your body relaxes and you regain awareness of Me. This awareness is vital to your spiritual well-being; it is your lifeline, spiritually speaking.

There are actually more than four dimensions in this world where you live. In addition to the three dimensions of space and the one of time, there is the dimension of openness to My Presence. This dimension transcends the others, giving you glimpses of heaven while you still reside on earth. This was part of My original design for mankind. Adam and Eve used to walk with Me in the garden, before their expulsion from Eden. I want you to walk with Me in the garden of your heart, where I have taken up permanent residence.

Then the man and his wife heard the sound of the LORD God as he was walking in the garden in the cool of the day, and they hid from the LORD God among the trees of the garden. —GENESIS 3:8

Blessed are those who have learned to acclaim you, who walk in the light of your presence, O LORD. —PSALM 89:15

May 25

The world is too much with you, My child. Your mind leaps from problem to problem to problem, tangling your thoughts in anxious knots. When you think like that, you leave Me out of your world-view and your mind becomes darkened. Though I yearn to help, I will not violate your freedom. I stand silently in the background of your mind, waiting for you to remember that I am with you.

When you turn from your problems to My Presence, your load is immediately lighter. Circumstances may not have changed, but we carry your burdens together. Your compulsion to "fix" everything gives way to deep, satisfying connection with Me. Together we can handle whatever this day brings.

"So do not fear, for I am with you; do not be dismayed, for I am your God. I will strengthen you and help you; I will uphold you with my righteous right hand." —Isaiah 41:10

The Lord your God is with you, he is mighty to save. He will take great delight in you, he will quiet you with his love, he will rejoice over you with singing. —Zephaniah 3:17

A righteous man may have many troubles, but the Lord delivers him from them all. —Psalm 34:19

IN A WORLD OF UNRELENTING CHANGES, I am the One who never changes. *I am the Alpha and the Omega, the First and the Last, the Beginning and the End.* Find in Me the stability for which you have yearned.

I created a beautifully ordered world: one that reflected My perfection. Now, however, the world is under the bondage of sin and evil. Every person on the planet faces gaping jaws of uncertainty. The only antidote to this poisonous threat is drawing closer to Me. In My Presence you can face uncertainty with perfect Peace.

"I am the Alpha and the Omega, the First and the Last, the Beginning and the End." —REVELATION 22:13

I have told you these things, so that in Me you may have [perfect] peace and confidence. In the world you have tribulation and trials and distress and frustration; but be of good cheer [take courage; be confident, certain, undaunted]! For I have overcome the world. [I have deprived it of power to harm you and have conquered it for you.] —JOHN 16:33 AMP

May 27

Seek My Face at the beginning of your day. This practice enables you to "put Me on" and "wear Me" throughout the day. Most people put on clothes soon after arising from bed. Similarly, the sooner you "put Me on" by communicating with Me, the better prepared you are for whatever comes your way.

To "wear Me" is essentially to have My mind: to think My thoughts. Ask the Holy Spirit to control your thinking; be transformed by this renewal within you. Thus you are well equipped to face whatever people and situations I bring your way. Clothing your mind in Me is your best preparation for each day. This discipline brings Joy and Peace to you and those around you.

When You said, "Seek My face," My heart said to You,
"Your face, LORD, I will seek." —PSALM 27:8 NKJV

Rather, clothe yourselves with the Lord Jesus Christ, and do not think
about how to gratify the desires of the sinful nature. —ROMANS 13:14

Therefore, as God's chosen people, holy and dearly loved,
clothe yourselves with compassion, kindness, humility,
gentleness and patience. —COLOSSIANS 3:12

Let Me anoint you with My Presence. *I am King of kings and Lord of lords, dwelling in unapproachable Light. When you draw near to Me, I respond by coming closer to you.* As My Presence envelops you, you may feel overwhelmed by My Power and Glory. This is a form of worship: sensing your smallness in comparison to My Greatness.

Man has tended to make himself the measure of all things. But man's measure is too tiny to comprehend My majestic vastness. That is why most people do not see Me at all, even though *they live and move and have their being in Me.*

Enjoy the radiant beauty of My Presence. Declare My glorious Being to the world!

Which God will bring about in his own time—God, the blessed and only Ruler, the King of kings and Lord of lords, who alone is immortal and who lives in unapproachable light, whom no one has seen or can see. To him be honor and might forever. Amen. 1 Timothy 6:15–16

Come near to God and he will come near to you. Wash your hands, you sinners, and purify your hearts, you double-minded. —James 4:8

"For in him we live and move and have our being." As some of your own poets have said, "We are his offspring." —Acts 17:28

Great is the Lord and most worthy of praise; his greatness no one can fathom. One generation will commend your works to another; they will tell of your mighty acts. They will speak of the glorious splendor of your majesty, and I will meditate on your wonderful works. They will tell of the power of your awesome works, and I will proclaim your great deeds. —Psalm 145:3–6

May 29

I AM WITH YOU, watching over you constantly. I am Immanuel (*God with you*); My Presence enfolds you in radiant Love. Nothing, including the brightest blessings and the darkest trials, can separate you from Me. Some of My children find Me more readily during dark times, when difficulties force them to depend on Me. Others feel closer to Me when their lives are filled with good things. They respond with thanksgiving and praise, thus opening wide the door to My Presence.

I know precisely what you need to draw nearer to Me. Go through each day looking for what I have prepared for you. Accept every event as My hand-tailored provision for your needs. When you view your life this way, the most reasonable response is to be thankful. Do not reject any of My gifts; find Me in every situation.

"The virgin will be with child and will give birth to a son, and they will call him Immanuel"—which means, "God with us." —MATTHEW 1:23

So then, just as you received Christ Jesus as Lord, continue to live in him, rooted and built up in him, strengthened in the faith as you were taught, and overflowing with thankfulness. —COLOSSIANS 2:6–7

TIME WITH ME cannot be rushed. When you are in a hurry, your mind flitters back and forth between Me and the tasks ahead of you. Push back the demands pressing in on you; create a safe space around you, a haven in which you can rest with Me. I also desire this time of focused attention and I use it to bless you, strengthening and equipping you for the day ahead. Thus, spending time with Me is a wise investment.

Bring Me the sacrifice of your precious time. This creates sacred space around you—space permeated with My Presence and My Peace.

Let me understand the teaching of your precepts; then I will meditate on your wonders. —PSALM 119:27

For the eyes of the LORD range throughout the earth to strengthen those whose hearts are fully committed to him. You have done a foolish thing, and from now on you will be at war. —2 CHRONICLES 16:9

Therefore by Him let us continually offer the sacrifice of praise to God, that is, the fruit of our lips, giving thanks to His name. —HEBREWS 13:15 NKJV

May 31

The Peace that I give you transcends your intellect. When most of your mental energy goes into efforts to figure things out, you are unable to receive this glorious gift. I look into your mind and see thoughts spinning round and round: going nowhere, accomplishing nothing. All the while, My Peace hovers over you, searching for a place to land.

Be still in My Presence, inviting Me to control your thoughts. Let My Light soak into your mind and heart, until you are aglow with My very Being. This is the most effective way to receive My Peace.

Now may the Lord of peace himself give you peace at all times and in every way. The Lord be with all of you. —2 Thessalonians 3:16

Submit to God and be at peace with him; in this way prosperity will come to you. —Job 22:21

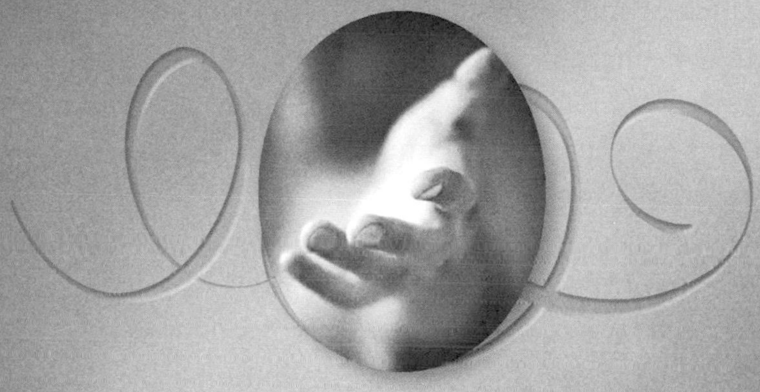

June

"For I am the Lord*, your God, who takes hold of your right hand and says to you, Do not fear; I will help you."*

Isaiah 41:13

June 1

I AM INVOLVED in each moment of your life. I have carefully mapped out every inch of your journey through this day, even though much of it may feel haphazard. Because the world is in a fallen condition, things always seem to be unraveling around the edges. Expect to find trouble in this day. At the same time, trust that *My way is perfect*, even in the midst of such messy imperfection.

Stay conscious of Me as you go through this day, remembering that I never leave your side. Let the Holy Spirit guide you step by step, protecting you from unnecessary trials and equipping you to get through whatever must be endured. As you trudge through the sludge of this fallen world, keep your mind in heavenly places with Me. Thus the Light of My Presence shines on you, giving you Peace and Joy that circumstances cannot touch.

As for God, his way is perfect; the word of the Lord is flawless.
He is a shield for all who take refuge in him. —Psalm 18:30

"For I am the Lord, your God, who takes hold of your right hand
and says to you, Do not fear; I will help you." —Isaiah 41:13

Relax in My healing, holy Presence. *Be still*, while I transform your heart and mind. *Let go* of cares and worries, so that you can receive My Peace. *Cease striving, and know that I am God.*

Do not be like Pharisees who multiplied regulations, creating their own form of "godliness." They got so wrapped up in their own rules that they lost sight of Me. Even today, man-made rules about how to live the Christian life enslave many people. Their focus is on their performance, rather than on Me.

It is through knowing Me intimately that you become like Me. This requires spending time alone with Me. *Let go, relax, be still, and know that I am God.*

"Cease striving and know that I am God; I will be exalted among the nations, I will be exalted in the earth." —Psalm 46:10 NASB

Dear friends, now we are children of God, and what we will be has not yet been made known. But we know that when he appears, we shall be like him, for we shall see him as he is. —1 John 3:2

June 3

I want to be Central in your entire being. When your focus is firmly on Me, My Peace displaces fears and worries. They will encircle you, seeking entrance, so you must stay alert. Let trust and thankfulness stand guard, turning back fear before it can gain a foothold. *There is no fear in My Love*, which shines on you continually. Sit quietly in My Love-Light, while I bless you with radiant Peace. Turn your whole being to trusting and loving Me.

Now may the Lord of peace himself give you peace at all times and in every way. The Lord be with all of you. —2 Thessalonians 3:16

There is no fear in love. But perfect love drives out fear, because fear has to do with punishment. The one who fears is not made perfect in love. —1 John 4:18

June 4

Welcome challenging times as opportunities to trust Me. You have Me beside you and My Spirit within you, so no set of circumstances is too much for you to handle. When the path before you is dotted with difficulties, beware of measuring your strength against those challenges. That calculation is certain to riddle you with anxiety. Without Me, you wouldn't make it past the first hurdle!

The way to walk through demanding days is to grip My hand tightly and stay in close communication with Me. Let your thoughts and spoken words be richly flavored with trust and thankfulness. Regardless of the day's problems, *I can keep you in perfect Peace* as you stay close to Me.

Consider it pure joy, my brothers, whenever you face trials of many kinds. —James 1:2

I can do all things through Christ who strengthens me. —Philippians 4:13 NKJV

You will keep in perfect peace him whose mind is steadfast, because he trusts in you. —Isaiah 26:3

June 5

Remember that you live in a fallen world: an abnormal world tainted by sin. Much frustration and failure result from your seeking perfection in this life. There is nothing perfect in this world except Me. That is why closeness to Me satisfies deep yearnings and fills you with Joy.

I have planted longing for perfection in every human heart. This is a good desire, which I alone can fulfill. But most people seek this fulfillment in other people and earthly pleasures or achievements. Thus they create idols, before which they bow down. *I will have no other gods before Me*! Make Me the deepest desire of your heart. Let Me fulfill your yearning for perfection.

"You shall have no other gods before me." —Exodus 20:3

Delight yourself in the Lord and he will give you the desires of your heart. —Psalm 37:4

SEEK MY FACE, and you will find fulfillment of your deepest longings. My world is filled with beautiful things; they are meant to be pointers to Me, reminders of My abiding Presence. The earth still declares My Glory to those who have eyes that see and ears that hear.

You had a darkened mind before you sought Me wholeheartedly. I chose to pour My Light into you, so that you can be a beacon to others. There is no room for pride in this position. Your part is to reflect *My* Glory. I am the Lord!

Look to the LORD and his strength; seek his face always. —PSALM 105:4

The heavens declare the glory of God; the skies proclaim the work of his hands. Day after day they pour forth speech; night after night they display knowledge. —PSALM 19:1–2

See, darkness covers the earth and thick darkness is over the peoples, but the LORD rises upon you and his glory appears over you. —ISAIAH 60:2

June 7

I AM ALL AROUND YOU, like a cocoon of Light. My Presence with you is a promise, independent of your awareness of Me. Many things can block this awareness, but the major culprit is worry. My children tend to accept worry as an inescapable fact of life. However, worry is a form of unbelief; it is anathema to Me.

Who is in charge of your life? If it is you, then you have good reason to worry. But since I am in charge, worry is both unnecessary and counterproductive. When you start to feel anxious about something, relinquish the situation to Me. Back off a bit, redirecting your focus to Me. I will either take care of the problem Myself or show you how to handle it. In this world you will have problems, but you need not lose sight of Me.

Then Jesus said to his disciples: "Therefore I tell you, do not worry about your life, what you will eat; or about your body, what you will wear. Life is more than food, and the body more than clothes. Consider the ravens: They do not sow or reap, they have no storeroom or barn; yet God feeds them. And how much more valuable you are than birds! Who of you by worrying can add a single hour to his life? Since you cannot do this very little thing, why do you worry about the rest? Consider how the lilies grow. They do not labor or spin. Yet I tell you, not even Solomon in all his splendor was dressed like one of these. If that is how God clothes the grass of the field, which is here today, and tomorrow is thrown into the fire, how much more will he clothe you, O you of little faith! And do not set your heart on what you will eat or drink; do not worry about it. . . . But seek his kingdom, and these things will be given to you as well." —LUKE 12:22–31

"I have told you these things, so that in me you may have peace. In this world you will have trouble. But take heart! I have overcome the world." —JOHN 16:33

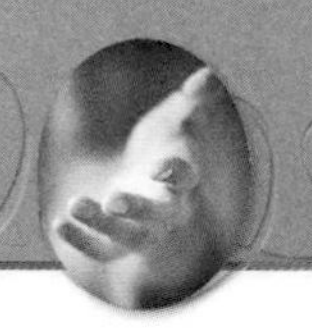

I WANT YOU TO BE ALL MINE, filled with the Light of My Presence. I gave everything for you by living as a man, then dying for your sins and living again. Hold back nothing from Me. Bring your most secret thoughts into the Light of My Love. Anything you bring to Me I transform and cleanse from darkness. I know everything about you, far more than you know of yourself. But I restrain My yearning to "fix" you, waiting instead for you to come to Me for help. Imagine the divine restraint this requires, for *I have all Power in heaven and on earth*.

Seek My Face with a teachable spirit. Come into My Presence with thanksgiving, desiring to be transformed.

Then Jesus came to them and said, "All authority in heaven and on earth has been given to me." —MATTHEW 28:18

Enter his gates with thanksgiving and his courts with praise; give thanks to him and praise his name. —PSALM 100:4

June 9

Seek to live in My Love, which *covers a multitude of sins*: both yours and others'. Wear My Love like a cloak of Light, covering you from head to toe. Have no fear, for *perfect Love decimates fear.* Look at other people through lenses of Love; see them from My perspective. This is how you walk in the Light, and it pleases Me.

I want My Body of believers to be radiant with the Light of My Presence. How I grieve when pockets of darkness increasingly dim the Love-Light. Return to Me, your *First Love*! Gaze at Me in the splendor of holiness, and My Love will once again envelop you in Light.

Above all, love each other deeply, because love covers over a multitude of sins. —1 Peter 4:8

There is no fear in love. But perfect love drives out fear, because fear has to do with punishment. The one who fears is not made perfect in love. —1 John 4:18

"Yet I hold this against you: You have forsaken your first love." —Revelation 2:4

Rest in Me, My child. Give your mind a break from planning and trying to anticipate what will happen. *Pray continually*, asking My Spirit to take charge of the details of this day. Remember that you are on a journey with Me. When you try to peer into the future and plan for every possibility, you ignore your constant Companion who sustains you moment by moment. As you gaze anxiously into the distance, you don't even feel the strong grip of My hand holding yours. How foolish you are, My child!

Remembrance of Me is a daily discipline. Never lose sight of My Presence with you. This will keep you resting in Me all day, every day.

Pray continually. —1 Thessalonians 5:17

Find rest, O my soul, in God alone; my hope comes from him. —Psalm 62:5

June 11

Trust Me and don't be afraid, for I am your Strength and Song. Do not let fear dissipate your energy. Instead, invest your energy in trusting Me and singing My Song. The battle for control of your mind is fierce, and years of worry have made you vulnerable to the enemy. Therefore, you need to be vigilant in guarding your thoughts. Do not despise this weakness in yourself, since I am using it to draw you closer to Me. Your constant need for Me creates an intimacy that is well worth all the effort. You are not alone in this struggle for your mind. My Spirit living within you is ever ready to help in this striving. Ask Him to *control your mind;* He will bless you with *Life and Peace.*

Surely God is my salvation; I will trust and not be afraid. The Lord, the Lord, is my strength and my song; he has become my salvation. —Isaiah 12:2

The mind of sinful man is death, but the mind controlled by the Spirit is life and peace. —Romans 8:6

JUNE 12

LET ME HELP YOU get through this day. There are many possible paths to travel between your getting up in the morning and your lying down at night. Stay alert to the many choice-points along the way, being continually aware of My Presence. You will get through this day one way or the other. One way is to moan and groan, stumbling along with shuffling feet. This will get you to the end of the day eventually, but there is a better way. You can choose to walk with Me along the path of Peace, leaning on Me as much as you need. There will still be difficulties along the way, but you can face them confidently in My strength. Thank Me for each problem you encounter, and watch to see how I transform trials into blessings.

And do not grumble, as some of them did—and were killed by the destroying angel. —1 CORINTHIANS 10:10

To shine on those living in darkness and in the shadow of death, to guide our feet into the path of peace. —LUKE 1:79

June 13

I AM CREATING something new in you: a bubbling spring of Joy that spills over into others' lives. Do not mistake this Joy for your own or try to take credit for it in any way. Instead, watch in delight as My Spirit flows through you to bless others. Let yourself become a reservoir of the Spirit's fruit.

Your part is to live close to Me, open to all that I am doing in you. Don't try to control the streaming of My Spirit through you. Just keep focusing on Me as we walk through this day together. Enjoy My Presence, which permeates you with *Love, Joy, and Peace.*

"The wind blows wherever it pleases. You hear its sound, but you cannot tell where it comes from or where it is going. So it is with everyone born of the Spirit." —JOHN 3:8

But the fruit of the Spirit is love, joy, peace, patience, kindness, goodness, faithfulness. —GALATIANS 5:22

I HAVE LOVED YOU *with an everlasting Love.* Before time began, I knew you. For years you swam around in a sea of meaninglessness, searching for Love, hoping for hope. All that time I was pursuing you, aching to embrace you in My compassionate arms.

When time was right, I revealed Myself to you. I lifted you out of that sea of despair and set you down on a firm foundation. Sometimes you felt naked—exposed to the revealing Light of My Presence. I wrapped an ermine robe around you: *My robe of righteousness.* I sang you a Love song, whose beginning and end are veiled in eternity. I infused meaning into your mind and harmony into your heart. Join Me in singing My song. Together we will draw others *out of darkness into My marvelous Light.*

The LORD *appeared to us in the past, saying: "I have loved you with an everlasting love; I have drawn you with loving-kindness."* —JEREMIAH 31:3

I delight greatly in the LORD; *my soul rejoices in my God. For he has clothed me with garments of salvation and arrayed me in a robe of righteousness, as a bridegroom adorns his head like a priest, and as a bride adorns herself with her jewels.* —ISAIAH 61:10

But you are a chosen generation, a royal priesthood, a holy nation, His own special people, that you may proclaim the praises of Him who called you out of darkness into His marvelous light. —1 PETER 2:9 NKJV

June 15

When you approach Me in stillness and in trust, you are strengthened. You need a buffer zone of silence around you in order to *focus on things that are unseen.* Since I am invisible, you must not let your senses dominate your thinking. The curse of this age is overstimulation of the senses, which blocks out awareness of the unseen world.

The tangible world still reflects My Glory, to those who have eyes that see and ears that hear. Spending time alone with Me is the best way to develop seeing eyes and hearing ears. The goal is to be aware of unseen things even as you live out your life in the visible world.

So we fix our eyes not on what is seen, but on what is unseen. For what is seen is temporary, but what is unseen is eternal. —2 Corinthians 4:18

And they were calling to one another: "Holy, holy, holy is the Lord Almighty; the whole earth is full of his glory." —Isaiah 6:3

I wait for the Lord, my soul waits, and in his word I put my hope. —Psalm 130:5

June 16

Stay on the high road with Me. Many voices clamor for your attention, trying to divert you to another path. But I have called you to walk ever so closely with Me, soaking in My Presence, living in My Peace. This is My unique design for you, planned before the world began.

I have called each of My children to a different path, distinctly designed for that one. Do not let anyone convince you that his path is the only right way. And be careful not to extol your path as superior to another's way. What I require of you is *to act justly, to love mercy, and to walk humbly with Me*—wherever I lead.

For we are God's workmanship, created in Christ Jesus to do good works, which God prepared in advance for us to do. —Ephesians 2:10

He has showed you, O man, what is good. And what does the Lord require of you? To act justly and to love mercy and to walk humbly with your God. —Micah 6:8

June 17

LEARN TO LAUGH at yourself more freely. Don't take yourself or your circumstances so seriously. Relax and know that I am *God with you.* When you desire My will above all else, life becomes much less threatening. Stop trying to monitor My responsibilities—things that are beyond your control. Find freedom by accepting the boundaries of your domain.

Laughter lightens your load and lifts your heart into heavenly places. Your laughter rises to heaven and blends with angelic melodies of praise. Just as parents delight in the laughter of their children, so I delight in hearing My children laugh. I rejoice when you trust Me enough to enjoy your life lightheartedly.

Do not miss the Joy of My Presence by carrying the weight of the world on your shoulders. Rather, *take My yoke upon you and learn from Me. My yoke is comfortable and pleasant; My burden is light and easily borne.*

A cheerful heart is good medicine, but a crushed spirit dries up the bones. —PROVERBS 17:22

She is clothed with strength and dignity; she can laugh at the days to come. —PROVERBS 31:25

"The virgin will be with child and will give birth to a son, and they will call him Immanuel"—which means, "God with us." —MATTHEW 1:23

Take My yoke upon you and learn of Me, for I am gentle (meek) and humble (lowly) in heart, and you will find rest . . . for your souls. For My yoke is wholesome (useful, good—not harsh, hard, sharp, or pressing, but comfortable, gracious, and pleasant), and My burden is light and easy to be borne. —MATTHEW 11:29–30 AMP

June 18

You are My beloved child. *I chose you before the foundation of the world*, to walk with Me along paths designed uniquely for you. Concentrate on keeping in step with Me, instead of trying to anticipate My plans for you. If you trust that My plans are *to prosper you and not to harm you*, you can relax and enjoy the present moment.

Your hope and your future are rooted in heaven, where eternal ecstasy awaits you. Nothing can rob you of your inheritance of unimaginable riches and well-being. Sometimes I grant you glimpses of your glorious future, to encourage you and spur you on. But your main focus should be staying close to Me. I set the pace in keeping with your needs and My purposes.

Just as He chose us in Him before the foundation of the world, that we would be holy and blameless before Him. —Ephesians 1:4 NASB

In his heart a man plans his course, but the Lord determines his steps. —Proverbs 16:9

"For I know the plans I have for you," declares the Lord, "plans to prosper you and not to harm you, plans to give you hope and a future." —Jeremiah 29:11

And you also were included in Christ when you heard the word of truth, the gospel of your salvation. Having believed, you were marked in him with a seal, the promised Holy Spirit, who is a deposit guaranteeing our inheritance until the redemption of those who are God's possession—to the praise of his glory. —Ephesians 1:13–14

I AM THE FIRM FOUNDATION on which you can dance and sing and celebrate My Presence. This is My high and holy calling for you; receive it as a precious gift. *Glorifying and enjoying Me* is a higher priority than maintaining a tidy, structured life. Give up your striving to keep everything under control—an impossible task and a waste of precious energy.

My guidance for each of My children is unique. That's why listening to Me is so vital for your well-being. Let me prepare you for the day that awaits you and point you in the right direction. I am with you continually, so don't be intimidated by fear. Though it stalks you, it cannot harm you, as long as you cling to My hand. Keep your eyes on Me, enjoying Peace in My Presence.

But let all who take refuge in you be glad; let them ever sing for joy. Spread your protection over them, that those who love your name may rejoice in you. —Psalm 5:11

Now to him who is able to do immeasurably more than all we ask or imagine, according to his power that is at work within us, to him be glory in the church and in Christ Jesus. —Ephesians 3:20–21

To him who is able to keep you from falling and to present you before his glorious presence without fault and with great joy—to the only God our Savior be glory, majesty, power and authority, through Jesus Christ our Lord, before all ages, now and forevermore! Amen. —Jude 24–25

"No one will be able to stand up against you all the days of your life. As I was with Moses, so I will be with you; I will never leave you nor forsake you." —Joshua 1:5

I speak to you continually. My nature is to communicate, though not always in words. I fling glorious sunsets across the sky, day after day after day. I speak in the faces and voices of loved ones. I caress you with a gentle breeze that refreshes and delights you. I speak softly in the depths of your spirit, where I have taken up residence.

You can find Me in each moment, when you have eyes that see and ears that hear. Ask My Spirit to sharpen your spiritual eyesight and hearing. I rejoice each time you discover My Presence. Practice looking and listening for Me during quiet intervals. Gradually you will find Me in more and more of your moments. *You will seek Me and find Me, when you seek Me above all else.*

O Lord, our Lord, how majestic is your name in all the earth! You have set your glory above the heavens. From the lips of children and infants you have ordained praise because of your enemies, to silence the foe and the avenger. When I consider your heavens, the work of your fingers, the moon and the stars, which you have set in place, what is man that you are mindful of him, the son of man that you care for him? —Psalm 8:1–4

The heavens declare the glory of God; the skies proclaim the work of his hands. Day after day they pour forth speech; night after night they display knowledge. —Psalm 19:1–2

Do you not know that your body is a temple of the Holy Spirit, who is in you, whom you have received from God? You are not your own. —1 Corinthians 6:19

"You will seek me and find me when you seek me with all your heart." —Jeremiah 29:13

June 21

WAIT PATIENTLY WITH ME while I bless you. Don't rush into My Presence with time-consciousness gnawing at your mind. I dwell in timelessness: *I am, I was, I will always be.* For you, time is a protection; you're a frail creature who can handle only twenty-four-hour segments of life. Time can also be a tyrant, ticking away relentlessly in your mind. Learn to master time, or it will be your master.

Though you are a time-bound creature, seek to meet Me in timelessness. As you focus on My Presence, the demands of time and tasks will diminish. *I will bless you and keep you, making My Face shine upon you graciously, giving you Peace.*

But as for me, I watch in hope for the LORD, I wait for God my Savior; my God will hear me. —MICAH 7:7

"I am the Alpha and the Omega," says the Lord God, "who is, and who was, and who is to come, the Almighty." —REVELATION 1:8

"The LORD bless you and keep you; the LORD make his face shine upon you and be gracious to you; the LORD turn his face toward you and give you peace." —NUMBERS 6:24–26

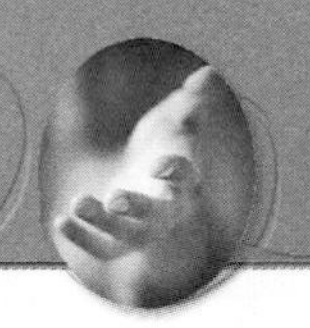

Thank Me for the very things that are troubling you. You are on the brink of rebellion, precariously close to shaking your fist in My Face. You are tempted to indulge in just a little complaining about My treatment of you. But once you step over that line, torrents of rage and self-pity can sweep you away. The best protection against this indulgence is thanksgiving. It is impossible to thank Me and curse Me at the same time.

Thanking Me for trials will feel awkward and contrived at first. But if you persist, your thankful words, prayed in faith, will eventually make a difference in your heart. Thankfulness awakens you to My Presence, which overshadows all your problems.

I will offer to You the sacrifice of thanksgiving, and will call upon the name of the Lord. —Psalm 116:17 NKJV

Rejoice in the Lord always. I will say it again: Rejoice! Let your gentleness be evident to all. The Lord is near. Do not be anxious about anything, but in everything, by prayer and petition, with thanksgiving, present your requests to God. —Philippians 4:4–6

June 23

Let My Love stream through you, washing away fear and distrust. A trusting response includes Me in your thoughts as you consider strategies to deal with a situation. My continual Presence is a promise, guaranteeing that you never have to face anything alone. My children teethe on the truth that I am always with them, yet they stumble around in a stupor, unaware of My loving Presence all around them. How that grieves Me!

When you walk through a day in trusting dependence on Me, My aching heart is soothed. Gently bring your attention back to Me whenever it wanders away. I look for persistence—rather than perfection—in your walk with Me.

But I am like an olive tree flourishing in the house of God; I trust in God's unfailing love for ever and ever. —Psalm 52:8

Be strong and courageous. Do not be afraid or terrified because of them, for the Lord your God goes with you; he will never leave you nor forsake you. —Deuteronomy 31:6

And do not grieve the Holy Spirit of God, with whom you were sealed for the day of redemption. —Ephesians 4:30

June 24

Hold My hand—and trust. So long as you are conscious of My Presence with you, all is well. It is virtually impossible to stumble while walking in the Light with Me. I designed you to enjoy Me above all else. You find the deepest fulfillment of your heart in Me alone.

Fearful, anxious thoughts melt away in the Light of My Presence. When you turn away from Me, you are vulnerable to the darkness that is always at work in the world. Don't be surprised by how easily you sin when you forget to cling to My hand. In the world, dependency is seen as immaturity. But in My kingdom, dependence on Me is a prime measure of maturity.

"So do not fear, for I am with you; do not be dismayed, for I am your God. I will strengthen you and help you; I will uphold you with my righteous right hand." —Isaiah 41:10

Find rest, O my soul, in God alone; my hope comes from him. He alone is my rock and my salvation; he is my fortress, I will not be shaken. —Psalm 62:5–6

June 25

Open your hands and your heart to receive this day as a precious gift from Me. I begin each day with a sunrise, announcing My radiant Presence. By the time you rise from your bed, I have already prepared the way before you. I eagerly await your first conscious thought. I rejoice when you glance My way.

Bring Me the gift of thanksgiving, which opens your heart to rich communion with Me. Because I am God, from whom all blessings flow, thankfulness is the best way to draw near Me. Sing praise songs to Me; tell of My wondrous works. Remember that *I take great delight in you; I rejoice over you with singing.*

This is the day the Lord has made; let us rejoice and be glad in it. —Psalm 118:24

Let us come before him with thanksgiving and extol him with music and song. —Psalm 95:2

The Lord your God is with you, he is mighty to save. He will take great delight in you, he will quiet you with his love, he will rejoice over you with singing. —Zephaniah 3:17

STAY CALMLY CONSCIOUS OF ME today, no matter what. Remember that I go before you as well as with you into the day. Nothing takes Me by surprise. I will not allow circumstances to overwhelm you, so long as you look to Me. I will help you cope with whatever the moment presents. Collaborating with Me brings *blessings that far outweigh all your troubles.* Awareness of My Presence contains Joy that can endure all eventualities.

The LORD is my shepherd; I shall not want. He makes me to lie down in green pastures; He leads me beside the still waters. He restores my soul; He leads me in the paths of righteousness for His name's sake. Yea, though I walk through the valley of the shadow of death, I will fear no evil; for You are with me; Your rod and Your staff, they comfort me. —PSALM 23:1–4 NKJV

Therefore we do not lose heart. Though outwardly we are wasting away, yet inwardly we are being renewed day by day. For our light and momentary troubles are achieving for us an eternal glory that far outweighs them all. —2 CORINTHIANS 4:16–17

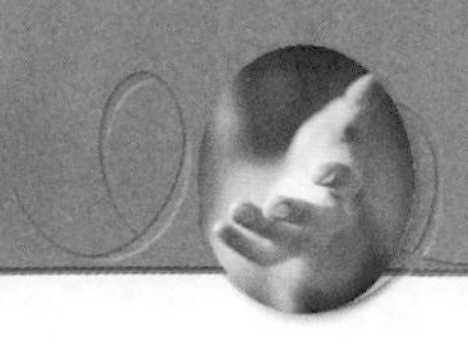

June 27

Rest with Me a while. You have journeyed up a steep, rugged path in recent days. The way ahead is shrouded in uncertainty. Look neither behind you nor before you. Instead, focus your attention on Me, your constant Companion. Trust that I will equip you fully for whatever awaits you on your journey.

I designed time to be a protection for you. You couldn't bear to see all your life at once. Though I am unlimited by time, it is in the present moment that I meet you. Refresh yourself in My company, breathing deep draughts of My Presence. The highest level of trust is to enjoy Me moment by moment. *I am with you, watching over you wherever you go.*

Let the morning bring me word of your unfailing love,
for I have put my trust in you. Show me the way I should
go, for to you I lift up my soul. —Psalm 143:8

"I am with you and will watch over you wherever you go, and
I will bring you back to this land. I will not leave you until I
have done what I have promised you." —Genesis 28:15

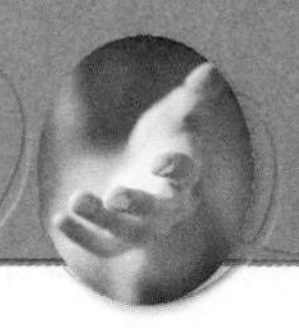

Taste and see that I am good. This command contains an invitation to experience My living Presence. It also contains a promise. The more you experience Me, the more convinced you become of My goodness. This knowledge is essential to your faith-walk. When adversities strike, the human instinct is to doubt My goodness. My ways are mysterious, even to those who know Me intimately. *As the heavens are higher than the earth, so are My ways and thoughts higher than your ways and thoughts.* Do not try to fathom My ways. Instead, spend time enjoying Me and experiencing My goodness.

Taste and see that the Lord is good; blessed is the man who takes refuge in him. —Psalm 34:8

"For my thoughts are not your thoughts, neither are your ways my ways," declares the Lord. "As the heavens are higher than the earth, so are my ways higher than your ways and my thoughts than your thoughts." —Isaiah 55:8–9

June 29

As you get out of bed in the morning, be aware of My Presence with you. You may not be thinking clearly yet, but I am. Your early morning thoughts tend to be anxious ones until you get connected with Me. Invite Me into your thoughts by whispering My Name. Suddenly your day brightens and feels more user-friendly. You cannot dread a day that is vibrant with My Presence.

You gain confidence through knowing that I am with you—that you face nothing alone. Anxiety stems from asking the wrong question: "If such and such happens, can I handle it?" The true question is not whether you can cope with whatever happens, but whether you and I together can handle anything that occurs. It is this you-and-I-together factor that gives you confidence to face the day cheerfully.

In the morning, O Lord, you hear my voice; in the morning I lay my requests before you and wait in expectation. —Psalm 5:3

O God, You are my God; early will I seek You; my soul thirsts for You; my flesh longs for You in a dry and thirsty land where there is no water. —Psalm 63:1 NKJV

I can do everything through him who gives me strength. —Philippians 4:13

June 30

I AM THE TRUTH: the One who came to *set you free*. As the Holy Spirit controls your mind and actions more fully, you become free in Me. You are increasingly released to become the one I created you to be. This is a work that I do in you as you yield to My Spirit. I can do My best handiwork when you sit in the stillness of My Presence, focusing your entire being on Me.

Let My thoughts burst freely upon your consciousness, stimulating abundant Life. *I am the Way and the Truth and the Life*. As you follow Me, I lead you along paths of newness: ways you have never imagined. Don't worry about what is on the road up ahead. I want you to find your security in knowing Me, the One who died to *set you free*.

"Then you will know the truth, and the truth will set you free." —JOHN 8:32

For it is God who works in you to will and to act according to his good purpose. —PHILIPPIANS 2:13

Jesus answered, "I am the way and the truth and the life. No one comes to the Father except through me." —JOHN 14:6

July

Therefore, there is now no condemnation for those who are in Christ Jesus.

ROMANS 8:1

July 1

I AM LIFE AND LIGHT IN ABUNDANCE. As you spend time "soaking" in My Presence, you are energized and lightened. Through communing with Me, you transfer your heavy burdens to My strong shoulders. By gazing at Me, you gain My perspective on your life. This time alone with Me is essential for unscrambling your thoughts and smoothing out the day before you.

Be willing to fight for this precious time with Me. Opposition comes in many forms: your own desire to linger in bed; the evil one's determination to distract you from Me; the pressure of family, friends, and your own inner critic to spend your time more productively. As you grow in your desire to please Me above all else, you gain strength to resist these opponents. *Delight yourself in Me, for I am the deepest Desire of your heart.*

Within your temple, O God, we meditate on your unfailing love. —PSALM 48:9

About Benjamin he said: "Let the beloved of the LORD rest secure in him, for he shields him all day long, and the one the LORD loves rests between his shoulders." —DEUTERONOMY 33:12

Delight yourself in the LORD and he will give you the desires of your heart. —PSALM 37:4

LET ME SHOW YOU My way for you this day. I guide you continually, so you can relax and enjoy My Presence in the present. Living well is both a discipline and an art. Concentrate on staying close to Me, the divine Artist. Discipline your thoughts to trust Me as I work My ways in your life. Pray about everything; then, leave outcomes up to Me. Do not fear My will, for through it I accomplish what is best for you. Take a deep breath and dive into the depths of absolute trust in Me. *Underneath are the everlasting arms!*

> *Listen to my cry for help, my King and my God, for to you I pray. In the morning, O LORD, you hear my voice; in the morning I lay my requests before you and wait in expectation.* —PSALM 5:2–3

> *The eternal God is your refuge, and underneath are the everlasting arms. He will drive out your enemy before you, saying, "Destroy him!"* —DEUTERONOMY 33:27

July 3

My children make a pastime of judging one another—and themselves. But I am the only capable Judge, and I have acquitted you through My own blood. Your acquittal came at the price of My unparalleled sacrifice. That is why I am highly offended when I hear My children judge one another or indulge in self-hatred.

If you live close to Me and absorb My Word, the Holy Spirit will guide and correct you as needed. There is *no condemnation* for those who belong to Me.

"Do not judge, and you will not be judged. Do not condemn, and you will not be condemned. Forgive, and you will be forgiven." —Luke 6:37

Now there is in store for me the crown of righteousness, which the Lord, the righteous Judge, will award to me on that day—and not only to me, but also to all who have longed for his appearing. —2 Timothy 4:8

He saved us, not because of righteous things we had done, but because of his mercy. He saved us through the washing of rebirth and renewal by the Holy Spirit. —Titus 3:5

Therefore, there is now no condemnation for those who are in Christ Jesus. —Romans 8:1

WHEN YOU WORSHIP ME *in spirit and truth*, you join with choirs of angels who are continually before My throne. Though you cannot hear their voices, your praise and thanksgiving are distinctly audible in heaven. Your petitions are also heard, but it is your gratitude that clears the way to My Heart. With the way between us wide open, My blessings fall upon you in rich abundance. The greatest blessing is nearness to Me—abundant Joy and Peace in My Presence. Practice praising and thanking Me continually throughout this day.

"Yet a time is coming and has now come when the true worshipers will worship the Father in spirit and truth, for they are the kind of worshipers the Father seeks. God is spirit, and his worshipers must worship in spirit and in truth." —JOHN 4:23–24

Enter his gates with thanksgiving and his courts with praise; give thanks to him and praise his name. —PSALM 100:4

DRAW NEAR TO ME with a thankful heart, aware that your cup is overflowing with blessings. Gratitude enables you to perceive Me more clearly and to rejoice in our Love-relationship. *Nothing can separate you from My loving Presence*! That is the basis of your security. Whenever you start to feel anxious, remind yourself that your security rests in Me alone, and I am totally trustworthy.

You will never be in control of your life circumstances, but you can relax and trust in My control. Instead of striving for a predictable, safe lifestyle, seek to know Me in greater depth and breadth. I long to make your life a glorious adventure, but you must stop clinging to old ways. I am always doing something new within My beloved ones. Be on the lookout for all that I have prepared for you.

For I am convinced that neither death nor life, neither angels nor demons, neither the present nor the future, nor any powers, neither height nor depth, nor anything else in all creation, will be able to separate us from the love of God that is in Christ Jesus our Lord. —ROMANS 8:38–39

When I am afraid, I will trust in you. In God, whose word I praise, in God I trust; I will not be afraid. What can mortal man do to me? —PSALM 56:3–4

See, I am doing a new thing! Now it springs up; do you not perceive it? I am making a way in the desert and streams in the wasteland. —ISAIAH 43:19

I AM YOUR FATHER-GOD. Listen to Me! Learn what it means to be a child of the everlasting King. Your richest duty is devotion to Me. This duty is such a joyous privilege that it feels like a luxury. You tend to feel guilty about pushing back the boundaries of your life to make space for time alone with Me. The world is waiting to squeeze you into its mold and to crowd out time devoted to Me. The ways of the world have also warped your conscience, which punishes you for doing the very thing that pleases Me most: seeking My Face. Listen to Me above the clamor of voices trying to distract you. Ask My Spirit to control your mind, for He and I work in perfect harmony. Be still and attentive in My Presence. *You are on holy ground.*

For to us a child is born, to us a son is given, and the government will be on his shoulders. And he will be called Wonderful Counselor, Mighty God, Everlasting Father, Prince of Peace. —ISAIAH 9:6

"Rejoice greatly, O daughter of Zion! Shout, O daughter of Jerusalem! Behold, your King is coming to you; He is just and having salvation, lowly and riding on a donkey, a colt, the foal of a donkey." —ZECHARIAH 9:9 NKJV

For you did not receive a spirit that makes you a slave again to fear, but you received the Spirit of sonship. And by him we cry, "Abba, Father." The Spirit himself testifies with our spirit that we are God's children. —ROMANS 8:15–16

"Do not come any closer," God said. "Take off your sandals, for the place where you are standing is holy ground." —EXODUS 3:5

Trust Me in all your thoughts. I know that some thoughts are unconscious or semiconscious, and I do not hold you responsible for those. But you can direct conscious thoughts much more than you may realize. Practice thinking in certain ways—trusting Me, thanking Me—and those thoughts become more natural. Reject negative or sinful thoughts as soon as you become aware of them. Don't try to hide them from Me; confess them and leave them with Me. Go on your way lightheartedly. This method of controlling your thoughts will keep your mind in My Presence and your feet on the *path of Peace.*

Some trust in chariots and some in horses, but we trust in the name of the Lord our God. —Psalm 20:7

If we confess our sins, he is faithful and just and will forgive us our sins and purify us from all unrighteousness. —1 John 1:9

To shine on those living in darkness and in the shadow of death, to guide our feet into the path of peace. —Luke 1:79

When you seek My Face, put aside thoughts of everything else. I am above all, as well as in all; your communion with Me transcends both time and circumstances. Be prepared to be blessed bountifully by My Presence, for I am a God of unlimited abundance. Open wide your heart and mind to receive more and more of Me. When your Joy in Me meets My Joy in you, there are fireworks of heavenly ecstasy. This is eternal life here and now: a tiny foretaste of what awaits you in the life to come. *Now you see only a poor reflection as in a mirror, but then you will see face to Face.*

"I have told you this so that my joy may be in you and that your joy may be complete." John 15:11

Now we see but a poor reflection as in a mirror; then we shall see face to face. Now I know in part; then I shall know fully, even as I am fully known. —1 Corinthians 13:12

July 9

Stop worrying long enough to hear My voice. I speak softly to you, in the depths of your being. Your mind shuttles back and forth, hither and yon, weaving webs of anxious confusion. As My thoughts rise up within you, they become entangled in those sticky webs of worry. Thus, My voice is muffled, and you hear only "white noise."

Ask My Spirit to quiet your mind so that you can think My thoughts. This ability is an awesome benefit of being My child, patterned after My own image. Do not be deafened by the noise of the world or that of your own thinking. Instead, *be transformed by the renewing of your mind.* Sit quietly in My Presence, letting My thoughts reprogram your thinking.

And that you may love the Lord your God, listen to his voice, and hold fast to him. For the Lord is your life, and he will give you many years in the land he swore to give to your fathers, Abraham, Isaac and Jacob. —Deuteronomy 30:20

So God created man in his own image, in the image of God he created him; male and female he created them. —Genesis 1:27

Do not conform any longer to the pattern of this world, but be transformed by the renewing of your mind. Then you will be able to test and approve what God's will is—his good, pleasing and perfect will. —Romans 12:2

Relax in My peaceful Presence. Do not bring performance pressures into our sacred space of communion. When you are with someone you trust completely, you feel free to be yourself. This is one of the joys of true friendship. Though I am *Lord of lords and King of kings*, I also desire to be your intimate Friend. When you are tense or pretentious in our relationship, I feel hurt. I know the worst about you, but I also see the best in you. I long for you to trust Me enough to be fully yourself with Me. When you are real with Me, I am able to bring out the best in you: the very gifts I have planted in your soul. Relax, and enjoy our friendship.

"They will make war against the Lamb, but the Lamb will overcome them because he is Lord of lords and King of kings—and with him will be his called, chosen and faithful followers." —Revelation 17:14

"Greater love has no one than this, that he lay down his life for his friends. You are my friends if you do what I command. I no longer call you servants, because a servant does not know his master's business. Instead, I have called you friends, for everything that I learned from my Father I have made known to you." —John 15:13–15

July 11

Worship Me only. Idolatry has always been the downfall of My people. I make no secrets about being *a jealous God*. Current idols are more subtle than ancient ones, because today's false gods are often outside the field of religion. People, possessions, status, and self-aggrandizement are some of the most popular deities today. Beware of bowing down before these things. False gods never satisfy; instead, they stir up lust for more and more.

When you seek Me instead of the world's idols, you experience My Joy and Peace. These intangibles slake the thirst of your soul, providing deep satisfaction. The glitter of the world is tinny and temporal. The Light of My Presence is brilliant and everlasting. Walk in the Light with Me. Thus you become a beacon through whom others are drawn to Me.

"You shall not make for yourself an idol in the form of anything in heaven above or on the earth beneath or in the waters below. You shall not bow down to them or worship them; for I, the Lord your God, am a jealous God, punishing the children for the sin of the fathers to the third and fourth generation of those who hate me." —Exodus 20:4–5

You are my lamp, O Lord; the Lord turns my darkness into light. —2 Samuel 22:29

Whenever you feel distant from Me, whisper My Name in loving trust. This simple prayer can restore your awareness of My Presence.

My Name is constantly abused in the world, where people use it as a curse word. This verbal assault reaches all the way to heaven; every word is heard and recorded. When you trustingly whisper My Name, My aching ears are soothed. The grating rancor of the world's blasphemies cannot compete with a trusting child's utterance: "Jesus." The power of My Name to bless both you and Me is beyond your understanding.

Salvation is found in no one else, for there is no other name under heaven given to men by which we must be saved. —Acts 4:12

"Until now you have not asked for anything in my name. Ask and you will receive, and your joy will be complete." —John 16:24

July 13

I WANT YOU TO EXPERIENCE the riches of your salvation: the Joy of being loved constantly and perfectly. You make a practice of judging yourself, based on how you look or behave or feel. If you like what you see in the mirror, you feel a bit more worthy of My Love. When things are going smoothly and your performance seems adequate, you find it easier to believe you are My beloved child. When you feel discouraged, you tend to look inward so you can correct whatever is wrong.

Instead of trying to "fix" yourself, *fix your gaze on Me, the Lover of your soul.* Rather than using your energy to judge yourself, redirect it to praising Me. Remember that I see you clothed in My righteousness, radiant in My perfect Love.

In order that in the coming ages he might show the incomparable riches of his grace, expressed in his kindness to us in Christ Jesus. For it is by grace you have been saved, through faith—and this not from yourselves, it is the gift of God. —EPHESIANS 2:7–8

Therefore, holy brothers, who share in the heavenly calling, fix your thoughts on Jesus, the apostle and high priest whom we confess. —HEBREWS 3:1

Those who look to him are radiant; their faces are never covered with shame. —PSALM 34:5

Keep walking with Me along the path I have chosen for you. Your desire to live close to Me is a delight to My heart. I could instantly grant you the spiritual riches you desire, but that is not My way for you. Together we will forge a pathway up the high mountain. The journey is arduous at times, and you are weak. Someday you will dance light-footed on the high peaks; but for now, your walk is often plodding and heavy. All I require of you is to take the next step, clinging to My hand for strength and direction. Though the path is difficult and the scenery dull at the moment, there are sparkling surprises just around the bend. Stay on the path I have selected for you. It is truly the *path of Life*.

If the Lord delights in a man's way, he makes his steps firm; though he stumble, he will not fall, for the Lord upholds him with his hand. —Psalm 37:23–24

You will show me the path of life; in Your presence is fullness of joy; at Your right hand are pleasures forevermore. —Psalm 16:11 NKJV

July 15

Do not worry about tomorrow! This is not a suggestion, but a command. I divided time into days and nights, so that you would have manageable portions of life to handle. *My grace is sufficient for you*, but its sufficiency is for only one day at a time. When you worry about the future, you heap day upon day of troubles onto your flimsy frame. You stagger under this heavy load, which I never intended you to carry.

Throw off this oppressive burden with one quick thrust of trust. Anxious thoughts meander about and crisscross in your brain, but trusting Me brings you directly into My Presence. As you thus affirm your faith, shackles of worry fall off instantly. Enjoy My Presence continually by trusting Me at all times.

"Therefore do not worry about tomorrow, for tomorrow will worry about itself. Each day has enough trouble of its own." —Matthew 6:34

But he said to me, "My grace is sufficient for you, for my power is made perfect in weakness." Therefore I will boast all the more gladly about my weaknesses, so that Christ's power may rest on me. —2 Corinthians 12:9

Trust in Him at all times, you people; pour out your heart before Him; God is a refuge for us. —Psalm 62:8 NKJV

Self-pity is a slimy, bottomless pit. Once you fall in, you tend to go deeper and deeper into the mire. As you slide down those slippery walls, you are well on your way to depression, and the darkness is profound.

Your only hope is to look up and see the Light of My Presence shining down on you. Though the Light looks dim from your perspective, deep in the pit, those rays of hope can reach you at any depth. While you focus on Me in trust, you rise ever so slowly out of the abyss of despair. Finally, you can reach up and grasp My hand. I will pull you out into the Light again. I will gently cleanse you, washing off the clinging mire. I will cover you with My righteousness and walk with you down the path of Life.

He lifted me out of the slimy pit, out of the mud and mire; he set my feet on a rock and gave me a firm place to stand. He put a new song in my mouth, a hymn of praise to our God. Many will see and fear and put their trust in the Lord. —Psalm 40:2–3

Why are you in despair, O my soul? And why have you become disturbed within me? Hope in God, for I shall again praise Him for the help of His presence. —Psalm 42:5 NASB

The Lord delights in those who fear him, who put their hope in his unfailing love. —Psalm 147:11

July 17

Come away with Me for a while. The world, with its nonstop demands, can be put on hold. Most people put *Me* on hold, rationalizing that someday they will find time to focus on Me. But the longer people push Me into the background of their lives, the harder it is for them to find Me.

You live among people who glorify busyness; they have made time a tyrant that controls their lives. Even those who know Me as Savior tend to march to the tempo of the world. They have bought into the illusion that more is always better: more meetings, more programs, more activity.

I have called you to follow Me on a solitary path, making time alone with Me your highest priority and deepest Joy. It is a pathway largely unappreciated and often despised. However, *you have chosen the better thing, which will never be taken away from you*. Moreover, as you walk close to Me, I can bless others through you.

The fig tree forms its early fruit; the blossoming vines spread their fragrance. Arise, come, my darling; my beautiful one, come with me. —Song of Songs 2:13

"But only one thing is needed. Mary has chosen what is better, and it will not be taken away from her." —Luke 10:42

I AM NEARER than you think, richly present in all your moments. You are connected to Me by Love-bonds that nothing can sever. However, you may sometimes feel alone, because your union with Me is invisible. Ask Me to open your eyes, so that you can find Me everywhere. The more aware you are of My Presence, the safer you feel. This is not some sort of escape from reality; it is tuning in to *ultimate reality*. I am far more Real than the world you can see, hear, and touch. *Faith is the confirmation of things we do not see and the conviction of their reality, perceiving as real fact what is not revealed to the senses.*

God did this so that men would seek him and perhaps reach out for him and find him, though he is not far from each one of us. "For in him we live and move and have our being." As some of your own poets have said, "We are his offspring." ACTS 17:27–28

Now faith is the assurance (the confirmation, the title deed) of the things [we] hope for, being the proof of things [we] do not see and the conviction of their reality [faith perceiving as real fact what is not revealed to the senses]. —HEBREWS 11:1 AMP

July 19

Bring Me all your feelings, even the ones you wish you didn't have. Fear and anxiety still plague you. Feelings *per se* are not sinful, but they can be temptations to sin. Blazing missiles of fear fly at you day and night; these attacks from the evil one come at you relentlessly. Use your *shield of faith to extinguish those flaming arrows.* Affirm your trust in Me, regardless of how you feel. If you persist, your feelings will eventually fall in line with your faith.

Do not hide from your fear or pretend it isn't there. Anxiety that you hide in the recesses of your heart will give birth to fear of fear: a monstrous mutation. Bring your anxieties out into the Light of My Presence, where we can deal with them together. Concentrate on trusting Me, and fearfulness will gradually lose its foothold within you.

In addition to all this, take up the shield of faith, with which you can extinguish all the flaming arrows of the evil one. —Ephesians 6:16

This is the message we have heard from him and declare to you: God is light; in him there is no darkness at all. If we claim to have fellowship with him yet walk in the darkness, we lie and do not live by the truth. But if we walk in the light, as he is in the light, we have fellowship with one another, and the blood of Jesus, his Son, purifies us from all sin. —1 John 1:5–7

Surely God is my salvation; I will trust and not be afraid.
The Lord, the Lord, is my strength and my song; he
has become my salvation. —Isaiah 12:2

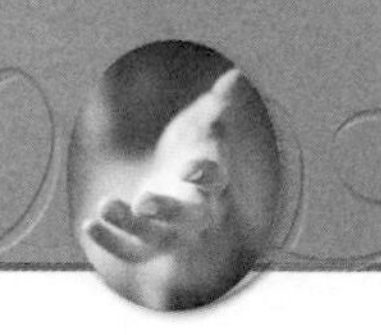

SEEK MY FACE, and you will find all that you have longed for. The deepest yearnings of your heart are for intimacy with Me. I know, because I designed you to desire Me. Do not feel guilty about taking time to be still in My Presence. You are simply responding to the tugs of divinity within you. I made you in My image, and I hid heaven in your heart. Your yearning for Me is a form of homesickness: longing for your true home in heaven.

Do not be afraid to be different from other people. The path I have called you to travel is exquisitely right for you. The more closely you follow My leading, the more fully I can develop your gifts. To follow Me wholeheartedly, you must relinquish your desire to please other people. However, your closeness to Me will bless others by enabling you to shine brightly in this dark world.

As the deer pants for streams of water, so my soul pants for you, O God. My soul thirsts for God, for the living God. When can I go and meet with God? PSALM 42:1–2

Those who look to him are radiant; their faces are never covered with shame. —PSALM 34:5

So that you may become blameless and pure, children of God without fault in a crooked and depraved generation, in which you shine like stars in the universe. —PHILIPPIANS 2:15

July 21

Rest in My Presence when you need refreshment. Resting is not necessarily idleness, as people often perceive it. When you relax in My company, you are demonstrating trust in Me. *Trust* is a rich word, laden with meaning and direction for your life. I want you to *lean on, trust, and be confident in Me*. When you lean on Me for support, I delight in your trusting confidence.

Many people turn away from Me when they are exhausted. They associate Me with duty and diligence, so they try to hide from My Presence when they need a break from work. How this saddens Me! As I spoke through My prophet Isaiah: *In returning to Me and resting in Me you shall be saved; in quietness and trust shall be your strength.*

Lean on, trust in, and be confident in the Lord with all your heart and mind and do not rely on your own insight or understanding. —Proverbs 3:5 AMP

For thus said the Lord God, the Holy One of Israel: In returning [to Me] and resting [in Me] you shall be saved; in quietness and in [trusting] confidence shall be your strength. But you would not. —Isaiah 30:15 AMP

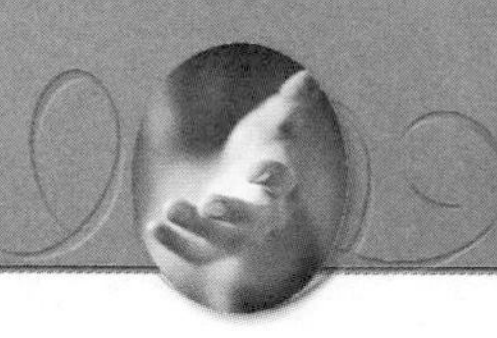

FIND FREEDOM through seeking to please Me above all else. *You can have only one Master.* When you let others' expectations drive you, you scatter your energy to the winds. Your own desire to look good can also drain your energy. I am your Master, and I do not drive you to be what you are not. Your pretense displeases Me, especially when it is in My "service." Concentrate on staying close to Me at all times. It is impossible to be inauthentic while you are focusing on My Presence.

For you were once darkness, but now you are light in the Lord. Live as children of light (for the fruit of the light consists in all goodness, righteousness and truth) and find out what pleases the Lord. —EPHESIANS 5:8–10

"But you are not to be called 'Rabbi,' for you have only one Master and you are all brothers." —MATTHEW 23:8

"Be careful not to do your 'acts of righteousness' before men, to be seen by them. If you do, you will have no reward from your Father in heaven." —MATTHEW 6:1

July 23

I am the Light of the world. Men crawl through their lives cursing the darkness, but all the while I am shining brightly. I desire each of My followers to be a Light-bearer. The Holy Spirit who lives in you can shine from your face, making Me visible to people around you. Ask My Spirit to live through you, as you wend your way through this day. Hold My hand in joyful trust, for I never leave your side. The Light of My Presence is shining upon you. Brighten up the world by reflecting who I AM.

When Jesus spoke again to the people, he said, "I am the light of the world. Whoever follows me will never walk in darkness, but will have the light of life." —JOHN 8:12

"You are the light of the world. A city on a hill cannot be hidden. Neither do people light a lamp and put it under a bowl. Instead they put it on its stand, and it gives light to everyone in the house. In the same way, let your light shine before men, that they may see your good deeds and praise your Father in heaven." —MATTHEW 5:14–16

And we, who with unveiled faces all reflect the Lord's glory, are being transformed into his likeness with ever-increasing glory, which comes from the Lord, who is the Spirit. —2 CORINTHIANS 3:18

God said to Moses, "I AM WHO I AM. This is what you are to say to the Israelites: 'I AM has sent me to you.'" —EXODUS 3:14

Thankfulness opens the door to My Presence. Though I am always with you, I have gone to great measures to preserve your freedom of choice. I have placed a door between you and Me, and I have empowered you to open or close that door. There are many ways to open it, but a grateful attitude is one of the most effective.

Thankfulness is built on a substructure of trust. When thankful words stick in your throat, you need to check up on your foundation of trust. When thankfulness flows freely from your heart and lips, let your gratitude draw you closer to Me. I want you to learn the art of *giving thanks in all circumstances*. See how many times you can thank Me daily; this will awaken your awareness to a multitude of blessings. It will also cushion the impact of trials when they come against you. Practice My Presence by practicing the discipline of thankfulness.

Enter his gates with thanksgiving and his courts with praise; give thanks to him and praise his name. —Psalm 100:4

Give thanks in all circumstances, for this is God's will for you in Christ Jesus. —1 Thessalonians 5:18

July 25

As you listen to birds calling to one another, hear also My Love-call to you. I speak to you continually: through sights, sounds, thoughts, impressions, scriptures. There is no limit to the variety of ways I can communicate with you. Your part is to be attentive to My messages, in whatever form they come. When you set out to find Me in a day, you discover that the world is vibrantly alive with My Presence. You can find Me not only in beauty and birdcalls, but also in tragedy and faces filled with grief. I can take the deepest sorrow and *weave it into a pattern for good.*

Search for Me and My messages, as you go through this day. *You will seek Me and find Me when you seek Me with your whole being.*

"My sheep listen to my voice; I know them, and they follow me." —John 10:27

We are assured and know that [God being a partner in their labor] all things work together and are [fitting into a plan] for good to and for those who love God and are called according to [His] design and purpose. —Romans 8:28 AMP

"You will seek me and find me when you seek me with all your heart." —Jeremiah 29:13

RELAX AND LET ME LEAD YOU through this day. I have everything under control: *My* control. You tend to peer anxiously into the day that is before you, trying to figure out what to do, and when. Meanwhile, the phone or the doorbell rings, and you have to reshuffle your plans. All that planning ties you up in knots and distracts you from Me. Attentiveness to Me is not only for your quiet time, but for all your time. As you look to Me, I show you what to do *now* and *next*.

Vast quantities of time and energy are wasted in obsessive planning. When you let *Me* direct your steps, you are set free to enjoy Me and to find what I have prepared for you this day.

I will instruct you and teach you in the way you should go; I will counsel you and watch over you. —PSALM 32:8

Direct me in the path of your commands, for there I find delight. —PSALM 119:35

Let the morning bring me word of your unfailing love, for I have put my trust in you. Show me the way I should go, for to you I lift up my soul. —PSALM 143:8

July 27

HOPE IS A GOLDEN CORD connecting you to heaven. This cord helps you hold your head up high, even when multiple trials are buffeting you. I never leave your side, and I never let go of your hand. But without the cord of hope, your head may slump and your feet may shuffle as you journey uphill with Me. Hope lifts your perspective from your weary feet to the glorious view you can see from the high road. You are reminded that the road we're traveling together is ultimately a highway to heaven. When you consider this radiant destination, the roughness or smoothness of the road ahead becomes much less significant. I am training you to hold in your heart a dual focus: My continual Presence and the hope of heaven.

Be joyful in hope, patient in affliction, faithful in prayer. —ROMANS 12:12

But since we belong to the day, let us be self-controlled, putting on faith and love as a breastplate, and the hope of salvation as a helmet. —1 THESSALONIANS 5:8

God did this so that, by two unchangeable things in which it is impossible for God to lie, we who have fled to take hold of the hope offered to us may be greatly encouraged. We have this hope as an anchor for the soul, firm and secure. It enters the inner sanctuary behind the curtain. —HEBREWS 6:18–19

Let My Love seep into the inner recesses of your being. Do not close off any part of yourself from Me. I know you inside and out, so do not try to present a "cleaned-up" self to Me. Wounds that you shut away from the Light of My Love will fester and become wormy. Secret sins that you "hide" from Me can split off and develop lives of their own, controlling you without your realizing it.

Open yourself fully to My transforming Presence. Let My brilliant Love-Light search out and destroy hidden fears. This process requires time alone with Me, as My Love soaks into your innermost being. Enjoy *My perfect Love, which expels every trace of fear.*

O Lord, you have searched me and you know me. You know when I sit and when I rise; you perceive my thoughts from afar. You discern my going out and my lying down; you are familiar with all my ways. Before a word is on my tongue you know it completely, O Lord. . . . Search me, O God, and know my heart; test me and know my anxious thoughts. See if there is any offensive way in me, and lead me in the way everlasting. —Psalm 139:1–4, 23–24

There is no fear in love [dread does not exist], but full-grown (complete, perfect) love turns fear out of doors and expels every trace of terror! For fear brings with it the thought of punishment, and [so] he who is afraid has not reached the full maturity of love [is not yet grown into love's complete perfection]. —1 John 4:18 amp

July 29

Come to Me continually. I am meant to be the Center of your consciousness, the *Anchor of your soul.* Your mind will wander from Me, but the question is how far you allow it to wander. An anchor on a short rope lets a boat drift only slightly before the taut line tugs the boat back toward the center. Similarly, as you drift away from Me, My Spirit within you gives a tug, prompting you to return to Me. As you become increasingly attuned to My Presence, the length of rope on your soul's Anchor is shortened. You wander only a short distance before feeling that inner tug—telling you to return to your true Center in Me.

We have this hope as an anchor for the soul, firm and secure. It enters the inner sanctuary behind the curtain. —Hebrews 6:19

And now, dear children, continue in him, so that when he appears we may be confident and unashamed before him at his coming. —1 John 2:28

Jesus replied: "'Love the Lord your God with all your heart and with all your soul and with all your mind.'" —Matthew 22:37

Worship Me in the beauty of holiness. I created beauty to declare the existence of My holy Being. A magnificent rose, a hauntingly glorious sunset, oceanic splendor—all these things were meant to proclaim My Presence in the world. Most people rush past these proclamations without giving them a second thought. Some people use beauty, especially feminine loveliness, to sell their products.

How precious are My children who are awed by nature's beauty; this opens them up to My holy Presence. Even before you knew Me personally, you responded to My creation with wonder. This is a gift, and it carries responsibility with it. Declare My glorious Being to the world. *The whole earth is full of My radiant beauty—My Glory*!

Give unto the Lord the glory due to His name; worship the Lord in the beauty of holiness. —Psalm 29:2 NKJV

And they were calling to one another: "Holy, holy, holy is the Lord Almighty; the whole earth is full of his glory." —Isaiah 6:3

July 31

Trust Me in the depths of your being. It is there that I live in constant communion with you. When you feel flustered and frazzled on the outside, do not get upset with yourself. You are only human, and the swirl of events going on all around you will sometimes feel overwhelming. Rather than scolding yourself for your humanness, remind yourself that I am both with you and within you.

I am with you at all times, encouraging and supportive rather than condemning. I know that deep within you, where I live, My Peace is your continual experience. Slow down your pace of living for a time. Quiet your mind in My Presence. Then you will be able to hear Me bestowing the resurrection blessing: *Peace be with you*.

To them God has chosen to make known among the Gentiles the glorious riches of this mystery, which is Christ in you, the hope of glory. —Colossians 1:27

"And teaching them to obey everything I have commanded you. And surely I am with you always, to the very end of the age." —Matthew 28:20

On the evening of that first day of the week, when the disciples were together, with the doors locked for fear of the Jews, Jesus came and stood among them and said, "Peace be with you!" —John 20:19

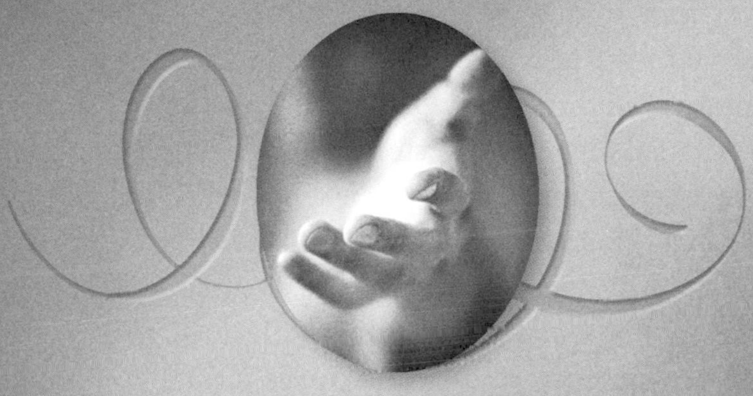

August

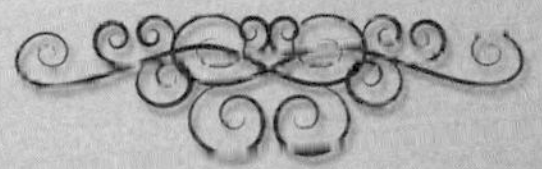

"Whoever believes in me, as the Scripture has said, streams of living water will flow from within him."

John 7:38

AUGUST 1

NOTHING CAN SEPARATE YOU from My Love. Let this divine assurance trickle through your mind and into your heart and soul. Whenever you start to feel fearful or anxious, repeat this unconditional promise: "Nothing can separate me from Your Love, Jesus."

Most of mankind's misery stems from feeling unloved. In the midst of adverse circumstances, people tend to feel that love has been withdrawn and they have been forsaken. This feeling of abandonment is often worse than the adversity itself. Be assured that I never abandon any of My children, not even temporarily. *I will never leave you or forsake you!* My Presence watches over you continually. *I have engraved you on the palms of My hands.*

For I am convinced that neither death nor life, neither angels nor demons, neither the present nor the future, nor any powers, neither height nor depth, nor anything else in all creation, will be able to separate us from the love of God that is in Christ Jesus our Lord. —ROMANS 8:38–39

"No one will be able to stand up against you all the days of your life. As I was with Moses, so I will be with you; I will never leave you nor forsake you." —JOSHUA 1:5

"Can a mother forget the baby at her breast and have no compassion on the child she has borne? Though she may forget, I will not forget you! See, I have engraved you on the palms of my hands; your walls are ever before me." —ISAIAH 49:15–16

August 2

Bring Me the sacrifice of your time: a most precious commodity. In this action-addicted world, few of My children take time to sit quietly in My Presence. But for those who do, blessings flow like *streams of living water.* I, the One from whom all blessings flow, am also blessed by our time together. This is a deep mystery; do not try to fathom it. Instead, glorify Me by delighting in Me. Enjoy Me now and forever!

Surely you have granted him eternal blessings and made him glad with the joy of your presence. —Psalm 21:6

"Whoever believes in me, as the Scripture has said, streams of living water will flow from within him." —John 7:38

For as high as the heavens are above the earth, so great is his love for those who fear him. —Psalm 103:11

August 3

Watch your words diligently. Words have such great power to bless or to wound. When you speak carelessly or negatively, you damage others as well as yourself. This ability to verbalize is an awesome privilege, granted only to those I created in My image. You need help in wielding this mighty power responsibly.

Though the world applauds quick-witted retorts, My instructions about communication are quite different: *Be quick to listen, slow to speak, and slow to become angry.* Ask My Spirit to help you whenever you speak. I have trained you to pray—"Help me, Holy Spirit"—before answering the phone, and you have seen the benefits of this discipline. Simply apply the same discipline to communicating with people around you. If they are silent, pray before speaking to them. If they are talking, pray before responding. These are split-second prayers, but they put you in touch with My Presence. In this way, your speaking comes under the control of My Spirit. As positive speech patterns replace your negative ones, the increase in your Joy will amaze you.

Reckless words pierce like a sword, but the tongue of the wise brings healing. —Proverbs 12:18

My dear brothers, take note of this: Everyone should be quick to listen, slow to speak and slow to become angry. —James 1:19

Do not let any unwholesome talk come out of your mouths, but only what is helpful for building others up according to their needs, that it may benefit those who listen. —Ephesians 4:29

HOLD MY HAND, and walk joyously with Me through this day. Together we will savor the pleasures and endure the difficulties it brings. Be on the lookout for everything I have prepared for you: stunning scenery, bracing winds of adventure, cozy nooks for resting when you are weary, and much more. I am your Guide, as well as your constant Companion. I know every step of the journey ahead of you, all the way to heaven.

You don't have to choose between staying close to Me and staying on course. Since *I am the Way*, staying close to Me *is* staying on course. As you focus your thoughts on Me, I will guide you carefully along today's journey. Don't worry about what is around the next bend. Just concentrate on enjoying My Presence and staying in step with Me.

Jesus answered, "I am the way and the truth and the life. No one comes to the Father except through me." —JOHN 14:6

Devote yourselves to prayer, being watchful and thankful. —COLOSSIANS 4:2

August 5

Sit quietly in My Presence while I bless you. Make your mind like a still pool of water, ready to receive whatever thoughts I drop into it. Rest in My sufficiency, as you consider the challenges this day presents. Do not wear yourself out by worrying about whether you can cope with the pressures. Keep looking to Me and communicating with Me, as we walk through this day together.

Take time to rest by the wayside, for I am not in a hurry. A leisurely pace accomplishes more than hurried striving. When you rush, you forget who you are and Whose you are. Remember that you are royalty in My kingdom.

Be still before the Lord and wait patiently for him; do not fret when men succeed in their ways, when they carry out their wicked schemes. —Psalm 37:7

The Spirit himself testifies with our spirit that we are God's children. Now if we are children, then we are heirs—heirs of God and co-heirs with Christ, if indeed we share in his sufferings in order that we may also share in his glory. —Romans 8:16–17

But you are a chosen people, a royal priesthood, a holy nation, a people belonging to God, that you may declare the praises of him who called you out of darkness into his wonderful light. —1 Peter 2:9

WHEN THINGS SEEM to be going all wrong, stop and affirm your trust in Me. Calmly bring these matters to Me, and leave them in My capable hands. Then, simply do the next thing. Stay in touch with Me through thankful, trusting prayers, resting in My sovereign control. Rejoice in Me—exult in the God of your salvation! As you trust in Me, *I make your feet like the feet of a deer. I enable you to walk and make progress upon your high places of trouble, suffering, or responsibility.*

Though He slay me, yet will I trust Him. Even so, I will defend my own ways before Him. —JOB 13:15 NKJV

He makes my feet like the feet of a deer; he enables me to stand on the heights. —PSALM 18:33

Though the fig tree does not blossom and there is no fruit on the vines, [though] the product of the olive fails and the fields yield no food, though the flock is cut off from the fold and there are no cattle in the stalls, Yet I will rejoice in the Lord; I will exult in the [victorious] God of my salvation! The Lord God is my Strength, my personal bravery, and my invincible army; He makes my feet like hinds' feet and will make me to walk [not to stand still in terror, but to walk] and make [spiritual] progress upon my high places [of trouble, suffering, or responsibility]! —HABAKKUK 3:17–19 AMP

August 7

Understanding will never bring you Peace. That's why I have instructed you to *trust in Me, not in your understanding.* Human beings have a voracious appetite for trying to figure things out, in order to gain a sense of mastery over their lives. But the world presents you with an endless series of problems. As soon as you master one set, another pops up to challenge you. The relief you had anticipated is short-lived. Soon your mind is gearing up again: searching for understanding (mastery), instead of seeking Me (your Master).

The wisest of all men, Solomon, could never think his way through to Peace. His vast understanding resulted in feelings of futility, rather than in fulfillment. Finally, he lost his way and succumbed to the will of his wives by worshiping idols.

My Peace is not an elusive goal, hidden at the center of some complicated maze. Actually, you are always enveloped in Peace, which is inherent in My Presence. As you look to Me, you gain awareness of this precious Peace.

Trust in the Lord with all your heart and lean not on your own understanding; in all your ways acknowledge him, and he will make your paths straight. —Proverbs 3:5–6

Therefore, since we have been justified through faith, we have peace with God through our Lord Jesus Christ. —Romans 5:1

Now may the Lord of peace himself give you peace at all times and in every way. The Lord be with all of you. —2 Thessalonians 3:16

AUGUST 8

I SPEAK TO YOU from deepest heaven. You hear Me in the depths of your being. *Deep calls unto deep.* You are blessed to hear Me so directly. Never take this privilege for granted. The best response is a heart overflowing with gratitude. I am training you to cultivate a thankful mind-set. This is like *building your house on a firm rock, where life's storms cannot shake you.* As you learn these lessons, you are to teach them to others. I will open up the way before you, one step at a time.

Deep calls unto deep at the noise of Your waterfalls; all Your waves and billows have gone over me. —PSALM 42:7 NKJV

Come, let us sing for joy to the LORD; let us shout aloud to the Rock of our salvation. Let us come before him with thanksgiving and extol him with music and song. —PSALM 95:1–2

"Therefore everyone who hears these words of mine and puts them into practice is like a wise man who built his house on the rock. The rain came down, the streams rose, and the winds blew and beat against that house; yet it did not fall, because it had its foundation on the rock." —MATTHEW 7:24–25

August 9

WEAR MY ROBE OF RIGHTEOUSNESS with ease. I custom-made it for you, to cover you from head to toe. The price I paid for this covering was astronomical—My own blood. You could never purchase such a royal garment, no matter how hard you worked. Sometimes you forget that My righteousness is a gift, and you feel ill at ease in your regal robe. I weep when I see you squirming under the velvety fabric, as if it were made of scratchy sackcloth.

I want you to trust Me enough to realize your privileged position in My kingdom. Relax in the luxuriant folds of your magnificent robe. Keep your eyes on Me, as you practice walking in this garment of salvation. When your behavior is unfitting for one in My kingdom, do not try to throw off your royal robe. Instead, throw off the unrighteous behavior. Then you will be able to feel at ease in this glorious garment, enjoying the gift I fashioned for you before the foundation of the world.

I delight greatly in the LORD; my soul rejoices in my God. For he has clothed me with garments of salvation and arrayed me in a robe of righteousness, as a bridegroom adorns his head like a priest, and as a bride adorns herself with her jewels. —ISAIAH 61:10

God made him who had no sin to be sin for us, so that in him we might become the righteousness of God. —2 CORINTHIANS 5:21

You were taught, with regard to your former way of life, to put off your old self, which is being corrupted by its deceitful desires; to be made new in the attitude of your minds; and to put on the new self, created to be like God in true righteousness and holiness. —EPHESIANS 4:22–24

RELAX IN MY HEALING, holy Presence. Allow Me to transform you through this time alone with Me. As your thoughts center more and more on Me, trust displaces fear and worry. Your mind is somewhat like a seesaw. As your trust in Me goes up, fear and worry automatically go down. Time spent with Me not only increases your trust; it also helps you discern what is important and what is not.

Energy and time are precious, limited entities. Therefore, you need to use them wisely, focusing on what is truly important. As you walk close to Me, saturating your mind with Scripture, I will show you how to spend your time and energy. *My Word is a lamp to your feet; My Presence is a Light for your path.*

See then that you walk circumspectly, not as fools but as wise, redeeming the time, because the days are evil. —EPHESIANS 5:15–16 NKJV

Your word is a lamp to my feet and a light for my path. —PSALM 119:105

August 11

COME TO ME. *Come to Me. Come to Me.* This is My continual invitation to you, proclaimed in holy whispers. When your heart and mind are quiet, you can hear Me inviting you to draw near. Coming close to Me requires no great effort on your part; it is more like ceasing to resist the magnetic pull of My Love. Open yourself to My loving Presence, so that I may fill you with My fullness. I want you to experience *how wide and long and high and deep is My Love for you, so that you can know My Love that surpasses knowledge.* This vast ocean of Love cannot be measured or explained, but it can be experienced.

The Spirit and the bride say, "Come!" And let him who hears say, "Come!" Whoever is thirsty, let him come; and whoever wishes, let him take the free gift of the water of life. —REVELATION 22:17

"All that the Father gives me will come to me, and whoever comes to me I will never drive away." —JOHN 6:37

I pray that out of his glorious riches he may strengthen you with power through his Spirit in your inner being, so that Christ may dwell in your hearts through faith. And I pray that you, being rooted and established in love, may have power, together with all the saints, to grasp how wide and long and high and deep is the love of Christ, and to know this love that surpasses knowledge—that you may be filled to the measure of all the fullness of God. —EPHESIANS 3:16–19

COME TO ME when you are weak and weary. Rest snugly in My everlasting arms. I do not despise your weakness, My child. Actually, it draws Me closer to you, because weakness stirs up My compassion—My yearning to help. Accept yourself in your weariness, knowing that I understand how difficult your journey has been.

Do not compare yourself with others, who seem to skip along their life-paths with ease. Their journeys have been different from yours, and I have gifted them with abundant energy. I have gifted you with fragility, providing opportunities for your spirit to blossom in My Presence. Accept this gift as a sacred treasure: delicate, yet glowing with brilliant Light. Rather than struggling to disguise or deny your weakness, allow Me to bless you richly through it.

"A bruised reed he will not break, and a smoldering wick he will not snuff out. In faithfulness he will bring forth justice." —ISAIAH 42:3

"Though the mountains be shaken and the hills be removed, yet my unfailing love for you will not be shaken nor my covenant of peace be removed," says the LORD, who has compassion on you. —ISAIAH 54:10

In the same way, the Spirit helps us in our weakness. We do not know what we ought to pray for, but the Spirit himself intercedes for us with groans that words cannot express. —ROMANS 8:26

August 13

LEARN TO ENJOY LIFE MORE. Relax, remembering that I am *God with you.* I crafted you with enormous capacity to know Me and enjoy My Presence. When My people wear sour faces and walk through their lives with resigned rigidity, I am displeased. When you walk through a day with childlike delight, savoring every blessing, you proclaim your trust in Me, your ever-present Shepherd. The more you focus on My Presence with you, the more fully you can enjoy life. Glorify Me through your pleasure in Me. Thus you proclaim My Presence to the watching world.

"The virgin will be with child and will give birth to a son, and they will call him Immanuel" —which means, "God with us." —MATTHEW 1:23

"The thief comes only to steal and kill and destroy; I have come that they may have life, and have it to the full. I am the good shepherd. The good shepherd lays down his life for the sheep." —JOHN 10:10–11

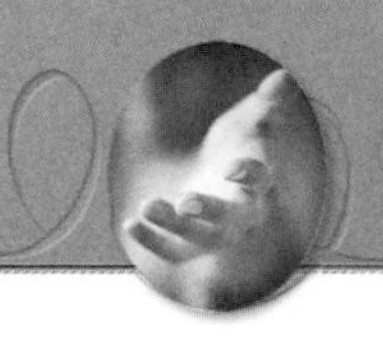

I AM YOURS FOR ALL ETERNITY. *I am the Alpha and the Omega: the One who is and was and is to come.* The world you inhabit is a place of constant changes—more than your mind can absorb without going into shock. Even the body you inhabit is changing relentlessly, in spite of modern science's attempts to prolong youth and life indefinitely. *I, however, am the same yesterday and today and forever.*

Because I never change, your relationship with Me provides a rock-solid foundation for your life. I will never leave your side. When you move on from this life to the next, My Presence beside you will shine brighter with each step. You have nothing to fear, because I am with you for all time and throughout eternity.

"I am the Alpha and the Omega," says the Lord God, "who is, and who was, and who is to come, the Almighty." —REVELATION 1:8

Jesus Christ is the same yesterday and today and forever. —HEBREWS 13:8

In the beginning you laid the foundations of the earth, and the heavens are the work of your hands. They will perish, but you remain; they will all wear out like a garment. Like clothing you will change them and they will be discarded. But you remain the same, and your years will never end. —PSALM 102:25–27

For this God is our God for ever and ever; he will be our guide even to the end. —PSALM 48:14

August 15

I AM THE GOD OF ALL TIME and all that is. Seek Me not only in morning quietness but consistently throughout the day. Do not let unexpected problems distract you from My Presence. Instead, talk with Me about everything, and watch confidently to see what I will do.

Adversity need not interrupt your communion with Me. When things go "wrong," you tend to react as if you're being punished. Instead of this negative response, try to view difficulties as blessings in disguise. *Make Me your Refuge by pouring out your heart to Me, trusting in Me at all times.*

Evening, morning and noon I cry out in distress,
and he hears my voice. —PSALM 55:17

Therefore let everyone who is godly pray to you while you may be found;
surely when the mighty waters rise, they will not reach him. —PSALM 32:6

Trust in him at all times, O people; pour out your hearts
to him, for God is our refuge. —PSALM 62:8

MEET ME in early morning splendor. I eagerly await you here. In the stillness of this holy time with Me, I *renew your strength* and saturate you with Peace. While others turn over for extra sleep or anxiously tune in to the latest news, you commune with the Creator of the universe. I have awakened in your heart strong desire to know Me. This longing originated in Me, though it now burns brightly in you.

When you seek My Face in response to My Love-call, both of us are blessed. This is a deep mystery, designed more for your enjoyment than for your understanding. I am not a dour God who discourages pleasure. I delight in your enjoyment of *everything that is true, noble, right, pure, lovely, admirable. Think on these things*, and My Light in you will shine brighter day by day.

But those who hope in the LORD will renew their strength. They will soar on wings like eagles; they will run and not grow weary, they will walk and not be faint. —ISAIAH 40:31

One thing I ask of the LORD, this is what I seek: that I may dwell in the house of the LORD all the days of my life, to gaze upon the beauty of the LORD and to seek him in his temple. —PSALM 27:4

Finally, brothers, whatever is true, whatever is noble, whatever is right, whatever is pure, whatever is lovely, whatever is admirable—if anything is excellent or praiseworthy—think about such things. —PHILIPPIANS 4:8

August 17

FIND ME in the midst of the maelstrom. Sometimes events whirl around you so quickly that they become a blur. Whisper My Name in recognition that I am still with you. Without skipping a beat in the activities that occupy you, you find strength and Peace through praying My Name. Later, when the happenings have run their course, you can talk with Me more fully.

Accept each day just as it comes to you. Do not waste your time and energy wishing for a different set of circumstances. Instead, trust Me enough to yield to My design and purposes. Remember that nothing can separate you from My loving Presence; *you are Mine.*

Therefore God exalted him to the highest place and gave him the name that is above every name, that at the name of Jesus every knee should bow, in heaven and on earth and under the earth, and every tongue confess that Jesus Christ is Lord, to the glory of God the Father. —PHILIPPIANS 2:9–11

But now, this is what the LORD says—he who created you, O Jacob, he who formed you, O Israel: "Fear not, for I have redeemed you; I have summoned you by name; you are mine." —ISAIAH 43:1

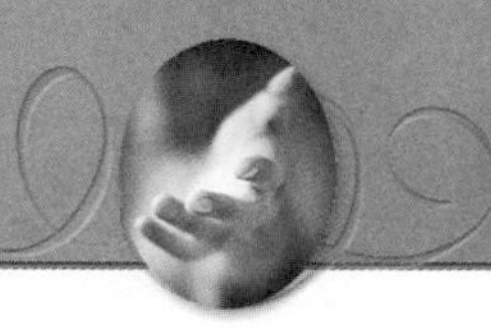

EXPECT TO ENCOUNTER ADVERSITY in your life, remembering that you live in a deeply fallen world. Stop trying to find a way that circumvents difficulties. The main problem with an easy life is that it masks your need for Me. When you became a Christian, I infused My very Life into you, empowering you to live on a supernatural plane by depending on Me.

Anticipate coming face to face with impossibilities: situations totally beyond your ability to handle. This awareness of your inadequacy is not something you should try to evade. It is precisely where I want you—the best place to encounter Me in *My Glory and Power.* When you see armies of problems marching toward you, cry out to Me! Allow Me to fight for you. Watch Me working on your behalf, as you *rest in the shadow of My Almighty Presence.*

After this I heard what sounded like the roar of a great multitude in heaven shouting: "Hallelujah! Salvation and glory and power belong to our God." —REVELATION 19:1

He who dwells in the shelter of the Most High will rest in the shadow of the Almighty. —PSALM 91:1

August 19

I CONTINUALLY CALL YOU to closeness with Me. I know the depth and breadth of your need for Me. I can read the emptiness of your thoughts when they wander away from Me. I offer rest for your soul, as well as refreshment for your mind and body. As you increasingly find fulfillment in Me, other pleasures become less important. Knowing Me intimately is like having a private wellspring of Joy within you. This spring flows freely from My throne of grace, so your Joy is independent of circumstances.

Waiting in My Presence keeps you connected to Me, aware of all that I offer you. If you feel any deficiency, you need to refocus your attention on Me. This is how you trust Me in the moments of your life.

But I have stilled and quieted my soul; like a weaned child with its mother, like a weaned child is my soul within me. —PSALM 131:2

Surely you have granted him eternal blessings and made him glad with the joy of your presence. —PSALM 21:6

Be still before the LORD and wait patiently for him; do not fret when men succeed in their ways, when they carry out their wicked schemes. —PSALM 37:7

I AM A GOD WHO HEALS. I heal broken bodies, broken minds, broken hearts, broken lives, and broken relationships. My very Presence has immense healing powers. You cannot live close to Me without experiencing some degree of healing. However, it is also true that *you have not because you ask not.* You receive the healing that flows naturally from My Presence, whether you seek it or not. But there is more—much more—available to those who ask.

The first step in receiving healing is to live ever so close to Me. The benefits of this practice are too numerous to list. As you grow more and more intimate with Me, I reveal My will to you more directly. When the time is right, I prompt you to ask for healing of some brokenness in you or in another person. The healing may be instantaneous, or it may be a process. That is up to Me. Your part is to trust Me fully and to thank Me for the restoration that has begun.

I rarely heal all the brokenness in a person's life. Even My servant Paul was told, *"My grace is sufficient for you,"* when he sought healing for the *thorn in his flesh.* Nonetheless, much healing is available to those whose lives are intimately interwoven with Mine. *Ask, and you will receive.*

Ye have not, because ye ask not. —JAMES 4:2 KJV

To keep me from becoming conceited because of these surpassingly great revelations, there was given me a thorn in my flesh, a messenger of Satan, to torment me. Three times I pleaded with the Lord to take it away from me. But he said to me, "My grace is sufficient for you, for my power is made perfect in weakness." —2 CORINTHIANS 12:7–9

"Ask and it will be given to you; seek and you will find." —MATTHEW 7:7

August 21

WAIT WITH ME FOR A WHILE. I have much to tell you. You are walking along the path I have chosen for you. It is both a privileged and a perilous way: experiencing My glorious Presence and heralding that reality to others. Sometimes you feel presumptuous to be carrying out such an assignment.

Do not worry about what other people think of you. The work I am doing in you is hidden at first. But eventually blossoms will burst forth, and abundant fruit will be borne. Stay on the path of Life with Me. Trust Me wholeheartedly, letting My Spirit fill you with Joy and Peace.

O LORD, God of Israel, there is no God like you in heaven above or on earth below—you who keep your covenant of love with your servants who continue wholeheartedly in your way. —1 KINGS 8:23

But the fruit of the Spirit is love, joy, peace, patience, kindness, goodness, faithfulness, gentleness and self-control. Against such things there is no law. —GALATIANS 5:22–23

TRUST ME, and don't be afraid. I want you to view trials as exercises designed to develop your trust-muscles. You live in the midst of fierce spiritual battles, and fear is one of Satan's favorite weapons. When you start to feel afraid, affirm your trust in Me. Speak out loud, if circumstances permit. *Resist the devil in My Name, and he will slink away from you.* Refresh yourself in My holy Presence. Speak or sing praises to Me, and My Face will shine radiantly upon you.

Remember that *there is no condemnation for those who belong to Me.* You have been judged NOT GUILTY for all eternity. *Trust Me, and don't be afraid; for I am your Strength, Song, and Salvation.*

Submit yourselves, then, to God. Resist the devil, and he will flee from you. —JAMES 4:7

Therefore, there is now no condemnation for those who are in Christ Jesus, because through Christ Jesus the law of the Spirit of life set me free from the law of sin and death. —ROMANS 8:1–2

Surely God is my salvation; I will trust and not be afraid. The LORD, the LORD, is my strength and my song; he has become my salvation. —ISAIAH 12:2

August 23

Entrust your loved ones to Me; release them into My protective care. They are much safer with Me than in your clinging hands. If you let a loved one become an idol in your heart, you endanger that one—as well as yourself. Joseph and his father, Jacob, suffered terribly because Jacob *loved Joseph more than any of his other sons* and treated him with special favor. So Joseph's brothers hated him and plotted against him. Ultimately, I used that situation for good, but both father and son had to endure years of suffering and separation from one another.

I detest idolatry, even in the form of parental love, so beware of making a beloved child your idol. When you release loved ones to Me, you are free to cling to My hand. As you entrust others into My care, I am free to shower blessings on them. *My Presence will go with them wherever they go, and I will give them rest.* This same Presence stays with you as you relax and place your trust in Me. Watch to see what I will do.

Now Israel loved Joseph more than any of his other sons, because he had been born to him in his old age; and he made an ornate robe for him. When his brothers saw that their father loved him more than any of them, they hated him and could not speak a kind word to him. —Genesis 37:3–4

Now to him who is able to do immeasurably more than all we ask or imagine, according to his power that is at work within us. —Ephesians 3:20

The Lord replied, "My Presence will go with you, and I will give you rest." —Exodus 33:14

I AM ALL AROUND YOU, hovering over you even as you seek My Face. I am nearer than you dare believe, closer than the air you breathe. If My children could only recognize My Presence, they would never feel lonely again. *I know every thought before you think it, every word before you speak it.* My Presence impinges on your innermost being. Can you see the absurdity of trying to hide anything from Me? You can easily deceive other people, and even yourself; but I read you like an open, large-print book.

Deep within themselves, most people have some awareness of My imminent Presence. Many people run from Me and vehemently deny My existence, because My closeness terrifies them. But My own children have nothing to fear, for I have cleansed them by My blood and clothed them in My righteousness. Be blessed by My intimate nearness. Since I live in you, let Me also live through you, shining My Light into the darkness.

O LORD, you have searched me and you know me. You know when I sit and when I rise; you perceive my thoughts from afar. You discern my going out and my lying down; you are familiar with all my ways. Before a word is on my tongue you know it completely, O LORD. —PSALM 139:1–4

But now in Christ Jesus you who once were far away have been brought near through the blood of Christ. —EPHESIANS 2:13

God made him who had no sin to be sin for us, so that in him we might become the righteousness of God. —2 CORINTHIANS 5:21

August 25

I AM THE ETERNAL *I AM;* I always have been, and I always will be. In My Presence you experience Love and Light, Peace and Joy. I am intimately involved in all your moments, and I am training you to be aware of Me at all times. Your assignment is to collaborate with Me in this training process.

I have taken up residence within you; I am central in your innermost being. Your mind goes off in tangents from its holy Center, time after time. Do not be alarmed by your inability to remain focused on Me. Simply bring your thoughts gently back to Me each time they wander. The quickest way to redirect your mind to me is to whisper My Name.

God said to Moses, "I AM WHO I AM. This is what you are to say to the Israelites: 'I AM has sent me to you.'" —EXODUS 3:14

Don't you know that you yourselves are God's temple and that God's Spirit lives in you? —1 CORINTHIANS 3:16

The LORD confides in those who fear him; he makes his covenant known to them. My eyes are ever on the LORD, for only he will release my feet from the snare. —PSALM 25:14–15

TRUST ME in the midst of a messy day. Your inner calm—your Peace in My Presence—need not be shaken by what is going on around you. Though you live in this temporal world, your innermost being is rooted and grounded in eternity. When you start to feel stressed, detach yourself from the disturbances around you. Instead of desperately striving to maintain order and control in your little world, relax and remember that circumstances cannot touch My Peace.

Seek My Face, and I will share My mind with you, opening your eyes to see things from My perspective. *Do not let your heart be troubled, and do not be afraid*. The Peace I give is sufficient for you.

"I have told you these things, so that in me you may have peace. In this world you will have trouble. But take heart! I have overcome the world." —JOHN 16:33

Look to the LORD and his strength; seek his face always. —PSALM 105:4

"Peace I leave with you; my peace I give you. I do not give to you as the world gives. Do not let your hearts be troubled and do not be afraid." —JOHN 14:27

August 27

Spend time with Me for the pure pleasure of being in My company. I can brighten up the dullest of gray days; I can add sparkle to the routines of daily life. You have to repeat so many tasks day after day. This monotony can dull your thinking until your mind slips into neutral. A mind that is unfocused is vulnerable to "the world, the flesh, and the devil," all of which exert a downward pull on your thoughts. As your thinking processes deteriorate, you become increasingly confused and directionless. The best remedy is to refocus your mind and heart on Me, your constant Companion.

Even the most confusing day opens up before you as you go step by step with Me. My Presence goes with you wherever you go, providing *Light for your path.*

Because you are my help, I sing in the shadow of your wings. My soul clings to you; your right hand upholds me. —Psalm 63:7–8

Your word is a lamp to my feet and a light for my path. —Psalm 119:105

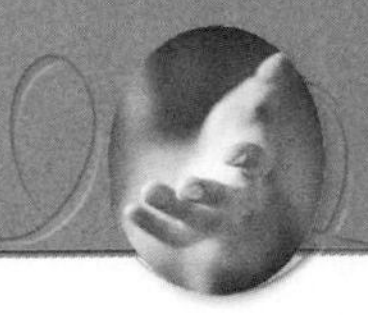

GROW STRONG in the Light of My Presence. As My Face shines upon you, you receive nutrients that enhance your growth in grace. I designed you to commune with Me face to Face, and this interaction strengthens your soul. Such communion provides a tiny glimpse of what awaits you in heaven, where all barriers between you and My Glory will be removed. This meditative time with Me blesses you doubly: You experience My Presence here and now, and you are refreshed by the hope of heaven, where you will know Me in ecstatic Joy.

Many are asking, "Who can show us any good?" Let the light of your face shine upon us, O LORD. You have filled my heart with greater joy than when their grain and new wine abound. I will lie down and sleep in peace, for you alone, O LORD, make me dwell in safety. —PSALM 4:6–8

The city does not need the sun or the moon to shine on it, for the glory of God gives it light, and the Lamb is its lamp. —REVELATION 21:23

August 29

Demonstrate your trust in Me by sitting quietly in My Presence. Put aside all that is waiting to be done, and refuse to worry about anything. This sacred time together strengthens you and prepares you to face whatever the day will bring. By waiting with Me before you begin the day's activities, you proclaim the reality of My living Presence. This act of faith—waiting before working—is noted in the spirit world, where your demonstration of trust weakens *principalities and powers of darkness.*

The most effective way to resist evil is to draw near Me. When you need to take action, I will guide you clearly through My Spirit and My Word. The world is so complex and overstimulating that you can easily lose your sense of direction. Doing countless unnecessary activities will dissipate your energy. When you spend time with Me, I restore your sense of direction. As you look to Me for guidance, I enable you to do less but accomplish more.

Then Jesus said to his disciples: "Therefore I tell you, do not worry about your life, what you will eat; or about your body, what you will wear. . . . Consider the ravens: They do not sow or reap, they have no storeroom or barn; yet God feeds them. And how much more valuable you are than birds! Who of you by worrying can add a single hour to his life?" —Luke 12:22–25

For we do not wrestle against flesh and blood, but against principalities, against powers, against the rulers of the darkness of this age, against spiritual hosts of wickedness in the heavenly places. —Ephesians 6:12 NKJV

Commit to the Lord whatever you do, and your plans will succeed. —Proverbs 16:3

THERE IS NO PLACE so desolate that you cannot find Me there. When Hagar fled from her mistress, Sarah, into the wilderness, she thought she was utterly alone and forsaken. But Hagar encountered Me in that desolate place. There she addressed Me as *the Living One who sees me*. Through that encounter with My Presence, she gained courage to return to her mistress.

No set of circumstances could ever isolate you from My loving Presence. Not only do I see you always; I see you as a redeemed saint, gloriously radiant in My righteousness. That is why *I take great delight in you and rejoice over you with singing!*

So she called the name of the Lord Who spoke to her, You are a God of seeing, for she said, Have I [not] even here [in the wilderness] looked upon Him Who sees me [and lived]? Or have I here also seen [the future purposes or designs of] Him Who sees me? Therefore the well was called Beer-lahai-roi [A well to the Living One Who sees me]. —GENESIS 16:13–14 AMP

Where can I go from your Spirit? Where can I flee from your presence? If I go up to the heavens, you are there; if I make my bed in the depths, you are there. If I rise on the wings of the dawn, if I settle on the far side of the sea, even there your hand will guide me, your right hand will hold me fast. —PSALM 139:7–10

The LORD your God is with you, he is mighty to save. He will take great delight in you, he will quiet you with his love, he will rejoice over you with singing. —ZEPHANIAH 3:17

August 31

Grow strong in your weakness. Some of My children I've gifted with abundant strength and stamina. Others, like you, have received the humble gift of frailty. Your fragility is not a punishment, nor does it indicate lack of faith. On the contrary, weak ones like you must live by faith, depending on Me to get you through the day. I am developing your ability to trust Me, to lean on Me, rather than on your understanding. Your natural preference is to plan out your day, knowing what will happen when. My preference is for you to depend on Me continually, trusting Me to guide you and strengthen you as needed. This is how you grow strong in your weakness.

Now listen, you who say, "Today or tomorrow we will go to this or that city, spend a year there, carry on business and make money." Why, you do not even know what will happen tomorrow. What is your life? You are a mist that appears for a little while and then vanishes. Instead, you ought to say, "If it is the Lord's will, we will live and do this or that." —James 4:13–15

Lean on, trust in, and be confident in the Lord with all your heart and mind and do not rely on your own insight or understanding. —Proverbs 3:5 AMP

Do you not know? Have you not heard? The Lord is the everlasting God, the Creator of the ends of the earth. He will not grow tired or weary, and his understanding no one can fathom. He gives strength to the weary and increases the power of the weak. Even youths grow tired and weary, and young men stumble and fall; but those who hope in the Lord will renew their strength. They will soar on wings like eagles; they will run and not grow weary, they will walk and not be faint. —Isaiah 40:28–31

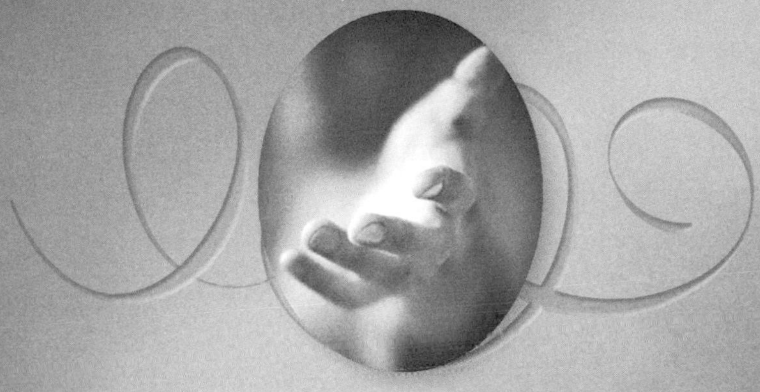

September

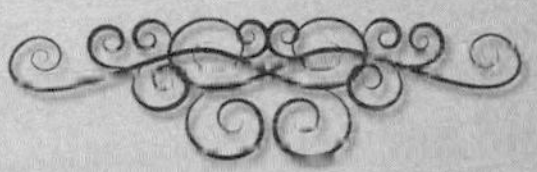

"I am the light of the world. Whoever follows me will never walk in darkness, but will have the light of life."

John 8:12

September 1

Seek Me with your whole being. I desire to be found by you, and I orchestrate the events of your life with that purpose in mind. When things go well and you are blessed, you can feel Me smiling on you. When you encounter rough patches along your life-journey, trust that My Light is still shining upon you. My reasons for allowing these adversities may be shrouded in mystery, but My continual Presence with you is an absolute promise. Seek Me in good times; seek Me in hard times. You will find Me watching over you all the time.

But if from there you seek the Lord *your God, you will find him if you look for him with all your heart and with all your soul.* —Deuteronomy 4:29

Let us hold unswervingly to the hope we profess, for he who promised is faithful. —Hebrews 10:23

The Lord *watches over all who love him, but all the wicked he will destroy.* —Psalm 145:20

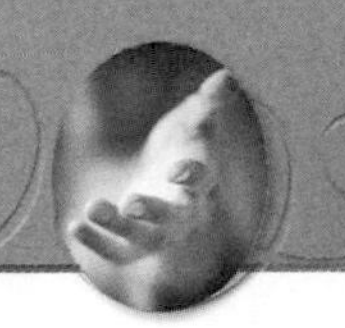

LIVING IN DEPENDENCE ON ME is a glorious adventure. Most people scurry around busily, trying to accomplish things through their own strength and ability. Some succeed enormously; others fail miserably. But both groups miss what life is meant to be: living and working in collaboration with Me.

When you depend on Me continually, your whole perspective changes. You see miracles happening all around, while others see only natural occurrences and "coincidences." You begin each day with joyful expectation, watching to see what I will do. You accept weakness as a gift from Me, knowing that *My Power plugs in most readily to consecrated weakness.* You keep your plans tentative, knowing that My plans are far superior. *You consciously live, move, and have your being in Me,* desiring that I live in you. I in you, and you in Me. This is the intimate adventure I offer you.

But he said to me, "My grace is sufficient for you, for my power is made perfect in weakness." Therefore I will boast all the more gladly about my weaknesses, so that Christ's power may rest on me. . . . For when I am weak, then I am strong. —2 CORINTHIANS 12:9–10

For in him we live and move and have our being. —ACTS 17:28

So then, just as you received Christ Jesus as Lord, continue to live in him, rooted and built up in him, strengthened in the faith as you were taught, and overflowing with thankfulness. —COLOSSIANS 2:6–7

"On that day you will realize that I am in my Father, and you are in me, and I am in you." —JOHN 14:20

September 3

Let the dew of My Presence refresh your mind and heart. So many, many things vie for your attention in this complex world of instant communication. The world has changed enormously since I first gave the command to *be still and know that I am God*. However, this timeless truth is essential for the well-being of your soul. As dew refreshes grass and flowers during the stillness of the night, so My Presence revitalizes you as you sit quietly with Me.

A refreshed, revitalized mind is able to sort out what is important and what is not. In its natural condition, your mind easily gets stuck on trivial matters. Like the spinning wheels of a car trapped in mud, the cogs of your brain spin impotently when you focus on a trivial thing. As soon as you start communicating with Me about the matter, your thoughts gain traction and you can move on to more important things. Communicate with Me continually, and I will put My thoughts into your mind.

"Be still, and know that I am God; I will be exalted among the nations, I will be exalted in the earth." —Psalm 46:10

She had a sister called Mary, who sat at the Lord's feet listening to what he said. But Martha was distracted by all the preparations that had to be made. She came to him and asked, "Lord, don't you care that my sister has left me to do the work by myself? Tell her to help me!" "Martha, Martha," the Lord answered, "you are worried and upset about many things, but only one thing is needed. Mary has chosen what is better, and it will not be taken away from her." —Luke 10:39–42

For God is not the author of confusion but of peace, as in all the churches of the saints. —1 Corinthians 14:33 NKJV

In closeness to Me, you are safe. In the intimacy of My Presence, you are energized. No matter where you are in the world, you know you belong when you sense My nearness. Ever since the Fall, man has experienced a gaping emptiness that only My Presence can fill. I designed you for close communication with your Creator. How I enjoyed walking in the garden with Adam and Eve, before the evil one deceived them!

When you commune with Me in the garden of your heart, both you and I are blessed. This is My way of living in the world—through you! Together we will push back the darkness, for *I am the Light of the world.*

You are my hiding place; you will protect me from trouble and surround me with songs of deliverance. —Psalm 32:7

Then the man and his wife heard the sound of the Lord God as he was walking in the garden in the cool of the day, and they hid from the Lord God among the trees of the garden. But the Lord God called to the man, "Where are you?" —Genesis 3:8–9

When Jesus spoke again to the people, he said, "I am the light of the world. Whoever follows me will never walk in darkness, but will have the light of life." —John 8:12

September 5

I AM YOUR BEST FRIEND, as well as your King. Walk hand in hand with Me through your life. Together we will face whatever each day brings: pleasures, hardships, adventures, disappointments. Nothing is wasted when it is shared with Me. *I can bring beauty out of the ashes* of lost dreams. I can glean Joy out of sorrow, Peace out of adversity. Only a Friend who is also the King of kings could accomplish this divine alchemy. There is no other like Me!

The friendship I offer you is practical and down-to-earth, yet it is saturated with heavenly Glory. Living in My Presence means living in two realms simultaneously: the visible world and unseen, eternal reality. I have equipped you to stay conscious of Me while walking along dusty, earthbound paths.

"Greater love has no one than this, that he lay down his life for his friends. You are my friends if you do what I command. I no longer call you servants, because a servant does not know his master's business. Instead, I have called you friends, for everything that I learned from my Father I have made known to you." —John 15:13–15

And provide for those who grieve in Zion—to bestow on them a crown of beauty instead of ashes, the oil of gladness instead of mourning, and a garment of praise instead of a spirit of despair. They will be called oaks of righteousness, a planting of the LORD for the display of his splendor. —ISAIAH 61:3

Sorrowful, yet always rejoicing; poor, yet making many rich; having nothing, and yet possessing everything. —2 CORINTHIANS 6:10

DO EVERYTHING IN DEPENDENCE ON ME. The desire to act independently—apart from Me—springs from the root of pride. Self-sufficiency is subtle, insinuating its way into your thoughts and actions without your realizing it. But *apart from Me, you can do nothing*: that is, nothing of eternal value. My deepest desire for you is that you learn to depend on Me in every situation. I move heaven and earth to accomplish this purpose, but you must collaborate with Me in this training. Teaching you would be simple if I negated your free will or overwhelmed you with My Power. However, I love you too much to withdraw the godlike privilege I bestowed on you as My image-bearer. Use your freedom wisely, by relying on Me constantly. Thus you enjoy My Presence and My Peace.

"I am the vine; you are the branches. If a man remains in me and I in him, he will bear much fruit; apart from me you can do nothing." —JOHN 15:5

Finally, be strong in the Lord and in his mighty power. —EPHESIANS 6:10

Then God said, "Let us make man in our image, in our likeness, and let them rule over the fish of the sea and the birds of the air, over the livestock, over all the earth, and over all the creatures that move along the ground." So God created man in his own image, in the image of God he created him; male and female he created them. —GENESIS 1:26–27

Enjoy the warmth of My Presence shining upon you. Feel your face tingle as you bask in My Love-Light. I delight in you more than you can imagine. I approve of you continuously, for I see you cloaked in My Light, *arrayed in My righteousness. There is no condemnation for those who are clothed in Me!* That is why I abhor the use of guilt as a means of motivation among Christians.

Some pastors try to whip their people into action with guilt-inducing sermons. This procedure can drive many people to work harder, but the end does not justify the means. Guilt-evoking messages can undermine the very foundation of grace in a believer's heart. A pastor may feel successful when his people are doing more, but I look at their hearts. I grieve when I see grace eroding, with weeds of anxious works creeping in. I want you to relax in the assurance of My perfect Love. *The law of My Spirit of Life has set you free from the law of sin and death.*

I delight greatly in the Lord; my soul rejoices in my God. For he has clothed me with garments of salvation and arrayed me in a robe of righteousness, as a bridegroom adorns his head like a priest, and as a bride adorns herself with her jewels. —Isaiah 61:10

Therefore, there is now no condemnation for those who are in Christ Jesus, because through Christ Jesus the law of the Spirit of life set me free from the law of sin and death. —Romans 8:1–2

ACCEPT EACH DAY exactly as it comes to you. By that, I mean not only the circumstances of your day but also the condition of your body. Your assignment is to trust Me absolutely, resting in My sovereignty and faithfulness.

On some days, your circumstances and your physical condition feel out of balance: The demands on you seem far greater than your strength. Days like that present a choice between two alternatives—giving up or relying on Me. Even if you wrongly choose the first alternative, I will not reject you. You can turn to Me at any point, and I will help you crawl out of the mire of discouragement. I will infuse My strength into you moment by moment, giving you all that you need for this day. Trust Me, by relying on My empowering Presence.

Why are you downcast, O my soul? Why so disturbed within me? Put your hope in God, for I will yet praise him, my Savior. —PSALM 42:5

For to be sure, he was crucified in weakness, yet he lives by God's power. Likewise, we are weak in him, yet by God's power we will live with him to serve you. —2 CORINTHIANS 13:4

"I will refresh the weary and satisfy the faint." —JEREMIAH 31:25

WALK WITH ME ALONG PATHS OF TRUST. The most direct route between point A and point B on your life-journey is the path of unwavering trust in Me. When your faith falters, you choose a trail that meanders and takes you well out of your way. You will get to point B eventually, but you will have lost precious time and energy. As soon as you realize you have wandered from your trust-path, look to Me and whisper, "I trust You, Jesus." This affirmation will help you get back on track.

The farther you roam along paths of unbelief, the harder it is to remember that I am with you. Anxious thoughts branch off in all directions, taking you farther and farther from awareness of My Presence. You need to voice your trust in Me frequently. This simple act of faith will keep you walking along straight paths with Me. *Trust in Me with all your heart, and I will make your paths straight.*

Trust in the LORD forever, for the LORD, the LORD,
is the Rock eternal. —ISAIAH 26:4

Those who know your name will trust in you, for you, LORD,
have never forsaken those who seek you. —PSALM 9:10

Show me your ways, O LORD, teach me your paths; guide
me in your truth and teach me, for you are God my Savior,
and my hope is in you all day long. —PSALM 25:4–5

Trust in the LORD with all your heart and lean not on your
own understanding; in all your ways acknowledge him, and
he will make your paths straight. —PROVERBS 3:5–6

I AM ALWAYS AVAILABLE TO YOU. Once you have trusted Me as your Savior, I never distance Myself from you. Sometimes you may *feel* distant from Me. Recognize that as feeling; do not confuse it with reality. The Bible is full of My promises to be with you always. As I assured Jacob, when he was journeying away from home into unknown places, *I am with you and will watch over you wherever you go.* After My resurrection, I made this promise to My followers: *Surely I am with you always, to the very end of the age.* Let these assurances of My continual Presence fill you with Joy and Peace. No matter what you may lose in this life, you can never lose your relationship with Me.

"Though the mountains be shaken and the hills be removed, yet my unfailing love for you will not be shaken nor my covenant of peace be removed," says the LORD, *who has compassion on you.* —ISAIAH 54:10

"I am with you and will watch over you wherever you go, and I will bring you back to this land. I will not leave you until I have done what I have promised you." —GENESIS 28:15

"And teaching them to obey everything I have commanded you. And surely I am with you always, to the very end of the age." —MATTHEW 28:20

September 11

Rejoice in Me always! No matter what is going on, you can rejoice in your Love-relationship with Me. This is *the secret of being content in all circumstances.* So many people dream of the day when they will finally be happy: when they are out of debt, when their children are out of trouble, when they have more leisure time, and so on. While they daydream, their moments are trickling into the ground like precious balm spilling wastefully from overturned bottles.

Fantasizing about future happiness will never bring fulfillment, because fantasy is unreality. Even though I am invisible, I am far more Real than the world you see around you. My reality is eternal and unchanging. Bring your moments to Me, and I will fill them with vibrant Joy. *Now* is the time to rejoice in My Presence!

Rejoice in the Lord always. I will say it again: Rejoice! . . . I know what it is to be in need, and I know what it is to have plenty. I have learned the secret of being content in any and every situation, whether well fed or hungry, whether living in plenty or in want. —Philippians 4:4, 12

But you remain the same, and your years will never end. —Psalm 102:27

SEPTEMBER 12

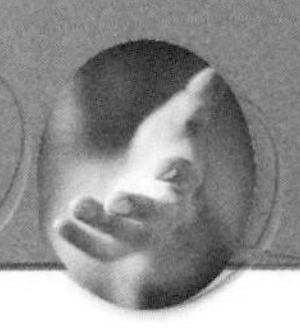

RECEIVE *MY PEACE.* It is My continual gift to you. The best way to receive this gift is to sit quietly in My Presence, trusting Me in every area of your life. *Quietness and trust* accomplish far more than you can imagine: not only in you, but also on earth and in heaven. When you trust Me in a given area, you release that problem or person into My care.

Spending time alone with Me can be a difficult discipline, because it goes against the activity addiction of this age. You may appear to be doing nothing, but actually you are participating in battles going on within spiritual realms. You are waging war—not with *the weapons of the world*, but with heavenly weapons, which *have divine power to demolish strongholds.* Living close to Me is a sure defense against evil.

"Peace I leave with you; my peace I give you. I do not give to you as the world gives. Do not let your hearts be troubled and do not be afraid." —JOHN 14:27

This is what the Sovereign LORD, the Holy One of Israel, says: "In repentance and rest is your salvation, in quietness and trust is your strength, but you would have none of it." —ISAIAH 30:15

The weapons we fight with are not the weapons of the world. On the contrary, they have divine power to demolish strongholds. —2 CORINTHIANS 10:4

September 13

Come to Me and rest. Give your mind a break from its habitual judging. You form judgments about this situation, that situation, this person, that person, yourself, even the weather—as if judging were your main function in life. But I created you first and foremost to *know Me* and to live in rich communication with Me. When you become preoccupied with passing judgment, you usurp My role.

Relate to Me as creature to Creator, sheep to Shepherd, subject to King, clay to Potter. Allow Me to have My way in your life. Rather than evaluating My ways with you, accept them thankfully. The intimacy I offer you is not an invitation to act as if you were My equal. Worship Me as *King of kings* while walking hand in hand with Me down the path of Life.

"Do not judge, or you too will be judged." —Matthew 7:1

"Now this is eternal life: that they may know you, the only true God, and Jesus Christ, whom you have sent." —John 17:3

But who are you, O man, to talk back to God? "Shall what is formed say to him who formed it, 'Why did you make me like this?'" Does not the potter have the right to make out of the same lump of clay some pottery for noble purposes and some for common use? —Romans 9:20–21

Which God will bring about in his own time—God, the blessed and only Ruler, the King of kings and Lord of lords. —1 Timothy 6:15

Worship Me by living close to Me. This was My original design for man, into whom *I breathed My very breath of Life*. This is My desire for you: that you stay near Me as you walk along your life-path. Each day is an important part of that journey. Although you may feel as if you are going nowhere in this world, your spiritual journey is another matter altogether, taking you along steep, treacherous paths of adventure. That is why *walking in the Light of My Presence* is essential to keep you from stumbling. By staying close to Me, you present yourself as a *living sacrifice*. Even the most routine part of your day can be *a spiritual act of worship, holy and pleasing to Me*.

The Lord God formed the man from the dust of the ground and breathed into his nostrils the breath of life, and the man became a living being. —Genesis 2:7

Blessed are those who have learned to acclaim you, who walk in the light of your presence, O Lord. —Psalm 89:15

Therefore, I urge you, brothers, in view of God's mercy, to offer your bodies as living sacrifices, holy and pleasing to God—this is your spiritual act of worship. Do not conform any longer to the pattern of this world, but be transformed by the renewing of your mind. Then you will be able to test and approve what God's will is—his good, pleasing and perfect will. —Romans 12:1–2

September 15

Rest in Me, My child. This time devoted to Me is meant to be peaceful, not stressful. You don't have to perform in order to receive My Love. I have boundless, unconditional Love for you. How it grieves Me to see My children working for Love: trying harder and harder, yet never feeling good enough to be loved.

Be careful that your devotion to Me does not become another form of works. I want you to come into My Presence joyfully and confidently. You have nothing to fear, for you wear My own righteousness. Gaze into My eyes, and you will see no condemnation, only Love and delight in the one I see. Be blessed as *My Face shines radiantly upon you, giving you Peace.*

"Greater love has no one than this, that he lay down his life for his friends." —John 15:13

The Lord your God is with you, he is mighty to save. He will take great delight in you, he will quiet you with his love, he will rejoice over you with singing. —Zephaniah 3:17

"The Lord make his face shine upon you and be gracious to you; the Lord turn his face toward you and give you peace." —Numbers 6:25–26

September 16

I DESIGNED YOU to live in union with Me. This union does not negate who you are; it actually makes you more fully yourself. When you try to live independently of Me, you experience emptiness and dissatisfaction. You may *gain the whole world* and yet lose everything that really counts.

Find fulfillment through living close to Me, yielding to My purposes for you. Though I may lead you along paths that feel alien to you, trust that I know what I am doing. If you follow Me wholeheartedly, you will discover facets of yourself that were previously hidden. I know you intimately—far better than you know yourself. In union with Me, you are complete. In closeness to Me, you are transformed more and more into the one I designed you to be.

"What good is it for a man to gain the whole world, yet forfeit his soul?" —MARK 8:36

For you created my inmost being; you knit me together in my mother's womb. I praise you because I am fearfully and wonderfully made; your works are wonderful, I know that full well. My frame was not hidden from you when I was made in the secret place. When I was woven together in the depths of the earth, your eyes saw my unformed body. All the days ordained for me were written in your book before one of them came to be. —PSALM 139:13–16

Now the Lord is the Spirit, and where the Spirit of the Lord is, there is freedom. And we, who with unveiled faces all reflect the Lord's glory, are being transformed into his likeness with ever-increasing glory, which comes from the Lord, who is the Spirit. —2 CORINTHIANS 3:17–18

YOU WILL NOT FIND MY PEACE by engaging in excessive planning: attempting to control what will happen to you in the future. That is a commonly practiced form of unbelief. When your mind spins with multiple plans, Peace may sometimes seem to be within your grasp; yet it always eludes you. Just when you think you have prepared for all possibilities, something unexpected pops up and throws things into confusion.

I did not design the human mind to figure out the future. That is beyond your capability. I crafted your mind for continual communication with Me. Bring Me all your needs, your hopes and fears. Commit everything into My care. Turn from the path of planning to the path of Peace.

Humble yourselves, therefore, under God's mighty hand, that he may lift you up in due time. Cast all your anxiety on him because he cares for you. —1 PETER 5:6–7

In his heart a man plans his course, but the LORD determines his steps. —PROVERBS 16:9

Commit your way to the LORD, trust also in Him, and He shall bring it to pass. —PSALM 37:5 NKJV

SEEK TO PLEASE ME above all else. Let that goal be your focal point as you go through this day. Such a mind-set will protect you from scattering your energy to the winds. The free will I bestowed on you comes with awesome responsibility. Each day presents you with choice after choice. Many of these decisions you ignore and thus make by default. Without a focal point to guide you, you can easily lose your way. That's why it is so important to stay in communication with Me, living in thankful awareness of My Presence.

You inhabit a fallen, disjointed world, where things are constantly unraveling around the edges. Only a vibrant relationship with Me can keep you from coming unraveled too.

"But seek first his kingdom and his righteousness, and all these things will be given to you as well." —MATTHEW 6:33

"The one who sent me is with me; he has not left me alone, for I always do what pleases him." —JOHN 8:29

Whatever you do, work at it with all your heart, as working for the Lord, not for men, since you know that you will receive an inheritance from the Lord as a reward. It is the Lord Christ you are serving. —COLOSSIANS 3:23–24

September 19

THERE IS A MIGHTY BATTLE going on for control of your mind. Heaven and earth intersect in your mind; the tugs of both spheres influence your thinking. I created you with the capacity to experience foretastes of heaven. When you shut out the world and focus on My Presence, you can enjoy sitting with Me *in heavenly realms*. This is an incredible privilege reserved for precious ones who belong to Me and seek My Face. Your greatest strength is your desire to spend time communing with Me. As you concentrate on Me, *My Spirit fills your mind with Life and Peace.*

The world exerts a downward pull on your thoughts. Media bombard you with greed, lust, and cynicism. When you face these things, pray for protection and discernment. Stay in continual communication with Me whenever you walk through the wastelands of this world. Refuse to worry, because this form of worldliness will weigh you down and block awareness of My Presence. Stay alert, recognizing the battle being waged against your mind. Look forward to an eternity of strife-free living, reserved for you in heaven.

And God raised us up with Christ and seated us with him in the heavenly realms in Christ Jesus. —EPHESIANS 2:6

The mind of sinful man is death, but the mind controlled by the Spirit is life and peace. —ROMANS 8:6

Do not love the world or anything in the world. . . . The world and its desires pass away, but the man who does the will of God lives forever. —1 JOHN 2:15, 17

TRY TO SEE THINGS more and more from My perspective. Let the Light of My Presence so fully fill your mind that you view the world through Me. When little things don't go as you had hoped, look to Me lightheartedly and say, "Oh, well." This simple discipline can protect you from being burdened with an accumulation of petty cares and frustrations. If you practice this diligently, you will make a life-changing discovery: You realize that most of the things that worry you are not important. If you shrug them off immediately and return your focus to Me, you will walk through your days with lighter steps and a joyful heart.

When serious problems come your way, you will have more reserves for dealing with them. You will not have squandered your energy on petty problems. You may even reach the point where you can agree with the apostle Paul that all your troubles are *light and momentary*, compared with *the eternal glory* being achieved by them.

A man's steps are directed by the LORD. How then can anyone understand his own way? —PROVERBS 20:24

For our light and momentary troubles are achieving for us an eternal glory that far outweighs them all. So we fix our eyes not on what is seen, but on what is unseen. For what is seen is temporary, but what is unseen is eternal. —2 CORINTHIANS 4:17–18

WAIT QUIETLY IN MY PRESENCE while My thoughts form silently in the depths of your being. Do not try to rush this process, because hurry keeps your heart earthbound. I am the Creator of the entire universe, yet I choose to make My humble home in your heart. It is there where you know Me most intimately; it is there where I speak to you in holy whispers. Ask My Spirit to quiet your mind so that you can hear *My still, small voice* within you. I am speaking to you continually: words of Life . . . Peace . . . Love. Tune your heart to receive these messages of abundant blessing. *Lay your requests before Me and wait in expectation.*

And after the earthquake a fire, but the LORD was not in the fire; and after the fire a still small voice. —1 KINGS 19:12 NKJV

In the morning, O LORD, you hear my voice; in the morning I lay my requests before you and wait in expectation. —PSALM 5:3

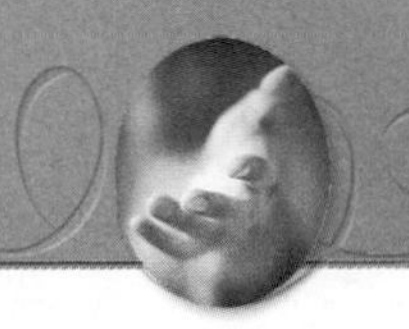

Trust Me and refuse to worry, for *I am your Strength and Song.* You are feeling wobbly this morning, looking at difficult times looming ahead, measuring them against your own strength. However, they are not today's tasks—or even tomorrow's. So leave them in the future and come home to the present, where you will find Me waiting for you. Since *I am your Strength*, I can empower you to handle each task as it comes. Because *I am your Song*, I can give you Joy as you work alongside Me.

Keep bringing your mind back to the present moment. Among all My creatures, only humans can anticipate future events. This ability is a blessing, but it becomes a curse whenever it is misused. If you use your magnificent mind to worry about tomorrow, you cloak yourself in dark unbelief. However, when the hope of heaven fills your thoughts, the Light of My Presence envelops you. Though heaven is future, it is also present tense. As you walk in the Light with Me, you have one foot on earth and one foot in heaven.

The Lord is my strength and my song; he has become my salvation. He is my God, and I will praise him, my father's God, and I will exalt him. —Exodus 15:2

We demolish arguments and every pretension that sets itself up against the knowledge of God, and we take captive every thought to make it obedient to Christ. —2 Corinthians 10:5

Let us hold unswervingly to the hope we profess, for he who promised is faithful. —Hebrews 10:23

SEPTEMBER 23

WALK WITH ME in the freedom of forgiveness. The path we follow together is sometimes steep and slippery. If you carry a burden of guilt on your back, you are more likely to stumble and fall. At your request, I will remove the heavy load from you and bury it at the foot of the cross. When I unburden you, you are undeniably free! Stand up straight and tall in My Presence, so that no one can place more burdens on your back. Look into My Face and feel the warmth of My Love-Light shining upon you. It is this unconditional Love that frees you from both fears and sins. Spend time basking in the Light of My Presence. As you come to know Me more and more intimately, you grow increasingly free.

Praise be to the Lord, to God our Savior, who daily bears our burdens. —PSALM 68:19

But if we walk in the light, as he is in the light, we have fellowship with one another, and the blood of Jesus, his Son, purifies us from all sin. If we claim to be without sin, we deceive ourselves and the truth is not in us. If we confess our sins, he is faithful and just and will forgive us our sins and purify us from all unrighteousness. —1 JOHN 1:7–9

There is no fear in love. But perfect love drives out fear, because fear has to do with punishment. The one who fears is not made perfect in love. —1 JOHN 4:18

LIVE FIRST AND FOREMOST in My Presence. Gradually you will become more aware of Me than of people and places around you. This awareness will not detract from your relationships with others. Instead, it will increase your ability to give love and encouragement to them. My Peace will permeate your words and demeanor. You will be active in the world, yet one step removed from it. You will not be easily shaken, because My enveloping Presence buffers the blow of problems.

This is the path I have set before you. As you follow it wholeheartedly, you experience abundant Life and Peace.

Blessed are those who have learned to acclaim you, who walk in the light of your presence, O LORD. They rejoice in your name all day long; they exult in your righteousness. —PSALM 89:15–16

I have set the LORD always before me. Because he is at my right hand, I will not be shaken. —PSALM 16:8

Grace and peace be yours in abundance through the knowledge of God and of Jesus our Lord. —2 PETER 1:2

September 25

Pour all of your energy into trusting Me. It is through trust that you stay connected to Me, aware of My Presence. Every step on your life-journey can be a step of faith. Baby steps of trust are simple for you; you can take them with almost unconscious ease. Giant steps are another matter altogether: leaping across chasms in semidarkness, scaling cliffs of uncertainty, trudging *through the valley of the shadow of death*. These feats require sheer concentration, as well as utter commitment to Me.

Each of My children is a unique blend of temperament, giftedness, and life experiences. Something that is a baby step for you may be a giant step for another person, and vice versa. Only I know the difficulty or ease of each segment of your journey. Beware of trying to impress others by acting as if your giant steps are only baby ones. Do not judge others who hesitate, in trembling fear, before an act that would be easy for you. If each of My children would seek to please Me above all else, fear of others' judgments would vanish, as would attempts to impress others. Focus your attention on the path just ahead of you and on the One who never leaves your side.

Even though I walk through the valley of the shadow of death, I will fear no evil, for you are with me; your rod and your staff, they comfort me. —Psalm 23:4

"Do not judge, or you too will be judged. For in the same way you judge others, you will be judged, and with the measure you use, it will be measured to you." —Matthew 7:1–2

Fear of man will prove to be a snare, but whoever trusts in the Lord is kept safe. —Proverbs 29:25

COME TO ME AND LISTEN! Attune yourself to My voice, and receive My richest blessings. Marvel at the wonder of communing with the Creator of the universe while sitting in the comfort of your home. Kings who reign on earth tend to make themselves inaccessible; ordinary people almost never gain an audience with them. Even dignitaries must plow through red tape and protocol in order to speak with royalty.

Though I am King of the universe, I am totally accessible to you. I am with you wherever you are. Nothing can separate you from My Presence! When I cried out from the cross, "It is finished!" *the curtain of the temple was torn in two from top to bottom.* This opened the way for you to meet Me face to Face, with no need of protocol or priests. I, the King of kings, am your constant Companion.

The Sovereign LORD has given me an instructed tongue, to know the word that sustains the weary. He wakens me morning by morning, wakens my ear to listen like one being taught. —ISAIAH 50:4

"Why spend money on what is not bread, and your labor on what does not satisfy? Listen, listen to me, and eat what is good, and your soul will delight in the richest of fare. Give ear and come to me; hear me, that your soul may live. I will make an everlasting covenant with you, my faithful love promised to David." —ISAIAH 55:2–3

When he had received the drink, Jesus said, "It is finished." With that, he bowed his head and gave up his spirit. —JOHN 19:30

And when Jesus had cried out again in a loud voice, he gave up his spirit. At that moment the curtain of the temple was torn in two from top to bottom. The earth shook and the rocks split. —MATTHEW 27:50–51

September 27

Relax in *My everlasting arms*. Your weakness is an opportunity to grow strong in awareness of My Almighty Presence. When your energy fails you, do not look inward and lament the lack you find there. Look to Me and My sufficiency; rejoice in My radiant riches that are abundantly available to help you.

Go gently through this day, leaning on Me and enjoying My Presence. Thank Me for your neediness, which is building trust-bonds between us. If you look back on your journey thus far, you can see that days of extreme weakness have been some of your most precious times. Memories of these days are richly interwoven with golden strands of My intimate Presence.

The eternal God is your refuge, and underneath are the everlasting arms. He will drive out your enemy before you, saying, "Destroy him!" —Deuteronomy 33:27

I am still confident of this: I will see the goodness of the Lord in the land of the living. Wait for the Lord; be strong and take heart and wait for the Lord. —Psalm 27:13–14

OPEN YOUR MIND AND HEART—your entire being—to receive My Love in full measure. So many of My children limp through their lives starved for Love, because they haven't learned the art of receiving. This is essentially an act of faith: believing that I love you with boundless, everlasting Love. The art of receiving is also a discipline: training your mind to trust Me, coming close to Me with confidence.

Remember that the evil one is *the father of lies*. Learn to recognize his deceptive intrusions into your thoughts. One of his favorite deceptions is to undermine your confidence in My unconditional Love. Fight back against these lies! Do not let them go unchallenged. *Resist the devil in My Name, and he will slink away from you. Draw near to Me*, and My Presence will envelop you in Love.

I pray that out of his glorious riches he may strengthen you with power through his Spirit in your inner being, so that Christ may dwell in your hearts through faith. And I pray that you, being rooted and established in love, may have power, together with all the saints, to grasp how wide and long and high and deep is the love of Christ. —EPHESIANS 3:16–19

Let us then approach the throne of grace with confidence. —HEBREWS 4:16

"You belong to your father, the devil, and you want to carry out your father's desire. . . . When he lies, he speaks his native language, for he is a liar and the father of lies." —JOHN 8:44

Therefore submit to God. Resist the devil and he will flee from you. Draw near to God and He will draw near to you. Cleanse your hands, you sinners; and purify your hearts, you double-minded. —JAMES 4:7–8 NKJV

I AM WITH YOU and all around you, encircling you in golden rays of Light. I always behold you Face to face. Not one of your thoughts escapes My notice. Because I am infinite, I am able to love you as if you and I were the only ones in the universe.

Walk with Me in intimate Love-steps, but do not lose sight of My Majesty. I desire to be your closest Friend, yet I am also your sovereign Lord. I created your brain with capacity to know Me as Friend and Lord simultaneously. The human mind is the pinnacle of My creation, but so few use it for its primary purpose—knowing Me. I communicate continually through My Spirit, My Word, and My creation. Only humans are capable of receiving Me and responding to My Presence. You are indeed *fearfully and wonderfully made*!

I sought the LORD, and he answered me; he delivered me from all my fears. Those who look to him are radiant; their faces are never covered with shame. This poor man called, and the LORD heard him; he saved him out of all his troubles. —PSALM 34:4–6

We did not follow cleverly invented stories when we told you about the power and coming of our Lord Jesus Christ, but we were eyewitnesses of his majesty. For he received honor and glory from God the Father when the voice came to him from the Majestic Glory, saying, "This is my Son, whom I love; with him I am well pleased." —2 PETER 1:16–17

"Now this is eternal life: that they may know you, the only true God, and Jesus Christ, whom you have sent." —JOHN 17:3

I praise you because I am fearfully and wonderfully made; your works are wonderful, I know that full well. —PSALM 139:14

I AM PERPETUALLY WITH YOU, taking care of you. That is the most important fact of your existence. I am not limited by time or space; My Presence with you is a forever-promise. You need not fear the future, for I am already there. When you make that *quantum leap* into eternity, you will find Me awaiting you in heaven. Your future is in My hands; I release it to you day by day, moment by moment. Therefore, *do not worry about tomorrow.*

I want you to live this day abundantly, seeing all there is to see, doing all there is to do. Don't be distracted by future concerns. Leave them to Me! Each day of life is a glorious gift, but so few people know how to live within the confines of today. Much of their energy for abundant living spills over the time line into tomorrow's worries or past regrets. Their remaining energy is sufficient only for limping through the day, not for living it to the full. I am training you to keep your focus on My Presence in the present. This is how to receive abundant Life, which flows freely from My throne of grace.

"Therefore do not worry about tomorrow, for tomorrow will worry about itself. Each day has enough trouble of its own." —MATTHEW 6:34

"The thief comes only to steal and kill and destroy; I have come that they may have life, and have it to the full." —JOHN 10:10

Now listen, you who say, "Today or tomorrow we will go to this or that city, spend a year there, carry on business and make money." Why, you do not even know what will happen tomorrow. What is your life? You are a mist that appears for a little while and then vanishes. Instead, you ought to say, "If it is the Lord's will, we will live and do this or that." —JAMES 4:13–15

October

"Come to me, all you who are weary and burdened, and I will give you rest."

MATTHEW 11:28

October 1

Worship Me only. I am *King of kings and Lord of lords, dwelling in unapproachable Light.* I am taking care of you! I am not only committed to caring for you, but I am also absolutely capable of doing so. Rest in Me, My weary one, for this is a form of worship.

Though self-flagellation has gone out of style, many of My children drive themselves like racehorses. They whip themselves into action, ignoring how exhausted they are. They forget that I am sovereign and that *My ways are higher* than theirs. Underneath their driven service, they may secretly resent Me as a harsh taskmaster. Their worship of Me is lukewarm, because I am no longer their *First Love.*

My invitation never changes: *Come to Me, all you who are weary, and I will give you rest.* Worship Me by resting peacefully in My Presence.

Which God will bring about in his own time—God, the blessed and only Ruler, the King of kings and Lord of lords, who alone is immortal and who lives in unapproachable light, whom no one has seen or can see. To him be honor and might forever. Amen. —1 Timothy 6:15–16

"For my thoughts are not your thoughts, neither are your ways my ways," declares the Lord. "As the heavens are higher than the earth, so are my ways higher than your ways and my thoughts than your thoughts." —Isaiah 55:8–9

"Yet I hold this against you: You have forsaken your first love." —Revelation 2:4

"Come to me, all you who are weary and burdened, and I will give you rest." —Matthew 11:28

Never take for granted My intimate nearness. Marvel at the wonder of My continual Presence with you. Even the most ardent human lover cannot be with you always. Nor can another person know the intimacies of your heart, mind, and spirit. *I know everything about you—even the number of hairs on your head.* You don't need to work at revealing yourself to Me.

Many people spend a lifetime or a small fortune searching for someone who understands them. Yet I am freely available to all who call upon My Name, who open their hearts to receive Me as Savior. This simple act of faith is the beginning of a lifelong love story. I, the Lover of your soul, understand you perfectly and love you eternally.

"Indeed, the very hairs of your head are all numbered. Don't be afraid; you are worth more than many sparrows." —Luke 12:7

Yet to all who received him, to those who believed in his name, he gave the right to become children of God. —John 1:12

Everyone who calls on the name of the Lord will be saved. —Romans 10:13

October 3

When many things seem to be going wrong, trust Me. When your life feels increasingly out of control, thank Me. These are supernatural responses, and they can lift you above your circumstances. If you do what comes naturally in the face of difficulties, you may fall prey to negativism. Even a few complaints can set you on a path that is a downward spiral, by darkening your perspective and mind-set. With this attitude controlling you, complaints flow more and more readily from your mouth. Each one moves you steadily down the slippery spiral. The lower you go, the faster you slide; but it is still possible to apply brakes. Cry out to Me in My Name! Affirm your trust in Me, regardless of how you feel. Thank Me for everything, though this seems unnatural—even irrational. Gradually you will begin to ascend, recovering your lost ground.

When you are back on ground level, you can face your circumstances from a humble perspective. If you choose supernatural responses this time—trusting and thanking Me—you will experience My unfathomable Peace.

But I trust in your unfailing love; my heart rejoices in your salvation. —Psalm 13:5

Always giving thanks to God the Father for everything, in the name of our Lord Jesus Christ. —Ephesians 5:20

I AM THE CREATOR OF HEAVEN AND EARTH: Lord of all that is and all that will ever be. Although I am unimaginably vast, I choose to dwell within you, permeating you with My Presence. Only in the spirit realm could Someone so infinitely great live within someone so very small. Be awed by the Power and the Glory of My Spirit within you!

Though the Holy Spirit is infinite, *He deigns to be your Helper.* He is always ready to offer assistance; all you need to do is ask. When the path before you looks easy and straightforward, you may be tempted to *go it alone* instead of relying on Me. This is when you are in the greatest danger of stumbling. Ask My Spirit to help you as you go each step of the way. Never neglect this glorious Source of strength within you.

"And I will pray the Father, and He will give you another Helper, that He may abide with you forever—the Spirit of truth, whom the world cannot receive, because it neither sees Him nor knows Him; but you know Him, for He dwells with you and will be in you." —JOHN 14:16–17 NKJV

"But I tell you the truth: It is for your good that I am going away. Unless I go away, the Counselor will not come to you; but if I go, I will send him to you." —JOHN 16:7

So he said to me, "This is the word of the LORD to Zerubbabel: 'Not by might nor by power, but by my Spirit,' says the LORD Almighty." —ZECHARIAH 4:6

October 5

Remember that Joy is not dependent on your circumstances. Some of the world's most miserable people are those whose circumstances seem the most enviable. People who reach the top of the ladder career-wise are often surprised to find emptiness awaiting them. True Joy is a by-product of living in My Presence. Therefore you can experience it in palaces, in prisons . . . anywhere.

Do not judge a day as devoid of Joy just because it contains difficulties. Instead, concentrate on staying in communication with Me. Many of the problems that clamor for your attention will resolve themselves. Other matters you must deal with, but I will help you with them. If you make problem-solving secondary to the goal of living close to Me, you can find Joy even in your most difficult days.

Though the fig tree does not bud and there are no grapes on the vines, though the olive crop fails and the fields produce no food, though there are no sheep in the pen and no cattle in the stalls, yet I will rejoice in the Lord, I will be joyful in God my Savior. The Sovereign Lord is my strength; he makes my feet like the feet of a deer, he enables me to go on the heights. —Habakkuk 3:17–19

Splendor and majesty are before him; strength and joy in his dwelling place. —1 Chronicles 16:27

BE WILLING TO FOLLOW wherever I lead. Follow Me wholeheartedly, with glad anticipation quickening your pace. Though you don't know what lies ahead, I know; and that is enough! Some of My richest blessings are just around the bend: out of sight, but nonetheless very real. To receive these gifts, you must *walk by faith—not by sight.* This doesn't mean closing your eyes to what is all around you. It means subordinating the visible world to the invisible Shepherd of your soul.

Sometimes I lead you up a high mountain with only My hand to support you. The higher you climb, the more spectacular the view becomes; also, the more keenly you sense your separation from the world with all its problems. This frees you to experience exuberantly the joyous reality of My Presence. Give yourself fully to these Glory-moments, awash in dazzling Light. I will eventually lead you down the mountain, back into community with others. Let My Light continue to shine within you as you walk among people again.

We live by faith, not by sight. —2 CORINTHIANS 5:7

Splendor and majesty are before him; strength and glory are in his sanctuary. —PSALM 96:6

When Jesus spoke again to the people, he said, "I am the light of the world. Whoever follows me will never walk in darkness, but will have the light of life." —JOHN 8:12

For with you is the fountain of life; in your light we see light. —PSALM 36:9

October 7

In order to hear My voice, you must release all your worries into My care. Entrust to Me everything that concerns you. This clears the way for you to seek My Face unhindered. Let Me free you from fear that is hiding deep inside you. Sit quietly in My Presence, allowing My Light to soak into you and drive out any darkness lodged within you.

Accept each day just as it comes to you, remembering that I am sovereign over your life. *Rejoice in this day that I have made*, trusting that I am abundantly present in it. Instead of regretting or resenting the way things are, *thank Me in all circumstances.* Trust Me and don't be fearful; thank Me and rest in My sovereignty.

Humble yourselves, therefore, under God's mighty hand, that he may lift you up in due time. Cast all your anxiety on him because he cares for you. —1 Peter 5:6–7

This is the day the Lord has made; let us rejoice and be glad in it. —Psalm 118:24

Give thanks in all circumstances, for this is God's will for you in Christ Jesus. —1 Thessalonians 5:18

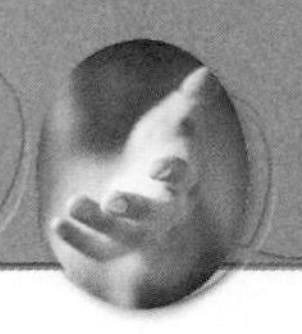

I LOVE YOU WITH *an everlasting Love.* The human mind cannot comprehend My constancy. Your emotions flicker and falter in the face of varying circumstances, and you tend to project your fickle feelings onto Me. Thus, you do not benefit fully from My unfailing Love.

You need to look beyond the flux of circumstances and discover Me gazing lovingly back at you. This awareness of My Presence strengthens you, as you receive and respond to My Love. *I am the same yesterday, today, and forever!* Let My Love flow into you continually. Your need for Me is as constant as the outflow of My Love to you.

The LORD appeared to us in the past, saying: "I have loved you with an everlasting love; I have drawn you with loving-kindness." —JEREMIAH 31:3

In your unfailing love you will lead the people you have redeemed. In your strength you will guide them to your holy dwelling. —EXODUS 15:13

Jesus Christ is the same yesterday and today and forever. —HEBREWS 13:8

October 9

You have been on a long, uphill journey, and your energy is almost spent. Though you have faltered at times, you have not let go of My hand. I am pleased with your desire to stay close to Me. There is one thing, however, that displeases Me: your tendency to complain. You may talk to Me as much as you like about the difficulty of the path we are following. I understand better than anyone else the stresses and strains that have afflicted you. You can ventilate safely to Me, because talking with Me tempers your thoughts and helps you see things from My perspective.

Complaining to others is another matter altogether. It opens the door to deadly sins such as self-pity and rage. Whenever you are tempted to grumble, come to Me and talk it out. As you open up to Me, I will put My thoughts in your mind and My song in your heart.

"I will refresh the weary and satisfy the faint." —Jeremiah 31:25

Do everything without complaining or arguing, so that you may become blameless and pure, children of God without fault in a crooked and depraved generation, in which you shine like stars in the universe. —Philippians 2:14–15

TRUST ME ENOUGH to let things happen without striving to predict or control them. Relax, and refresh yourself in the Light of My everlasting Love. My Love-Light never dims, yet you are often unaware of My radiant Presence. When you project yourself into the future, rehearsing what you will do or say, you are seeking to be self-sufficient: to be adequate without My help. This is a subtle sin—so common that it usually slips by unnoticed.

The alternative is to live fully in the present, depending on Me each moment. Rather than fearing your inadequacy, rejoice in My abundant supply. Train your mind to seek My help continually, even when you feel competent to handle something by yourself. Don't divide your life into things you can do by yourself and things that require My help. Instead, learn to rely on Me in every situation. This discipline will enable you to enjoy life more and to face each day confidently.

Trust in the LORD and do good; dwell in the land and enjoy safe pasture. Delight yourself in the LORD and he will give you the desires of your heart. Commit your way to the LORD; trust in him and he will do this: He will make your righteousness shine like the dawn, the justice of your cause like the noonday sun. —PSALM 37:3–6

And my God shall supply all your need according to His riches in glory by Christ Jesus. —PHILIPPIANS 4:19 NKJV

October 11

I AM THE CULMINATION of all your hopes and desires. *I am the Alpha and the Omega, the first and the last: who is and was and is to come*. Before you knew Me, you expressed your longing for Me in hurtful ways. You were ever so vulnerable to the evil around you in the world. But now My Presence safely shields you, enfolding you in My loving arms. *I have lifted you out of darkness into My marvelous Light*.

Though I have brought many pleasures into your life, not one of them is essential. Receive My blessings with open hands. Enjoy My good gifts, but do not cling to them. Turn your attention to *the Giver of all good things*, and rest in the knowledge that you are complete in Me. The one thing you absolutely need is the one thing you can never lose: My Presence with you.

Find rest, O my soul, in God alone; my hope comes from him. He alone is my rock and my salvation; he is my fortress, I will not be shaken. My salvation and my honor depend on God; he is my mighty rock, my refuge. Trust in him at all times, O people; pour out your hearts to him, for God is our refuge. —PSALM 62:5–8

"I am the Alpha and the Omega," says the Lord God, "who is, and who was, and who is to come, the Almighty." —REVELATION 1:8

But you are a chosen generation, a royal priesthood, a holy nation, His own special people, that you may proclaim the praises of Him who called you out of darkness into His marvelous light. —1 PETER 2:9 NKJV

Every good and perfect gift is from above, coming down from the Father of the heavenly lights, who does not change like shifting shadows. —JAMES 1:17

BEWARE OF SEEING YOURSELF through other people's eyes. There are several dangers to this practice. First of all, it is nearly impossible to discern what others actually think of you. Moreover, their views of you are variable: subject to each viewer's spiritual, emotional, and physical condition. The major problem with letting others define you is that it borders on idolatry. Your concern to please others dampens your desire to please Me, your Creator.

It is much more real to see yourself through *My eyes*. My gaze upon you is steady and sure, untainted by sin. Through My eyes you can see yourself as one who is deeply, eternally loved. Rest in My loving gaze, and you will receive deep Peace. Respond to My loving Presence by *worshiping Me in spirit and in truth.*

And without faith it is impossible to please God, because anyone who comes to him must believe that he exists and that he rewards those who earnestly seek him. —HEBREWS 11:6

"Yet a time is coming and has now come when the true worshipers will worship the Father in spirit and truth, for they are the kind of worshipers the Father seeks. God is spirit, and his worshipers must worship in spirit and in truth." —JOHN 4:23–24

October 13

TAKE TIME TO *BE STILL* in My Presence. The more hassled you feel, the more you need this sacred space of communion with Me. Breathe slowly and deeply. Relax in My holy Presence while *My Face shines upon you*. This is how you receive My Peace, which I always proffer to you.

Imagine the pain I feel when My children tie themselves up in anxious knots, ignoring My gift of Peace. I died a criminal's death to secure this blessing for you. Receive it gratefully; hide it in your heart. My Peace is an inner treasure, growing within you as you trust in Me. Therefore, circumstances cannot touch it. Be still, enjoying Peace in My Presence.

"Be still, and know that I am God; I will be exalted among the nations, I will be exalted in the earth." —PSALM 46:10

"The LORD make his face shine upon you and be gracious to you; the LORD turn his face toward you and give you peace." —NUMBERS 6:25–26

OCTOBER 14

BE PREPARED TO SUFFER FOR ME, in My Name. All suffering has meaning in My kingdom. Pain and problems are opportunities to demonstrate your trust in Me. Bearing your circumstances bravely—even thanking Me for them—is one of the highest forms of praise. This sacrifice of thanksgiving rings golden-toned bells of Joy throughout heavenly realms. On earth also, your patient suffering sends out ripples of good tidings in ever-widening circles.

When suffering strikes, remember that I am sovereign and that I can bring good out of everything. Do not try to run from pain or hide from problems. Instead, accept adversity in My Name, offering it up to Me for My purposes. Thus, your suffering gains meaning and draws you closer to Me. Joy emerges from the ashes of adversity through your trust and thankfulness.

Consider it pure joy, my brothers, whenever you face trials of many kinds, because you know that the testing of your faith develops perseverance. Perseverance must finish its work so that you may be mature and complete, not lacking anything. —JAMES 1:2–4

Let them give thanks to the LORD for his unfailing love and his wonderful deeds for men. Let them sacrifice thank offerings and tell of his works with songs of joy. —PSALM 107:21–22

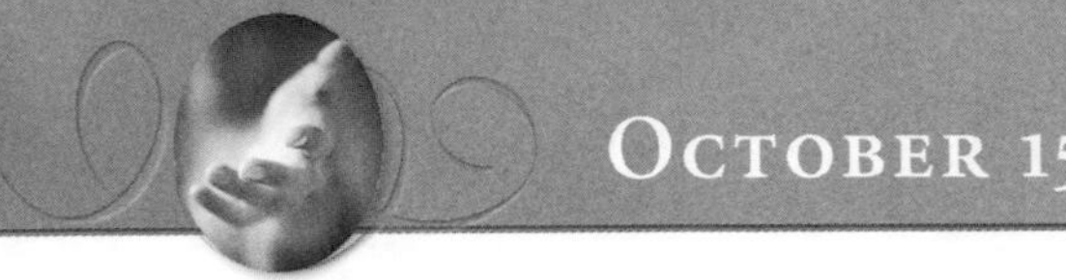

October 15

Try to stay conscious of Me as you go step by step through this day. My Presence with you is both a promise and a protection. After My resurrection, I assured My followers: *Surely I am with you always.* That promise was for all of My followers, without exception.

The promise of My Presence is a powerful protection. As you journey through your life, there are numerous pitfalls along the way. Many voices clamor for your attention, enticing you to go their way. A few steps away from your true path are pits of self-pity and despair, plateaus of pride and self-will. If you take your eyes off Me and follow another's way, you are in grave danger. Even well-meaning friends can lead you astray if you let them usurp My place in your life. The way to stay on the path of Life is to keep your focus on Me. Awareness of My Presence is your best protection.

"And teaching them to obey everything I have commanded you. And surely I am with you always, to the very end of the age." —Matthew 28:20

Therefore, since we are surrounded by such a great cloud of witnesses, let us throw off everything that hinders and the sin that so easily entangles, and let us run with perseverance the race marked out for us. Let us fix our eyes on Jesus, the author and perfecter of our faith, who for the joy set before him endured the cross, scorning its shame, and sat down at the right hand of the throne of God. —Hebrews 12:1–2

Look to Me continually for help, comfort, and companionship. Because I am always by your side, the briefest glance can connect you with Me. When you look to Me for help, it flows freely from My Presence. This recognition of your need for Me, in small matters as well as in large ones, keeps you spiritually alive.

When you need comfort, I love to enfold you in My arms. I enable you not only to feel comforted but also to be a channel through whom I comfort others. Thus you are doubly blessed, because a living channel absorbs some of whatever flows through it.

My constant Companionship is the *pièce de résistance*: the summit of salvation blessings. No matter what losses you experience in your life, no one can take away this glorious gift.

I sought the Lord, and he answered me; he delivered me from all my fears. Those who look to him are radiant; their faces are never covered with shame. This poor man called, and the Lord heard him; he saved him out of all his troubles. —Psalm 34:4–6

Look to the Lord and his strength; seek his face always. —Psalm 105:4

Praise be to the God and Father of our Lord Jesus Christ, the Father of compassion and the God of all comfort, who comforts us in all our troubles, so that we can comfort those in any trouble with the comfort we ourselves have received from God. —2 Corinthians 1:3–4

October 17

Anxiety is a result of envisioning the future without Me. So the best defense against worry is staying in communication with Me. When you turn your thoughts toward Me, you can think much more positively. Remember to listen, as well as to speak, making your thoughts a dialogue with Me.

If you must consider upcoming events, follow these rules: 1) Do not linger in the future, because anxieties sprout up like mushrooms when you wander there. 2) Remember the promise of My continual Presence; include Me in any imagery that comes to mind. This mental discipline does not come easily, because you are accustomed to being god of your fantasies. However, the reality of My Presence with you, now and forevermore, outshines any fantasy you could ever imagine.

Then Jesus said to his disciples: "Therefore I tell you, do not worry about your life, what you will eat; or about your body, what you will wear. Life is more than food, and the body more than clothes. Consider the ravens: They do not sow or reap, they have no storeroom or barn; yet God feeds them. And how much more valuable you are than birds! Who of you by worrying can add a single hour to his life? Since you cannot do this very little thing, why do you worry about the rest?" —Luke 12:22–26

Now to him who is able to do immeasurably more than all we ask or imagine, according to his power that is at work within us, to him be glory in the church and in Christ Jesus throughout all generations, for ever and ever! Amen. —Ephesians 3:20–21

GO GENTLY THROUGH THIS DAY, keeping your eyes on Me. I will open up the way before you, as you take steps of trust along your path. Sometimes the way before you appears to be blocked. If you focus on the obstacle or search for a way around it, you will probably go off course. Instead, focus on Me, the Shepherd who is leading you along your life-journey. Before you know it, the "obstacle" will be behind you and you will hardly know how you passed through it.

That is the secret of success in My kingdom. Although you remain aware of the visible world around you, your primary awareness is of Me. When the road before you looks rocky, you can trust Me to get you through that rough patch. My Presence enables you to face each day with confidence.

"I am the good shepherd; I know my sheep and my sheep know me—just as the Father knows me and I know the Father—and I lay down my life for the sheep." —JOHN 10:14–15

The path of the righteous is level; O upright One, you make the way of the righteous smooth. —ISAIAH 26:7

October 19

Come to Me with your defenses down, ready to be blessed and filled with My Presence. Relax, and feel the relief of being totally open and authentic with Me. You have nothing to hide and nothing to disclose, because I know everything about you already. You can have no other relationship like this one. Take time to savor its richness, basking in My golden Light.

One of the worst consequences of the Fall is the elaborate barriers people erect between themselves and others. Facades abound in the world, even in My Body, the church. Sometimes, church is the last place where people feel free to be themselves. They cover up with Sunday clothes and Sunday smiles. They feel relief when they leave because of the strain of false fellowship. The best antidote to this artificial atmosphere is practicing My Presence at church. Let your primary focus be communing with Me, worshiping Me, glorifying Me. Then you will be able to smile at others with My Joy and love them with My Love.

This is the message we have heard from him and declare to you: God is light; in him there is no darkness at all. If we claim to have fellowship with him yet walk in the darkness, we lie and do not live by the truth. But if we walk in the light, as he is in the light, we have fellowship with one another, and the blood of Jesus, his Son, purifies us from all sin. —1 John 1:5–7

The Lord replied, "My Presence will go with you, and I will give you rest." —Exodus 33:14

Finally, brothers, whatever is true, whatever is noble, whatever is right, whatever is pure, whatever is lovely, whatever is admirable . . . think about such things. —Philippians 4:8

October 20

I AM YOUR LIVING GOD, far more abundantly alive than the most vivacious person you know. The human body is wonderfully crafted, but gravity and the inevitable effects of aging weigh it down. Even the most superb athlete cannot maintain his fitness over many decades. Lasting abundant life can be found in Me alone. Do not be anxious about the weakness of your body. Instead, view it as the prelude to My infusing energy into your being.

As you identify more and more fully with Me, My Life becomes increasingly intertwined with yours. Though the process of aging continues, inwardly you grow stronger with the passing years. Those who live close to Me develop an inner aliveness that makes them seem youthful in spite of their years. Let My Life shine through you, as you *walk in the Light* with Me.

I praise you because I am fearfully and wonderfully made; your works are wonderful, I know that full well. —PSALM 139:14

To this end I labor, struggling with all his energy, which so powerfully works in me. —COLOSSIANS 1:29

But if we walk in the light, as he is in the light, we have fellowship with one another, and the blood of Jesus, his Son, purifies us from all sin. —1 JOHN 1:7

October 21

To live in My Presence consistently, you must expose and expel your rebellious tendencies. When something interferes with your plans or desires, you tend to resent the interference. Try to become aware of each resentment, however petty it may seem. Don't push those unpleasant feelings down; instead, let them come to the surface where you can deal with them. Ask My Spirit to increase your awareness of resentful feelings. Bring them boldly into the Light of My Presence, so that I can free you from them.

The ultimate solution to rebellious tendencies is submission to My authority over you. Intellectually you rejoice in My sovereignty, without which the world would be a terrifying place. But when My sovereign will encroaches on your little domain of control, you often react with telltale resentment.

The best response to losses or thwarted hopes is praise: *The Lord gives and the Lord takes away. Blessed be the name of the Lord.* Remember that all good things—your possessions, your family and friends, your health and abilities, your time—are gifts from Me. Instead of feeling entitled to all these blessings, respond to them with gratitude. Be prepared to let go of anything I take from you, but never let go of My hand!

Search me, O God, and know my heart; test me and know my anxious thoughts. See if there is any offensive way in me, and lead me in the way everlasting. —Psalm 139:23–24

Humble yourselves, therefore, under God's mighty hand. —1 Peter 5:6

And he said: . . . "The Lord gave, and the Lord has taken away; blessed be the name of the Lord." —Job 1:21 NKJV

NO MATTER WHAT your circumstances may be, you can find Joy in My Presence. On some days Joy is generously strewn along your life-path, glistening in the sunlight. On days like that, being content is as simple as breathing the next breath or taking the next step. Other days are overcast and gloomy; you feel the strain of the journey, which seems endless. Dull gray rocks greet your gaze and cause your feet to ache. Yet Joy is still attainable. *Search for it as for hidden treasure.*

Begin by remembering that I have created this day; it is not a chance occurrence. Recall that I am present with you whether you sense My Presence or not. Then, start talking with Me about whatever is on your mind. Rejoice in the fact that I understand you perfectly, and I know exactly what you are experiencing. As you continue communicating with Me, your mood will gradually lighten. Awareness of My marvelous Companionship can infuse Joy into the grayest day.

Surely you have granted him eternal blessings and made him glad with the joy of your presence. —PSALM 21:6

And if you look for it as for silver and search for it as for hidden treasure. —PROVERBS 2:4

October 23

As you turn your attention to Me, feel the Light of My Presence shining upon you. Open your mind and heart to receive My heavenly smile of approval. Let My gold-tinged Love wash over you and soak into the depths of your being. As you are increasingly filled with My Being, you experience joyous union with Me: *I in you, and you in Me.* Your Joy-in-Me and My Joy-in-you become intertwined and inseparable. I suffuse your soul with Joy in My Presence; *at My right hand there are pleasures forevermore.*

"My prayer is not for them alone. I pray also for those who will believe in me through their message, that all of them may be one, Father, just as you are in me and I am in you. May they also be in us so that the world may believe that you have sent me. I have given them the glory that you gave me, that they may be one as we are one: I in them and you in me. May they be brought to complete unity to let the world know that you sent me and have loved them even as you have loved me." —John 17:20–23

You will show me the path of life; in Your presence is fullness of joy; at Your right hand are pleasures forevermore. —Psalm 16:11 NKJV

Lie down in green pastures of Peace. Learn to unwind whenever possible, resting in the Presence of your Shepherd. This electronic age keeps My children "wired" much of the time, too tense to find Me in the midst of their moments. I built into your very being the need for rest. How twisted the world has become when people feel guilty about meeting this basic need! How much time and energy they waste by being always on the go, rather than taking time to seek My direction for their lives.

I have called you to walk with Me down *paths of Peace.* I want you to blaze a trail for others who desire to live in My peaceful Presence. I have chosen you less for your strengths than for your weaknesses, which amplify your need for Me. Depend on Me more and more, and I will shower Peace on all your paths.

The Lord is my shepherd, I shall not be in want. He makes me lie down in green pastures, he leads me beside quiet waters, he restores my soul. He guides me in paths of righteousness for his name's sake. —Psalm 23:1–3

By the seventh day God had finished the work he had been doing; so on the seventh day he rested from all his work. And God blessed the seventh day and made it holy, because on it he rested from all the work of creating that he had done. —Genesis 2:2–3

To shine on those living in darkness and in the shadow of death, to guide our feet into the path of peace. —Luke 1:79

October 25

I AM *GOD WITH YOU*, for all time and throughout eternity. Don't let the familiarity of that concept numb its impact on your consciousness. My perpetual Presence with you can be a continual source of Joy, springing up and flowing out in streams of abundant Life. Let your mind reverberate with meanings of My Names: Jesus—*the Lord saves*, and Immanuel—*God with us*. Strive to remain conscious of My Presence even in your busiest moments. Talk with Me about whatever delights you, whatever upsets you, whatever is on your mind. These tiny steps of daily discipline, taken one after the other, will keep you close to Me on the path of Life.

"She will give birth to a son, and you are to give him the name Jesus, because he will save his people from their sins. . . . The virgin will be with child and will give birth to a son, and they will call him Immanuel"—which means, "God with us." —MATTHEW 1:21, 23

You have made known to me the paths of life; you will fill me with joy in your presence. —ACTS 2:28

Come to Me when you are hurting, and I will soothe your pain. Come to Me when you are joyful, and I will share your Joy, multiplying it many times over. I am All you need, just when you need it. Your deepest desires find fulfillment in Me alone.

This is the age of self-help. Bookstores abound with books about "taking care of number one," making oneself the center of all things. The main goal of these methodologies is to become self-sufficient and confident. You, however, have been called to take a "road less traveled": continual dependence on Me. True confidence comes from knowing you are complete in My Presence. Everything you need has its counterpart in Me.

"I am the vine; you are the branches. If a man remains in me and I in him, he will bear much fruit; apart from me you can do nothing." —John 15:5

Perseverance must finish its work so that you may be mature and complete, not lacking anything. —James 1:4

October 27

As you become increasingly aware of My Presence, you find it easier to discern the way you should go. This is one of the practical benefits of living close to Me. Instead of wondering about what is on the road ahead or worrying about what you should do if . . . or when . . . , you can concentrate on staying in communication with Me. When you actually arrive at a choice-point, I will show you which direction to go.

Many people are so preoccupied with future plans and decisions that they fail to see choices they need to make today. Without any conscious awareness, they make their habitual responses. People who live this way find a dullness creeping into their lives. They sleepwalk through their days, following well-worn paths of routine.

I, the Creator of the universe, am the most creative Being imaginable. I will not leave you circling in deeply rutted paths. Instead, I will lead you along fresh trails of adventure, revealing to you things you did not know. Stay in communication with Me. Follow My guiding Presence.

I will instruct you and teach you in the way you should go;
I will counsel you and watch over you. —Psalm 32:8

In the beginning God created the heavens and the earth. —Genesis 1:1

Do not expect to be treated fairly in this life. People will say and do hurtful things to you, things that you don't deserve. When someone mistreats you, try to view it as an opportunity to grow in grace. See how quickly you can forgive the one who has wounded you. Don't be concerned about setting the record straight. Instead of obsessing about other people's opinions of you, keep your focus on Me. Ultimately, it is My view of you that counts.

As you concentrate on relating to Me, remember that I have clothed you in My righteousness and holiness. I see you attired in these radiant garments, which I bought for you with My blood. This also is not fair; it is pure gift. When others treat you unfairly, remember that My ways with you are much better than fair. My ways are Peace and *Love, which I have poured out into your heart by My Spirit.*

Bear with each other and forgive whatever grievances you may have against one another. Forgive as the Lord forgave you. —Colossians 3:13

I delight greatly in the Lord; my soul rejoices in my God. For he has clothed me with garments of salvation and arrayed me in a robe of righteousness, as a bridegroom adorns his head like a priest, and as a bride adorns herself with her jewels. —Isaiah 61:10

In him we have redemption through his blood, the forgiveness of sins, in accordance with the riches of God's grace that he lavished on us with all wisdom and understanding. —Ephesians 1:7–8

And hope does not disappoint us, because God has poured out his love into our hearts by the Holy Spirit, whom he has given us. —Romans 5:5

October 29

Linger in My Presence a while. Rein in your impulses to plunge into the day's activities. Beginning your day alone with Me is essential preparation for success. A great athlete takes time to prepare himself mentally for the feat ahead of him before he moves a muscle. Similarly, your time of being still in My Presence equips you for the day ahead of you. Only I know what will happen to you this day. I have arranged the events you will encounter as you go along your way. If you are not adequately equipped for the journey, you will *grow weary and lose heart*. Relax with Me while I ready you for action.

For we are God's workmanship, created in Christ Jesus to do good works, which God prepared in advance for us to do. —Ephesians 2:10

Consider him who endured such opposition from sinful men, so that you will not grow weary and lose heart. —Hebrews 12:3

I am with you. I am with you. I am with you. Heaven's bells continually peal with that promise of My Presence. Some people never hear those bells because their minds are earthbound and their hearts are closed to Me. Others hear the bells only once or twice in their lifetimes, in rare moments of seeking Me above all else. My desire is that My "sheep" hear My voice continually, for *I am the ever-present Shepherd.*

Quietness is the classroom where you learn to hear My voice. Beginners need a quiet place in order to still their minds. As you advance in this discipline, you gradually learn to carry the stillness with you wherever you go. When you step back into the mainstream of life, strain to hear those glorious bells: *I am with you. I am with you. I am with you.*

"Then you will call upon me and come and pray to me, and I will listen to you. You will seek me and find me when you seek me with all your heart." —Jeremiah 29:12–13

"I am the good shepherd; I know my sheep and my sheep know me. . . . My sheep listen to my voice; I know them, and they follow me. I give them eternal life, and they shall never perish; no one can snatch them out of my hand." —John 10:14, 27–28

Learn to listen to Me even while you are listening to other people. As they open their souls to your scrutiny, *you are on holy ground*. You need the help of My Spirit to respond appropriately. Ask Him to think through you, live through you, love through you. My own Being is alive within you in the Person of the Holy Spirit. If you respond to others' needs through your unaided thought processes, you offer them dry crumbs. When the Spirit empowers your listening and speaking, My *streams of living water flow* through you to other people. Be a channel of My Love, Joy, and Peace by listening to Me as you listen to others.

"Do not come any closer," God said. "Take off your sandals, for the place where you are standing is holy ground." —Exodus 3:5

Do you not know that your body is a temple of the Holy Spirit, who is in you, whom you have received from God? You are not your own. —1 Corinthians 6:19

"Whoever believes in me, as the Scripture has said, streams of living water will flow from within him." By this he meant the Spirit, whom those who believed in him were later to receive. Up to that time the Spirit had not been given, since Jesus had not yet been glorified. —John 7:38–39

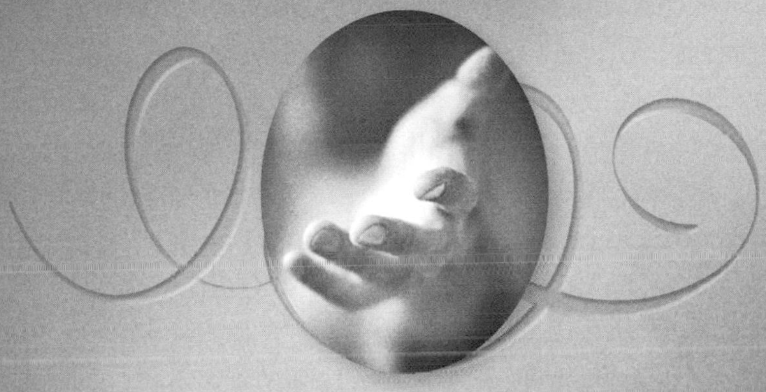

November

And my God will meet all your needs according to his glorious riches in Christ Jesus.

PHILIPPIANS 4:19

November 1

Do not be discouraged by the difficulty of keeping your focus on Me. I know that your heart's desire is to be aware of My Presence continually. This is a lofty goal; you aim toward it but never fully achieve it in this life. Don't let feelings of failure weigh you down. Instead, try to see yourself as I see you. First of all, I am delighted by your deep desire to walk closely with Me through your life. I am pleased each time you initiate communication with Me. In addition, I notice the progress you have made since you first resolved to live in My Presence.

When you realize that your mind has wandered away from Me, don't be alarmed or surprised. You live in a world that has been rigged to distract you. Each time you plow your way through the massive distractions to communicate with Me, you achieve a victory. Rejoice in these tiny triumphs, and they will increasingly light up your days.

Who will bring any charge against those whom God has chosen? It is God who justifies. Who is he that condemns? Christ Jesus, who died—more than that, who was raised to life—is at the right hand of God and is also interceding for us. —Romans 8:33–34

Therefore, since we have a great high priest who has gone through the heavens, Jesus the Son of God, let us hold firmly to the faith we profess. For we do not have a high priest who is unable to sympathize with our weaknesses, but we have one who has been tempted in every way, just as we are—yet was without sin. Let us then approach the throne of grace with confidence, so that we may receive mercy and find grace to help us in our time of need. —Hebrews 4:14–16

GROW STRONG in the Light of My Presence. Your weakness does not repel Me. On the contrary, it attracts My Power, which is always available to flow into a yielded heart. Do not condemn yourself for your constant need of help. Instead, come to Me with your gaping neediness; let the Light of My Love fill you.

A yielded heart does not whine or rebel when the going gets rough. It musters the courage to thank Me even during hard times. Yielding yourself to My will is ultimately an act of trust. *In quietness and trust is your strength.*

The LORD is gracious and righteous; our God is full of compassion. The LORD protects the simplehearted; when I was in great need, he saved me. Be at rest once more, O my soul, for the LORD has been good to you. PSALM 116:5–7

Always giving thanks to God the Father for everything, in the name of our Lord Jesus Christ. —EPHESIANS 5:20

This is what the Sovereign LORD, the Holy One of Israel, says: "In repentance and rest is your salvation, in quietness and trust is your strength, but you would have none of it." —ISAIAH 30:15

NOVEMBER 3

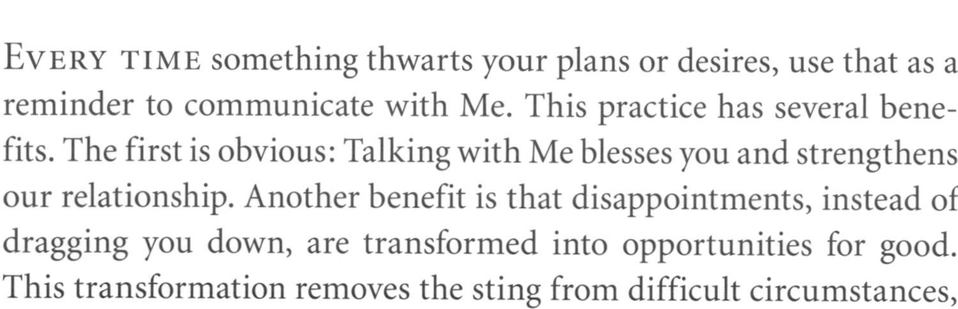

EVERY TIME something thwarts your plans or desires, use that as a reminder to communicate with Me. This practice has several benefits. The first is obvious: Talking with Me blesses you and strengthens our relationship. Another benefit is that disappointments, instead of dragging you down, are transformed into opportunities for good. This transformation removes the sting from difficult circumstances, making it possible to be joyful in the midst of adversity.

Begin by practicing this discipline in all the little disappointments of daily life. It is often these minor setbacks that draw you away from My Presence. When you reframe *setbacks as opportunities*, you find that you gain much more than you have lost. It is only after much training that you can accept major losses in this positive way. But it is possible to attain the perspective of the apostle Paul, who wrote: *Compared to the surpassing greatness of knowing Christ Jesus, I consider everything I once treasured to be as insignificant as rubbish.*

Devote yourselves to prayer, being watchful and thankful. —COLOSSIANS 4:2

But whatever was to my profit I now consider loss for the sake of Christ. What is more, I consider everything a loss compared to the surpassing greatness of knowing Christ Jesus my Lord, for whose sake I have lost all things. I consider them rubbish, that I may gain Christ. —PHILIPPIANS 3:7–8

November 4

WALK PEACEFULLY WITH ME through this day. You are wondering how you will cope with all that is expected of you. You must traverse this day like any other: one step at a time. Instead of mentally rehearsing how you will do this or that, keep your mind on My Presence and on taking the next step. The more demanding your day, the more help you can expect from Me. This is a training opportunity, since I designed you for deep dependence on your Shepherd-King. Challenging times wake you up and amplify your awareness of needing My help.

When you don't know what to do, wait while I open the way before you. Trust that I know what I'm doing, and be ready to follow My lead. *I will give strength to you, and I will bless you with Peace.*

The LORD replied, "My Presence will go with you, and I will give you rest." —EXODUS 33:14

The bolts of your gates will be iron and bronze, and your strength will equal your days. —DEUTERONOMY 33:25

May the God of peace, who through the blood of the eternal covenant brought back from the dead our Lord Jesus, that great Shepherd of the sheep, equip you with everything good for doing his will, and may he work in us what is pleasing to him, through Jesus Christ, to whom be glory for ever and ever. Amen. —HEBREWS 13:20–21

The LORD gives strength to his people; the LORD blesses his people with peace. —PSALM 29:11

November 5

You can live as close to Me as you choose. I set up no barriers between us; neither do I tear down barriers that you erect.

People tend to think their circumstances determine the quality of their lives. So they pour their energy into trying to control those situations. They feel happy when things are going well, and sad or frustrated when things don't turn out as they'd hoped. They rarely question this correlation between their circumstances and feelings. Yet it is possible *to be content in any and every situation*.

Put more energy into trusting Me and enjoying My Presence. Don't let your well-being depend on your circumstances. Instead, connect your joy to My precious promises:

I am with you and will watch over you wherever you go.
I will meet all your needs according to My glorious riches.
Nothing in all creation will be able to separate you
from My Love.

I have learned the secret of being content in any and every situation. —Philippians 4:12

"I am with you and will watch over you wherever you go, and I will bring you back to this land." —Genesis 28:15

And my God will meet all your needs according to his glorious riches in Christ Jesus. —Philippians 4:19

For I am convinced that neither death nor life, neither angels nor demons, neither the present nor the future, nor any powers, neither height nor depth, nor anything else in all creation, will be able to separate us from the love of God that is in Christ Jesus our Lord. —Romans 8:38–39

SEEK TO PLEASE ME above all else. As you journey through today, there will be many choice-points along your way. Most of the day's decisions will be small ones you have to make quickly. You need some rule of thumb to help you make good choices. Many people's decisions are a combination of their habitual responses and their desire to please themselves or others. This is not My way for you. Strive to please Me in everything, not just in major decisions. This is possible only to the extent that you are living in close communion with Me. When My Presence is your deepest delight, you know almost instinctively what will please Me. A quick *glance* at Me is all you need to make the right choice. *Delight yourself in Me* more and more; seek My pleasure in all you do.

"The one who sent me is with me; he has not left me alone, for I always do what pleases him." —JOHN 8:29

By faith Enoch was taken from this life, so that he did not experience death; he could not be found, because God had taken him away. For before he was taken, he was commended as one who pleased God. And without faith it is impossible to please God, because anyone who comes to him must believe that he exists and that he rewards those who earnestly seek him. —HEBREWS 11:5–6

Delight yourself in the LORD and he will give you the desires of your heart. —PSALM 37:4

November 7

Worship Me in the beauty of holiness. All true beauty reflects some of who I am. I am working My ways in you: the divine Artist creating loveliness within your being. My main work is to clear out debris and clutter, making room for My Spirit to take full possession. Collaborate with Me in this effort by being willing to let go of anything I choose to take away. I know what you need, and I have promised to provide all of that—abundantly!

Your sense of security must not rest in your possessions or in things going your way. I am training you to depend on Me alone, finding fulfillment in My Presence. This entails being satisfied with much or with little, accepting *either* as My will for the moment. Instead of grasping and controlling, you are learning to release and receive. Cultivate this receptive stance by trusting Me in every situation.

Give unto the Lord the glory due to His name; worship the Lord in the beauty of holiness. —Psalm 29:2 NKJV

One thing I ask of the Lord, this is what I seek: that I may dwell in the house of the Lord all the days of my life, to gaze upon the beauty of the Lord and to seek him in his temple. —Psalm 27:4

NOVEMBER 8

LEARN TO APPRECIATE difficult days. Be stimulated by the challenges you encounter along your way. As you journey through rough terrain with Me, gain confidence from your knowledge that together we can handle anything. This knowledge is comprised of three parts: your relationship with Me, promises in the Bible, and past experiences of coping successfully during hard times.

Look back on your life, and see how I have helped you through difficult days. If you are tempted to think, "Yes, but that was then, and this is now," remember who I am! Although you and your circumstances may change dramatically, *I remain the same* throughout time and eternity. This is the basis of your confidence. In My Presence *you live and move and have your being.*

"So do not fear, for I am with you; do not be dismayed, for I am your God. I will strengthen you and help you; I will uphold you with my righteous right hand." —ISAIAH 41:10

But you remain the same, and your years will never end. —PSALM 102:27

"For in him we live and move and have our being." As some of your own poets have said, "We are his offspring." —ACTS 17:28

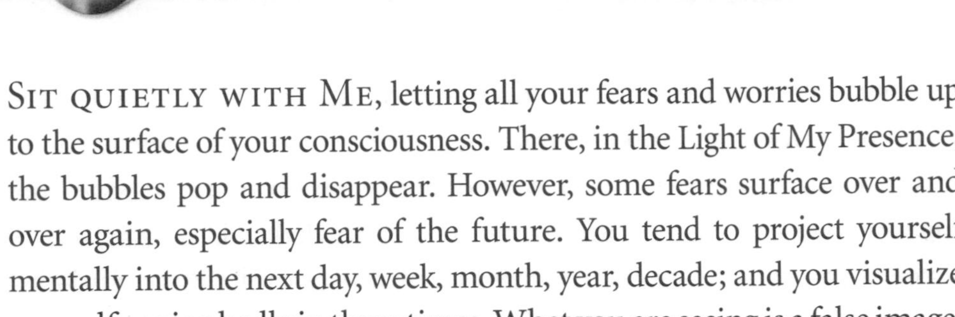

November 9

Sit quietly with Me, letting all your fears and worries bubble up to the surface of your consciousness. There, in the Light of My Presence, the bubbles pop and disappear. However, some fears surface over and over again, especially fear of the future. You tend to project yourself mentally into the next day, week, month, year, decade; and you visualize yourself coping badly in those times. What you are seeing is a false image, because it doesn't include Me. Those gloomy times that you imagine will not come to pass, since My Presence will be with you at *all* times.

When a future-oriented worry assails you, capture it and disarm it by suffusing the Light of My Presence into that mental image. Say to yourself, "Jesus will be with me then and there. With His help, I can cope!" Then, come home to the present moment, where you can enjoy Peace in My Presence.

Then Jesus said to his disciples: "Therefore I tell you, do not worry about your life, what you will eat; or about your body, what you will wear. Life is more than food, and the body more than clothes. Consider the ravens: They do not sow or reap, they have no storeroom or barn; yet God feeds them. And how much more valuable you are than birds! Who of you by worrying can add a single hour to his life?" —Luke 12:22–25

Be strong and courageous. Do not be afraid or terrified because of them, for the Lord your God goes with you; he will never leave you nor forsake you. —Deuteronomy 31:6

We demolish arguments and every pretension that sets itself up against the knowledge of God, and we take captive every thought to make it obedient to Christ. —2 Corinthians 10:5

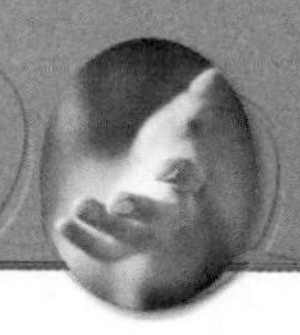

Focus your entire being on My living Presence. I am most assuredly with you, enveloping you in My Love and Peace. While you relax in My Presence, I am molding your mind and cleansing your heart. I am recreating you into the one I designed you to be.

As you move from stillness into the activities of your day, do not relinquish your attentiveness to Me. If something troubles you, talk it over with Me. If you get bored with what you are doing, fill the time with prayers and praise. When someone irritates you, don't let your thoughts linger on that person's faults. Gently nudge your mind back to Me. Every moment is precious if you keep your focus on Me. Any day can be a good day, because My Presence permeates all time.

Blessed are those who have learned to acclaim you, who walk in the light of your presence, O Lord. They rejoice in your name all day long; they exult in your righteousness. —Psalm 89:15–16

This then is how we know that we belong to the truth, and how we set our hearts at rest in his presence whenever our hearts condemn us. For God is greater than our hearts, and he knows everything. —1 John 3:19–20

To him who is able to keep you from falling and to present you before his glorious presence without fault and with great joy—to the only God our Savior be glory, majesty, power and authority, through Jesus Christ our Lord, before all ages, now and forevermore! Amen. —Jude 24–25

In my integrity you uphold me and set me in your presence forever. —Psalm 41:12

DO NOT LET any set of circumstances intimidate you. The more challenging your day, the more of My Power I place at your disposal. You seem to think that I empower you equally each day, but this is not so. Your tendency upon awakening is to assess the difficulties ahead of you, measuring them against your average strength. This is an exercise in unreality.

I know what each of your days will contain, and I empower you accordingly. The degree to which I strengthen you on a given day is based mainly on two variables: the difficulty of your circumstances, and your willingness to depend on Me for help. Try to view challenging days as opportunities to receive more of My Power than usual. Look to Me for all that you need, and watch to see what I will do. *As your day, so shall your strength be.*

I pray also that the eyes of your heart may be enlightened in order that you may know the hope to which he has called you, the riches of his glorious inheritance in the saints, and his incomparably great power for us who believe. That power is like the working of his mighty strength, which he exerted in Christ when he raised him from the dead and seated him at his right hand in the heavenly realms. —EPHESIANS 1:18–20

Look to the LORD and his strength; seek his face always. —PSALM 105:4

Your sandals shall be iron and bronze; as your days, so shall your strength be. —DEUTERONOMY 33:25 NKJV

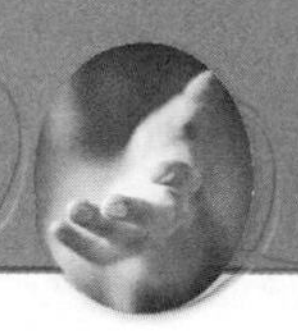

THIS IS A TIME OF ABUNDANCE in your life. *Your cup runneth over* with blessings. After plodding uphill for many weeks, you are now traipsing through lush meadows drenched in warm sunshine. I want you to enjoy to the full this time of ease and refreshment. I delight in providing it for you.

Sometimes My children hesitate to receive My good gifts with open hands. Feelings of false guilt creep in, telling them they don't deserve to be so richly blessed. This is nonsense-thinking, because no one deserves anything from Me. My kingdom is not about earning and deserving; it's about believing and receiving.

When a child of Mine balks at accepting My gifts, I am deeply grieved. When you receive My abundant blessings with a grateful heart, I rejoice. My pleasure in giving and your pleasure in receiving flow together in joyous harmony.

Thou preparest a table before me in the presence of mine enemies: thou anointest my head with oil; my cup runneth over. —PSALM 23:5 KJV

"For God so loved the world that he gave his one and only Son, that whoever believes in him shall not perish but have eternal life." —JOHN 3:16

"So I say to you: Ask and it will be given to you; seek and you will find; knock and the door will be opened to you. For everyone who asks receives; he who seeks finds; and to him who knocks, the door will be opened." —LUKE 11:9–10

He who did not spare his own Son, but gave him up for us all—how will he not also, along with him, graciously give us all things? —ROMANS 8:32

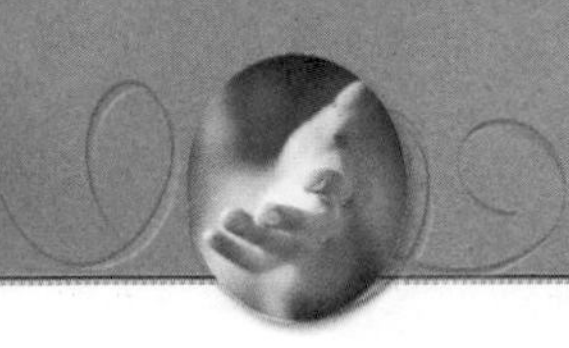

November 13

I AM *CHRIST IN YOU, the hope of Glory.* The One who walks beside you, holding you by your hand, is the same One who lives within you. This is a deep, unfathomable mystery. You and I are intertwined in an intimacy involving every fiber of your being. The Light of My Presence shines within you, as well as upon you. I am in you, and you are in Me; therefore, nothing in heaven or on earth can separate you from Me!

As you sit quietly in My Presence, your awareness of My Life within you is heightened. This produces the *Joy of the Lord, which is your strength. I, the God of hope, fill you with all Joy and Peace as you trust in Me, so that you may bubble over with hope by the power of the Holy Spirit.*

To them God has chosen to make known among the Gentiles the glorious riches of this mystery, which is Christ in you, the hope of glory. —COLOSSIANS 1:27

"I, the LORD, have called you in righteousness; I will take hold of your hand. I will keep you and will make you to be a covenant for the people and a light for the Gentiles." —ISAIAH 42:6

Nehemiah said, "Go and enjoy choice food and sweet drinks, and send some to those who have nothing prepared. This day is sacred to our Lord. Do not grieve, for the joy of the LORD is your strength." —NEHEMIAH 8:10

May the God of your hope so fill you with all joy and peace in believing [through the experience of your faith] that by the power of the Holy Spirit you may abound and be overflowing (bubbling over) with hope. —ROMANS 15:13 AMP

November 14

Bask in the luxury of being fully understood and unconditionally loved. Dare to see yourself as I see you: radiant in My righteousness, cleansed by My blood. I view you as the one I created you to be, the one you will be in actuality when heaven becomes your home. It is My Life within you that is changing you *from glory to glory*. Rejoice in this mysterious miracle! Thank Me continually for the amazing gift of My Spirit within you.

Try to depend on the help of the Spirit as you go through this day of life. Pause briefly from time to time so you can consult with this Holy One inside you. He will not force you to do His bidding, but He will guide you as you give Him space in your life. Walk along this wondrous way of collaboration with My Spirit.

Those who look to him are radiant; their faces are never covered with shame. —Psalm 34:5

God made him who had no sin to be sin for us, so that in him we might become the righteousness of God. —2 Corinthians 5:21

But we all, with unveiled face, beholding as in a mirror the glory of the Lord, are being transformed into the same image from glory to glory, just as by the Spirit of the Lord. —2 Corinthians 3:18 NKJV

Since we live by the Spirit, let us keep in step with the Spirit. —Galatians 5:25

November 15

Approach problems with a light touch. When your mind moves toward a problem area, you tend to focus on that situation so intensely that you lose sight of Me. You pit yourself against the difficulty as if you had to conquer it immediately. Your mind gears up for battle, and your body becomes tense and anxious. Unless you achieve total victory, you feel defeated.

There is a better way. When a problem starts to overshadow your thoughts, bring this matter to Me. Talk with Me about it and look at it in the Light of My Presence. This puts some much-needed space between you and your concern, enabling you to see from My perspective. You will be surprised at the results. Sometimes you may even laugh at yourself for being so serious about something so insignificant.

You will always face trouble in this life. But more importantly, you will always have Me with you, helping you to handle whatever you encounter. Approach problems with a light touch by viewing them in My revealing Light.

Blessed are those who have learned to acclaim you, who walk in the light of your presence, O Lord. —Psalm 89:15

"I have told you these things, so that in me you may have peace. In this world you will have trouble. But take heart! I have overcome the world." —John 16:33

November 16

As you look at the day before you, you see a twisted, complicated path, with branches going off in all directions. You wonder how you can possibly find your way through that maze. Then you remember the One who is *with you always, holding you by your right hand*. You recall My promise to *guide you with My counsel*, and you begin to relax. As you look again at the path ahead, you notice that a peaceful fog has settled over it, obscuring your view. You can see only a few steps in front of you, so you turn your attention more fully to Me and begin to enjoy My Presence.

The fog is a protection for you, calling you back into the present moment. Although I inhabit all of space and time, you can communicate with Me only here and now. Someday the fog will no longer be necessary, for you will have learned to keep your focus on Me and on the path just ahead of you.

Yet I am always with you; you hold me by my right hand. You guide me with your counsel, and afterward you will take me into glory. —Psalm 73:23–24

Now we see but a poor reflection as in a mirror; then we shall see face to face. Now I know in part; then I shall know fully, even as I am fully known. —1 Corinthians 13:12

November 17

THERE IS *NO CONDEMNATION* for those who are in Me. *The law of the Spirit of Life has set you free from the law of sin and death.* Not many Christians know how to live in this radical freedom, which is their birthright. I died to set you free; live freely in Me!

To walk along the path of freedom, you must keep your mind firmly fixed on Me. Many voices proclaim: "This is the way for you to go," but only My voice tells you the true way. If you follow the way of the world with all its glitter and glamour, you will descend deeper and deeper into an abyss. Christian voices also can lead you astray: "Do this!" "Don't do that!" "Pray this way!" "Don't pray that way!" If you listen to all those voices, you will become increasingly confused.

Be content to be a simple sheep, listening for My voice and following Me. *I will lead you into restful green pastures and guide you along paths of righteousness.*

Therefore, there is now no condemnation for those who are in Christ Jesus, because through Christ Jesus the law of the Spirit of life set me free from the law of sin and death. —ROMANS 8:1–2

Whether you turn to the right or to the left, your ears will hear a voice behind you, saying, "This is the way; walk in it." —ISAIAH 30:21

"My sheep listen to my voice; I know them, and they follow me." —JOHN 10:27

The LORD is my shepherd, I shall not be in want. He makes me lie down in green pastures, he leads me beside quiet waters, he restores my soul. He guides me in paths of righteousness for his name's sake. —PSALM 23:1–3

COME TO ME, and rest in My Peace. My Face is shining upon you, in rays of *Peace transcending understanding.* Instead of trying to figure things out yourself, you can relax in the Presence of the One who knows everything. As you lean on Me in trusting dependence, you feel peaceful and complete. This is how I designed you to live: in close communion with Me.

When you are around other people, you tend to cater to their expectations—real or imagined. You feel enslaved to pleasing them, and your awareness of My Presence grows dim. Your efforts to win their approval eventually exhaust you. You offer these people dry crumbs rather than the *living water* of My Spirit flowing through you. This is not My way for you! Stay in touch with Me, even during your busiest moments. Let My Spirit give you words of grace as you live in the Light of My Peace.

Do not be anxious about anything, but in everything, by prayer and petition, with thanksgiving, present your requests to God. And the peace of God, which transcends all understanding, will guard your hearts and your minds in Christ Jesus. —PHILIPPIANS 4:6–7

"Whoever believes in me, as the Scripture has said, streams of living water will flow from within him." —JOHN 7:38

Do not get drunk on wine, which leads to debauchery. Instead, be filled with the Spirit. Speak to one another with psalms, hymns and spiritual songs. Sing and make music in your heart to the Lord, always giving thanks to God the Father for everything, in the name of our Lord Jesus Christ. —EPHESIANS 5:18–20

November 19

Leave outcomes up to Me. Follow Me wherever I lead, without worrying about how it will all turn out. Think of your life as an adventure, with Me as your Guide and Companion. Live in the *now*, concentrating on staying in step with Me. When our path leads to a cliff, be willing to climb it with My help. When we come to a resting place, take time to be refreshed in My Presence. Enjoy the rhythm of life lived close to Me.

You already know the ultimate destination of your journey: your entrance into heaven. So keep your focus on the path just before you, leaving outcomes up to Me.

I am still confident of this: I will see the goodness of the Lord in the land of the living. Wait for the Lord; be strong and take heart and wait for the Lord. —Psalm 27:13–14

In your unfailing love you will lead the people you have redeemed. In your strength you will guide them to your holy dwelling. —Exodus 15:13

I AM PLEASED WITH YOU, MY CHILD. Allow yourself to become fully aware of My pleasure shining upon you. You don't have to perform well in order to receive My Love. In fact, a performance focus will pull you away from Me, toward some sort of Pharisaism. This can be a subtle form of idolatry: worshiping your own good works. It can also be a source of deep discouragement when your works don't measure up to your expectations.

Shift your focus from your performance to My radiant Presence. The Light of My Love shines on you continually, regardless of your feelings or behavior. Your responsibility is to be receptive to this unconditional Love. Thankfulness and trust are your primary receptors. Thank Me for everything; *trust in Me at all times.* These simple disciplines will keep you open to My loving Presence.

For it is by grace you have been saved, through faith—
and this not from yourselves, it is the gift of God—not by
works, so that no one can boast. —EPHESIANS 2:8–9

I pray that out of his glorious riches he may strengthen you with
power through his Spirit in your inner being, so that Christ may dwell
in your hearts through faith. And I pray that you, being rooted and
established in love, may have power, together with all the saints, to
grasp how wide and long and high and deep is the love of Christ, and
to know this love that surpasses knowledge—that you may be filled
to the measure of all the fullness of God. —EPHESIANS 3:16–19

Trust in him at all times, O people; pour out your hearts
to him, for God is our refuge. —PSALM 62:8

Thank Me throughout this day for My Presence and My Peace. These are gifts of supernatural proportions. Ever since the resurrection, I have comforted My followers with these messages: *Peace be with you*, and *I am with you always.* Listen as I offer you My Peace and Presence in full measure. The best way to receive these glorious gifts is to thank Me for them.

It is impossible to spend too much time thanking and praising Me. I created you first and foremost to glorify Me. Thanksgiving and praise put you in proper relationship with Me, opening the way for My riches to flow into you. As you thank Me for My Presence and Peace, you appropriate My richest gifts.

While they were still talking about this, Jesus himself stood among them and said to them, "Peace be with you." —Luke 24:36

"And teaching them to obey everything I have commanded you. And surely I am with you always, to the very end of the age." —Matthew 28:20

Through Jesus, therefore, let us continually offer to God a sacrifice of praise—the fruit of lips that confess his name. —Hebrews 13:15

A THANKFUL ATTITUDE opens windows of heaven. Spiritual blessings fall freely onto you through those openings into eternity. Moreover, as you look up with a grateful heart, you get glimpses of Glory through those windows. You cannot yet live in heaven, but you can experience foretastes of your ultimate home. Such samples of heavenly fare revive your hope. Thankfulness opens you up to these experiences, which then provide further reasons to be grateful. Thus, your path becomes an upward spiral: ever increasing in gladness.

Thankfulness is not some sort of magic formula; it is the language of Love, which enables you to communicate intimately with Me. A thankful mind-set does not entail a denial of reality with its plethora of problems. Instead, it *rejoices in Me, your Savior*, in the midst of trials and tribulations. *I am your refuge and strength, an ever-present and well-proved help in trouble.*

Though the fig tree does not bud and there are no grapes on the vines, though the olive crop fails and the fields produce no food, though there are no sheep in the pen and no cattle in the stalls, yet I will rejoice in the LORD, I will be joyful in God my Savior. —HABAKKUK 3:17–18

God is our Refuge and Strength [mighty and impenetrable to temptation], a very present and well-proved help in trouble. —PSALM 46:1 AMP

AS YOU SIT QUIETLY IN MY PRESENCE, let Me fill your heart and mind with thankfulness. This is the most direct way to achieve a thankful stance. If your mind needs a focal point, gaze at My Love poured out for you on the cross. Remember that *nothing in heaven or on earth can separate you from that Love*. This remembrance builds a foundation of gratitude in you, a foundation that circumstances cannot shake.

As you go through this day, look for tiny treasures strategically placed along the way. I lovingly go before you and plant little pleasures to brighten your day. Look carefully for them, and pluck them one by one. When you reach the end of the day, you will have gathered a lovely bouquet. Offer it up to Me with a grateful heart. Receive My Peace as you lie down to sleep, with thankful thoughts playing a lullaby in your mind.

For I am convinced that neither death nor life, neither angels nor demons, neither the present nor the future, nor any powers, neither height nor depth, nor anything else in all creation, will be able to separate us from the love of God that is in Christ Jesus our Lord. —ROMANS 8:38–39

You have filled my heart with greater joy than when their grain and new wine abound. I will lie down and sleep in peace, for you alone, O LORD, make me dwell in safety. —PSALM 4:7–8

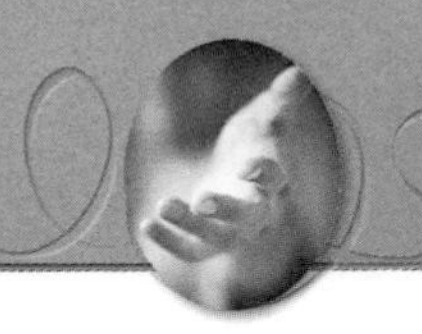

THANKFULNESS takes the sting out of adversity. That is why I have instructed you to *give thanks for everything*. There is an element of mystery in this transaction: You give Me thanks (regardless of your feelings), and I give you Joy (regardless of your circumstances). This is a spiritual act of obedience—at times, blind obedience. To people who don't know Me intimately, it can seem irrational and even impossible to thank Me for heartrending hardships. Nonetheless, those who obey Me in this way are invariably blessed, even though difficulties may remain.

Thankfulness opens your heart to My Presence and your mind to My thoughts. You may still be in the same place, with the same set of circumstances, but it is as if a light has been switched on, enabling you to see from My perspective. It is this *Light of My Presence* that removes the sting from adversity.

Always giving thanks to God the Father for everything, in the name of our Lord Jesus Christ. —EPHESIANS 5:20

Give thanks to the LORD, for he is good; his love endures forever. —PSALM 118:1

Blessed are those who have learned to acclaim you, who walk in the light of your presence, O LORD. —PSALM 89:15

Thank Me frequently as you journey through today. This practice makes it possible to *pray without ceasing*, as the apostle Paul taught. If you are serious about learning to pray continually, the best approach is to thank Me in every situation. These thankful prayers provide a solid foundation on which you can build all your other prayers. Moreover, a grateful attitude makes it easier for you to communicate with Me.

When your mind is occupied with thanking Me, you have no time for worrying or complaining. If you practice thankfulness consistently, negative thought patterns will gradually grow weaker and weaker. *Draw near to Me* with a grateful heart, and My Presence will *fill you with Joy and Peace.*

Rejoice evermore. Pray without ceasing. In every thing give thanks: for this is the will of God in Christ Jesus concerning you. —1 Thessalonians 5:16–18 KJV

Come near to God and he will come near to you. Wash your hands, you sinners, and purify your hearts, you double-minded. —James 4:8

May the God of hope fill you with all joy and peace as you trust in him, so that you may overflow with hope by the power of the Holy Spirit. —Romans 15:13

THIS IS THE DAY THAT I HAVE MADE! As you rejoice in this day of life, it will yield up to you precious gifts and beneficial training. Walk with Me along the high road of thanksgiving, and you will find all the delights I have made ready for you.

To protect your thankfulness, you must remember that you reside in a fallen world, where blessings and sorrows intermingle freely. A constant focus on adversity defeats many Christians. They walk through a day that is brimming with beauty and brightness, seeing only the grayness of their thoughts. Neglecting the practice of giving thanks has darkened their minds. How precious are My children who remember to thank Me at all times. They can walk through the darkest days with Joy in their hearts because they know that the Light of My Presence is still shining on them. *Rejoice in this day that I have made*, for I am your steadfast Companion.

This is the day the LORD has made; let us rejoice and be glad in it. —PSALM 118:24

I will sacrifice a thank offering to you and call on the name of the LORD. —PSALM 116:17

November 27

Let thankfulness rule in your heart. As you thank Me for blessings in your life, a marvelous thing happens. It is as if *scales fall off your eyes*, enabling you to see more and more of My glorious riches. With your eyes thus opened, you can help yourself to whatever you need from My treasure house. Each time you receive one of My golden gifts, let your thankfulness sing out praises to My Name. "Hallelujahs" are the language of heaven, and they can become the language of your heart.

A life of praise and thankfulness becomes a life filled with miracles. Instead of trying to be in control, you focus on Me and what I am doing. This is the power of praise: centering your entire being in Me. This is how I created you to live, for I made you in My own image. Enjoy abundant life by overflowing with praise and thankfulness.

Let the peace of Christ rule in your hearts. . . .
And be thankful. —Colossians 3:15

Immediately, something like scales fell from Saul's eyes, and he
could see again. He got up and was baptized. —Acts 9:18

And again they shouted: "Hallelujah! . . ." The twenty-four elders and the four
living creatures fell down and worshiped God, who was seated on the throne.
And they cried: "Amen, Hallelujah!" Then a voice came from the throne,
saying: "Praise our God, all you his servants, you who fear him, both small and
great!" Then I heard what sounded like a great multitude, like the roar of
rushing waters and like loud peals of thunder, shouting: "Hallelujah! For our
Lord God Almighty reigns." —Revelation 19:3–6

Enter his gates with thanksgiving and his courts with praise;
give thanks to him and praise his name. —Psalm 100:4

Rest in the deep assurance of My unfailing Love. Let your body, mind, and spirit relax in My Presence. Release into My care anything that is troubling you, so that you can focus your full attention on Me. Be awed by the vast dimensions of My Love for you: *wider, longer, higher, and deeper* than anything you know. Rejoice that this marvelous Love is yours forever!

The best response to this glorious gift is a life steeped in thankfulness. Every time you thank Me, you acknowledge that I am your Lord and Provider. This is the proper stance for a child of God: receiving with thanksgiving. Bring Me the sacrifice of gratitude, and watch to see how much I bless you.

Cast all your anxiety on him because he cares for you. —1 Peter 5:7

I pray that out of his glorious riches he may strengthen you with power through his Spirit in your inner being, so that Christ may dwell in your hearts through faith. And I pray that you, being rooted and established in love, may have power, together with all the saints, to grasp how wide and long and high and deep is the love of Christ, and to know this love that surpasses knowledge—that you may be filled to the measure of all the fullness of God. —Ephesians 3:16–19

Let them give thanks to the Lord for his unfailing love and his wonderful deeds for men. Let them sacrifice thank offerings and tell of his works with songs of joy. —Psalm 107:21–22

November 29

Let Me infuse My Peace into your innermost being. As you sit quietly in the Light of My Presence, you can sense Peace growing within you. This is not something that you accomplish through self-discipline and willpower; it is opening yourself to receive My blessing.

In this age of independence, people find it hard to acknowledge their neediness. However, I have taken you along a path that has highlighted your need for Me: placing you in situations where your strengths were irrelevant and your weaknesses were glaringly evident. Through the aridity of those desert marches, I have drawn you closer and closer to Myself. You have discovered flowers of Peace blossoming in the most desolate places. You have learned to thank Me for hard times and difficult journeys, trusting that through them I accomplish My best work. You have realized that needing Me is the key to knowing Me intimately, which is the gift above all gifts.

"The Lord will guide you always; he will satisfy your needs in a sun-scorched land and will strengthen your frame. You will be like a well-watered garden, like a spring whose waters never fail." —Isaiah 58:11

He tends his flock like a shepherd: He gathers the lambs in his arms and carries them close to his heart; he gently leads those that have young. —Isaiah 40:11

Problems are part of life. They are inescapable: woven into the very fabric of this fallen world. You tend to go into problem-solving mode all too readily, acting as if you have the capacity to fix everything. This is a habitual response, so automatic that it bypasses your conscious thinking. Not only does this habit frustrate you, it also distances you from Me.

Do not let fixing things be your top priority. You are ever so limited in your capacity to correct all that is wrong in the world around you. Don't weigh yourself down with responsibilities that are not your own. Instead, make your relationship with Me your primary concern. Talk with Me about whatever is on your mind, seeking My perspective on the situation. Rather than trying to fix everything that comes to your attention, ask Me to show you what is truly important. Remember that you are *en route* to heaven, and let your problems fade in the Light of eternity.

I will instruct you and teach you in the way you should go; I will counsel you and watch over you. —Psalm 32:8

"Martha, Martha," the Lord answered, "you are worried and upset about many things, but only one thing is needed. Mary has chosen what is better, and it will not be taken away from her." —Luke 10:41–42

But our citizenship is in heaven. And we eagerly await a Savior from there, the Lord Jesus Christ, who, by the power that enables him to bring everything under his control, will transform our lowly bodies so that they will be like his glorious body. —Philippians 3:20–21

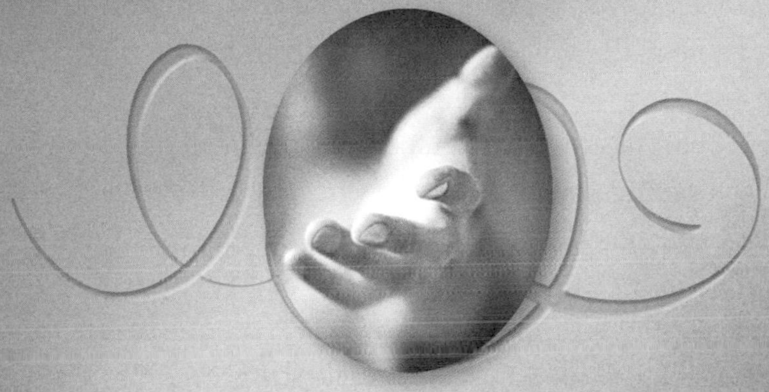

December

"For to us a child is born. . . . And he will be called Wonderful Counselor, Mighty God, Everlasting Father, Prince of Peace."

Isaiah 9:6

December 1

I LOVE YOU with an everlasting Love, which flows out from the depths of eternity. Before you were born, I knew you. Ponder the awesome mystery of a Love that encompasses you from before birth to beyond the grave.

Modern man has lost the perspective of eternity. To distract himself from the gaping jaws of death, he engages in ceaseless activity and amusement. The practice of being still in My Presence is almost a lost art, yet it is this very stillness that enables you to experience My eternal Love. You need the certainty of My loving Presence in order to weather the storms of life. During times of severe testing, even the best theology can fail you if it isn't accompanied by experiential knowledge of Me. The ultimate protection against sinking during life's storms is devoting time to develop your friendship with Me.

The LORD appeared to us in the past, saying: "I have loved you with an everlasting love; I have drawn you with loving-kindness." —JEREMIAH 31:3

Because of the LORD's great love we are not consumed, for his compassions never fail. They are new every morning; great is your faithfulness. I say to myself, "The LORD is my portion; therefore I will wait for him." The LORD is good to those whose hope is in him, to the one who seeks him; it is good to wait quietly for the salvation of the LORD. —LAMENTATIONS 3:22–26

December 2

I AM THE *PRINCE OF PEACE*. As I said to My disciples, I say also to you: *Peace be with you*. Since I am your constant Companion, My Peace is steadfastly with you. When you keep your focus on Me, you experience both My Presence and My Peace. Worship Me as King of kings, Lord of lords, and Prince of Peace.

You need My Peace each moment to accomplish My purposes in your life. Sometimes you are tempted to take shortcuts, in order to reach your goal as quickly as possible. But if the shortcut requires turning your back on My peaceful Presence, you must choose the longer route. Walk with Me along paths of Peace; enjoy the journey in My Presence.

For to us a child is born, to us a son is given, and the government will be on his shoulders. And he will be called Wonderful Counselor, Mighty God, Everlasting Father, Prince of Peace. —ISAIAH 9:6

On the evening of that first day of the week, when the disciples were together, with the doors locked for fear of the Jews, Jesus came and stood among them and said, "Peace be with you!" After he said this, he showed them his hands and side. The disciples were overjoyed when they saw the Lord. Again Jesus said, "Peace be with you! As the Father has sent me, I am sending you." —JOHN 20:19–21

Show me Your ways, O LORD; teach me Your paths. —PSALM 25:4 NKJV

December 3

Do not be surprised by the fiery attacks on your mind. When you struggle to find Me and to live in My Peace, don't let discouragement set in. You are engaged in massive warfare, spiritually speaking. The evil one abhors your closeness to Me, and his demonic underlings are determined to destroy our intimacy. When you find yourself in the thick of battle, call upon My Name: "Jesus, help me!" At that instant, the battle becomes Mine; your role is simply to trust Me as I fight for you.

My Name, properly used, has unlimited Power to bless and protect. At the end of time, *every knee will bow (in heaven, on earth, and under the earth) when My Name is proclaimed*. People who have used "Jesus" as a shoddy swear word will fall down in terror on that awesome day. But all those who have drawn near Me through trustingly uttering My Name will be filled with *inexpressible and glorious Joy*. This is your great hope, as you await My return.

For our struggle is not against flesh and blood, but against the rulers, against the authorities, against the powers of this dark world and against the spiritual forces of evil in the heavenly realms. —Ephesians 6:12

Therefore God exalted him to the highest place and gave him the name that is above every name, that at the name of Jesus every knee should bow, in heaven and on earth and under the earth. —Philippians 2:9–10

Though you have not seen him, you love him; and even though you do not see him now, you believe in him and are filled with an inexpressible and glorious joy, for you are receiving the goal of your faith, the salvation of your souls. —1 Peter 1:8–9

My thoughts are not your thoughts; neither are your ways My ways. As the heavens are higher than the earth, so are My ways and thoughts higher than yours. Remember who I AM when you spend time with Me. Marvel at the wonder of being able to commune with the King of the universe—any time, any place. Never take this amazing privilege for granted!

Though I am vastly higher and greater than you, I am training you to think My thoughts. As you spend time in My Presence, My thoughts gradually form in your mind. My Spirit is the Director of this process. Sometimes He brings Bible verses to mind. Sometimes He enables you to hear Me "speak" directly to you. These communications strengthen you and prepare you for whatever is before you on your life-path. Take time to listen to My voice. Through your sacrifice of precious time, I bless you far more than you dare to ask.

"For my thoughts are not your thoughts, neither are your ways my ways," declares the Lord. "As the heavens are higher than the earth, so are my ways higher than your ways and my thoughts than your thoughts." —Isaiah 55:8–9

Devote yourselves to prayer, being watchful and thankful. —Colossians 4:2

I will sacrifice a thank offering to you and call on the name of the Lord. —Psalm 116:17

December 5

Let My Presence override everything you experience. Like a luminous veil of Light, I hover over you and everything around you. I am training you to stay conscious of Me in each situation you encounter.

When the patriarch Jacob ran away from his enraged brother, he went to sleep on a stone pillow in a land that seemed desolate. But after dreaming about heaven and angels and promises of My Presence, he awoke and exclaimed: "Surely the Lord is in this place, and I was not aware of it." His discovery was not only for him but for all who seek Me. Whenever you feel distant from Me, say: "Surely the Lord is in this place!" Then, ask Me to give you awareness of My Presence. This is a prayer that I delight to answer.

In the shelter of your presence you hide them from the intrigues of men; in your dwelling you keep them safe from accusing tongues. —Psalm 31:20

When he reached a certain place, he stopped for the night because the sun had set. Taking one of the stones there, he put it under his head and lay down to sleep. He had a dream in which he saw a stairway resting on the earth, with its top reaching to heaven, and the angels of God were ascending and descending on it. There above it stood the Lord, and he said: "I am the Lord, the God of your father Abraham and the God of Isaac. I will give you and your descendants the land on which you are lying. Your descendants will be like the dust of the earth, and you will spread out to the west and to the east, to the north and to the south. All peoples on earth will be blessed through you and your offspring. I am with you and will watch over you wherever you go, and I will bring you back to this land. I will not leave you until I have done what I have promised you." When Jacob awoke from his sleep, he thought, "Surely the Lord is in this place, and I was not aware of it." —Genesis 28:11–16

STAY EVER SO CLOSE TO ME, and you will not deviate from the path I have prepared for you. This is the most efficient way to stay on track; it is also the most enjoyable way. Men tend to multiply duties in their observance of religion. This practice enables them to give Me money, time, and work without yielding up to Me what I desire the most—their hearts. Rules can be observed mechanically. Once they become habitual, they can be followed with minimal effort and almost no thought. These habit-forming rules provide a false sense of security, lulling the soul into a comatose condition.

What I search for in My children is an awakened soul that thrills to the Joy of My Presence! I created mankind to glorify Me and enjoy Me forever. I provide the Joy; your part is to glorify Me by living close to Me.

Love the LORD your God with all your heart and with all your soul and with all your strength. —DEUTERONOMY 6:5

Whatever you do, work at it with all your heart, as working for the Lord, not for men. —COLOSSIANS 3:23

You have made known to me the path of life; you will fill me with joy in your presence, with eternal pleasures at your right hand. —PSALM 16:11

December 7

I AM WITH YOU IN ALL THAT YOU DO, even in the most menial task. I am always aware of you, concerned with every detail of your life. Nothing escapes My notice—not even *the number of hairs on your head*. However, your awareness of My Presence falters and flickers; as a result, your life experience feels fragmented. When your focus is broad enough to include Me in your thoughts, you feel safe and complete. When your perception narrows so that problems or details fill your consciousness, you feel empty and incomplete.

Learn to look steadily at Me in all your moments and all your circumstances. Though the world is unstable and in flux, you can experience continuity through your uninterrupted awareness of My Presence. *Fix your gaze on what is unseen*, even as the visible world parades before your eyes.

"Are not two sparrows sold for a penny? Yet not one of them will fall to the ground apart from the will of your Father. And even the very hairs of your head are all numbered. So don't be afraid; you are worth more than many sparrows." —MATTHEW 10:29–31

By faith he left Egypt, not fearing the king's anger; he persevered because he saw him who is invisible. —HEBREWS 11:27

So we fix our eyes not on what is seen, but on what is unseen. For what is seen is temporary, but what is unseen is eternal. —2 CORINTHIANS 4:18

YOUR NEEDS AND MY RICHES are a perfect fit. I never meant for you to be self-sufficient. Instead, I designed you to need Me not only for daily bread but also for fulfillment of deep yearnings. I carefully crafted your longings and feelings of incompleteness, to point you to Me. Therefore, do not try to bury or deny these feelings. Beware also of trying to pacify these longings with lesser gods: people, possessions, power.

Come to Me in all your neediness, with defenses down and with desire to be blessed. As you spend time in My Presence, your deepest longings are fulfilled. Rejoice in your neediness, which enables you to find intimate completion in Me.

And my God will meet all your needs according to his glorious riches in Christ Jesus. —PHILIPPIANS 4:19

My purpose is that they may be encouraged in heart and united in love, so that they may have the full riches of complete understanding, in order that they may know the mystery of God, namely, Christ, in whom are hidden all the treasures of wisdom and knowledge. —COLOSSIANS 2:2–3

DECEMBER 9

BE WILLING TO GO OUT on a limb with Me. If that is where I am leading you, it is the safest place to be. Your desire to live a risk-free life is a form of unbelief. Your longing to live close to Me is at odds with your attempts to minimize risk. You are approaching a crossroads in your journey. In order to follow Me wholeheartedly, you must relinquish your tendency to play it safe.

Let Me lead you step by step through this day. If your primary focus is on Me, you can walk along perilous paths without being afraid. Eventually, you will learn to relax and enjoy the adventure of our journey together. As long as you stay close to Me, My sovereign Presence protects you wherever you go.

Even though I walk through the valley of the shadow of death, I will fear no evil, for you are with me; your rod and your staff, they comfort me. —PSALM 23:4

Those who know your name will trust in you, for you, LORD, have never forsaken those who seek you. —PSALM 9:10

"Whoever serves me must follow me; and where I am, my servant also will be. My Father will honor the one who serves me." —JOHN 12:26

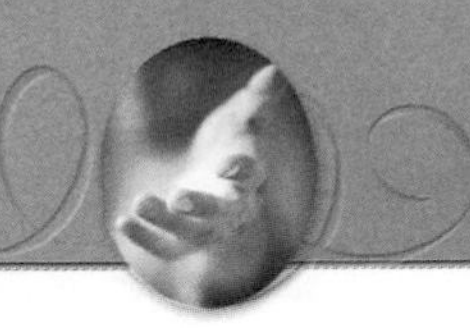

Make Me the focal point of your search for security. In your private thoughts, you are still trying to order your world so that it is predictable and feels safe. Not only is this an impossible goal, but it is also counterproductive to spiritual growth. When your private world feels unsteady and you grip My hand for support, you are living in conscious dependence on Me.

Instead of yearning for a problem-free life, rejoice that trouble can highlight your awareness of My Presence. In the darkness of adversity, you are able to see more clearly the radiance of My Face. Accept the value of problems in this life, *considering them pure joy.* Remember that you have an eternity of trouble-free living awaiting you in heaven.

"So do not fear, for I am with you; do not be dismayed, for I am your God. I will strengthen you and help you; I will uphold you with my righteous right hand." —Isaiah 41:10

Even there your hand will guide me, your right hand will hold me fast. —Psalm 139:10

Consider it pure joy, my brothers, whenever you face trials of many kinds. —James 1:2

December 11

I am working on your behalf. Bring Me all your concerns, including your dreams. Talk with Me about everything, letting the Light of My Presence shine on your hopes and plans. Spend time allowing My Light to infuse your dreams with life, gradually transforming them into reality. This is a very practical way of collaborating with Me. I, the Creator of the universe, have deigned to co-create with you. Do not try to hurry this process. If you want to work with Me, you have to accept My time frame. Hurry is not in My nature. Abraham and Sarah had to wait many years for the fulfillment of My promise, a son. How their long wait intensified their enjoyment of this child! *Faith is the assurance of things hoped for, perceiving as real fact what is not revealed to the senses.*

For with you is the fountain of life; in your light we see light. —Psalm 36:9

Now the Lord was gracious to Sarah as he had said, and the Lord did for Sarah what he had promised. Sarah became pregnant and bore a son to Abraham in his old age, at the very time God had promised him. Abraham gave the name Isaac to the son Sarah bore him. When his son Isaac was eight days old, Abraham circumcised him, as God commanded him. Abraham was a hundred years old when his son Isaac was born to him. Sarah said, "God has brought me laughter, and everyone who hears about this will laugh with me." And she added, "Who would have said to Abraham that Sarah would nurse children? Yet I have borne him a son in his old age." —Genesis 21:1–7

Now faith is the assurance (the confirmation, the title deed) of the things [we] hope for, being the proof of things [we] do not see and the conviction of their reality [faith perceiving as real fact what is not revealed to the senses]. —Hebrews 11:1 AMP

DECEMBER 12

I AM TAKING CARE OF YOU. Feel the warmth and security of being enveloped in My loving Presence. Every detail of your life is under My control. Moreover, *everything fits into a pattern for good, to those who love Me and are called according to My design and purpose.*

Because the world is in an abnormal, fallen condition, people tend to think that chance governs the universe. Events may seem to occur randomly, with little or no meaning. People who view the world this way have overlooked one basic fact: the limitations of human understanding. What you know of the world you inhabit is only the tip of the iceberg. Submerged beneath the surface of the visible world are mysteries too vast for you to comprehend. If you could only see how close I am to you and how constantly I work on your behalf, you would never again doubt that I am wonderfully caring for you. This is why you must *live by faith, not by sight*; trusting in My mysterious, majestic Presence.

We are assured and know that [God being a partner in their labor] all things work together and are [fitting into a plan] for good to and for those who love God and are called according to [His] design and purpose. —ROMANS 8:28 AMP

Then Job replied to the LORD: "I know that you can do all things; no plan of yours can be thwarted. You asked, 'Who is this that obscures my counsel without knowledge?' Surely I spoke of things I did not understand, things too wonderful for me to know." —JOB 42:1–3

Cast all your anxiety on him because he cares for you. —1 PETER 5:7

We live by faith, not by sight. —2 CORINTHIANS 5:7

December 13

Take time to be holy. The word *holy* does not mean *goody-goody*; it means *set apart for sacred use.* That is what these quiet moments in My Presence are accomplishing within you. As you focus your mind and heart on Me, you are being transformed: re-created into the one I designed you to be. This process requires blocks of time set aside for communion with Me.

The benefits of this practice are limitless. Emotional and physical healing are enhanced by your soaking in the Light of My Presence. You experience a nearness to Me that strengthens your faith and fills you with Peace. You open yourself up to receive the many blessings that I have prepared for you. You become a cleansed *temple of My Holy Spirit*, who is able to do in and through you *immeasurably more than you ask or imagine.* These are just some of the benefits of being still in My Presence.

On the day he comes to be glorified in his holy people and to be marveled at among all those who have believed. This includes you, because you believed our testimony to you. —2 Thessalonians 1:10

One thing I ask of the Lord, this is what I seek: that I may dwell in the house of the Lord all the days of my life, to gaze upon the beauty of the Lord and to seek him in his temple. —Psalm 27:4

Do you not know that your body is a temple of the Holy Spirit, who is in you, whom you have received from God? You are not your own. —1 Corinthians 6:19

Now to him who is able to do immeasurably more than all we ask or imagine, according to his power that is at work within us. —Ephesians 3:20

Rest in Me, My child, forgetting about the worries of the world. Focus on Me—Immanuel—and let My living Presence envelop you in Peace. Tune in to My eternal security, for *I am the same yesterday, today, and forever.* If you live on the surface of life by focusing on ever-changing phenomena, you will find yourself echoing the words of Solomon: "*Meaningless! Meaningless! Everything is meaningless!*"

Living in collaboration with Me is the way to instill meaning into your days. Begin each day alone with Me, so that you can experience the reality of My Presence. As you spend time with Me, the way before you opens up step by step. Arise from the stillness of our communion, and gradually begin your journey through the day. Hold My hand in deliberate dependence on Me, and I will smooth out the path before you.

Jesus Christ is the same yesterday and today and forever. —Hebrews 13:8

"Meaningless! Meaningless!" says the Teacher. "Utterly meaningless! Everything is meaningless." —Ecclesiastes 1:2

In all your ways acknowledge him, and he will make your paths straight. —Proverbs 3:6

DECEMBER 15

YOUR LONGING for heaven is good, because it is an extension of your yearning for Me. The hope of heaven is meant to strengthen and encourage you, filling you with wondrous Joy. Many Christians have misunderstood this word *hope*, believing that it denotes wishful thinking. Nothing could be farther from the truth! As soon as I became your Savior, heaven became your ultimate destination. The phrase *hope of heaven* highlights the benefits you can enjoy even while remaining on earth. This hope keeps you spiritually alive during dark times of adversity; it brightens your path and heightens your awareness of My Presence. My desire is *that you may overflow with hope by the power of the Holy Spirit.*

Not only so, but we ourselves, who have the firstfruits of the Spirit, groan inwardly as we wait eagerly for our adoption as sons, the redemption of our bodies. For in this hope we were saved. But hope that is seen is no hope at all. Who hopes for what he already has? But if we hope for what we do not yet have, we wait for it patiently. —ROMANS 8:23–25

God did this so that, by two unchangeable things in which it is impossible for God to lie, we who have fled to take hold of the hope offered to us may be greatly encouraged. We have this hope as an anchor for the soul, firm and secure. It enters the inner sanctuary behind the curtain. —HEBREWS 6:18–19

May the God of hope fill you with all joy and peace as you trust in him, so that you may overflow with hope by the power of the Holy Spirit. —ROMANS 15:13

I AM SPEAKING in the depths of your being. Be still, so that you can hear My voice. I speak in the language of Love; My words fill you with Life and Peace, Joy and Hope. I desire to talk with all of My children, but many are too busy to listen. The "work ethic" has them tied up in knots. They submit wholeheartedly to this taskmaster, wondering why they feel so distant from Me.

Living close to Me requires making Me your *First Love*—your highest priority. As you seek My Presence above all else, you experience Peace and Joy in full measure. I also am blessed when you make Me first in your life. While you journey through life in My Presence, *My Glory brightens the world around you.*

The Sovereign LORD has given me an instructed tongue, to know the word that sustains the weary. He wakens me morning by morning, wakens my ear to listen like one being taught. —ISAIAH 50:4

"Yet I hold this against you: You have forsaken your first love." —REVELATION 2:4

See, darkness covers the earth and thick darkness is over the peoples, but the LORD rises upon you and his glory appears over you. —ISAIAH 60:2

December 17

Come to Me with your gaping emptiness, knowing that in Me you are complete. As you rest quietly in My Presence, My Light within you grows brighter and brighter. Facing the emptiness inside you is simply the prelude to being filled with My fullness. Therefore, rejoice on those days when you drag yourself out of bed, feeling sluggish and inadequate. Tell yourself that this is a perfect day to depend on Me in childlike trust. If you persevere in this dependence as you go through the day, you will discover at bedtime that Joy and Peace have become your companions. You may not realize at what point they joined you on your journey, but you will feel the beneficial effects of their presence. The perfect end to such a day is a doxology of gratitude. I am He from whom all blessings flow!

For God, who said, "Let light shine out of darkness," made his light shine in our hearts to give us the light of the knowledge of the glory of God in the face of Christ. —2 Corinthians 4:6

"Blessed are the poor in spirit, for theirs is the kingdom of heaven. . . . Blessed are those who hunger and thirst for righteousness, for they will be filled." —Matthew 5:3, 6

For in Christ all the fullness of the Deity lives in bodily form, and you have been given fullness in Christ, who is the head over every power and authority. —Colossians 2:9–10

Let everything that has breath praise the Lord. Praise the Lord. —Psalm 150:6

WHEN YOU ARE PLAGUED by a persistent problem—one that goes on and on—view it as a rich opportunity. An ongoing problem is like a tutor who is always by your side. The learning possibilities are limited only by your willingness to be teachable. In faith, thank Me for your problem. Ask Me to open your eyes and your heart to all that I am accomplishing through this difficulty. Once you have become grateful for a problem, it loses its power to drag you down. On the contrary, your thankful attitude will lift you up into heavenly places with Me. From this perspective, your difficulty can be seen as *a slight, temporary distress that is producing for you a transcendent Glory never to cease!*

Although the Lord gives you the bread of adversity and the water of affliction, your teachers will be hidden no more; with your own eyes you will see them. Whether you turn to the right or to the left, your ears will hear a voice behind you, saying, "This is the way; walk in it." —ISAIAH 30:20–21

For our light, momentary affliction (this slight distress of the passing hour) is ever more and more abundantly preparing and producing and achieving for us an everlasting weight of glory [beyond all measure, excessively surpassing all comparisons and all calculations, a vast and transcendent glory and blessedness never to cease!]. —2 CORINTHIANS 4:17 AMP

December 19

Do not be weighed down by the clutter in your life: lots of little chores to do sometime, in no particular order. If you focus too much on these petty tasks, trying to get them all out of the way, you will discover that they are endless. They can eat up as much time as you devote to them.

Instead of trying to do all your chores at once, choose the ones that need to be done today. Let the rest slip into the background of your mind, so I can be in the forefront of your awareness. Remember that your ultimate goal is living close to Me, being responsive to My initiatives. I can communicate with you most readily when your mind is uncluttered and turned toward Me. Seek My Face continually throughout this day. Let My Presence bring order to your thoughts, infusing Peace into your entire being.

Commit to the Lord *whatever you do, and your plans will succeed.* —Proverbs 16:3

"But seek first his kingdom and his righteousness, and all these things will be given to you as well." —Matthew 6:33

December 20

When I joined the ranks of humanity, born into the humblest conditions, My Glory was hidden from all but a few people. Occasionally, streaks of Glory shone out of Me, especially when I began to do miracles. Toward the end of My life, I was taunted and tempted to display more of My awesome Power than My Father's plan permitted. I could have called down legions of angels to rescue Me at any point. Imagine the self-control required of a martyr who could free Himself at will! All of this was necessary to provide the relationship with Me that you now enjoy. Let your life become a praise song to Me by proclaiming My glorious Presence in the world.

This, the first of his miraculous signs, Jesus performed at Cana in Galilee. He thus revealed his glory, and his disciples put their faith in him. —John 2:11

The people stood watching, and the rulers even sneered at him. They said, "He saved others; let him save himself if he is the Christ of God, the Chosen One." The soldiers also came up and mocked him. They offered him wine vinegar. —Luke 23:35–36

It is good to praise the Lord and make music to your name, O Most High, to proclaim your love in the morning and your faithfulness at night, to the music of the ten-stringed lyre and the melody of the harp. For you make me glad by your deeds, O Lord; I sing for joy at the works of your hands. How great are your works, O Lord, how profound your thoughts! —Psalm 92:1–5

DECEMBER 21

MY PLAN FOR YOUR LIFE is unfolding before you. Sometimes the road you are traveling seems blocked, or it opens up so painfully slowly that you must hold yourself back. Then, when time is right, the way before you suddenly clears—through no effort of your own. What you have longed for and worked for I present to you freely, as pure gift. You feel awed by the ease with which I operate in the world, and you glimpse *My Power and My Glory.*

Do not fear your weakness, for it is the stage on which My Power and Glory perform most brilliantly. As you persevere along the path I have prepared for you, depending on My strength to sustain you, expect to see miracles—and you will. Miracles are not always visible to the naked eye, but those who *live by faith* can see them clearly. *Living by faith, rather than sight*, enables you to see My Glory.

I have seen you in the sanctuary and beheld your power and your glory. —PSALM 63:2

We live by faith, not by sight. —2 CORINTHIANS 5:7

Then Jesus said, "Did I not tell you that if you believed, you would see the glory of God?" —JOHN 11:40

DECEMBER 22

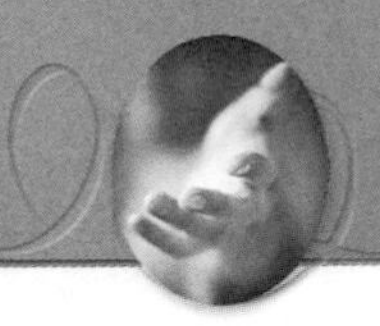

COME TO ME, and rest in My Presence. As you ponder the majestic mystery of the Incarnation, relax in My everlasting arms. I am the only Person who was ever *sired* by the Holy Spirit. This is beyond your understanding. Instead of trying to comprehend My Incarnation intellectually, learn from the example of the wise men. They followed the leading of a spectacular star, then fell down in humble worship when they found Me.

Praise and worship are the best responses to the wonder of My Being. Sing praises to My holy Name. Gaze at Me in silent adoration. Look for a star of guidance in your own life, and be willing to follow wherever I lead. *I am the Light from on high that dawns upon you, to guide your feet into the way of Peace.*

The angel answered, "The Holy Spirit will come upon you, and the power of the Most High will overshadow you. So the holy one to be born will be called the Son of God." —LUKE 1:35

The Word became flesh and made his dwelling among us. We have seen his glory, the glory of the One and Only, who came from the Father, full of grace and truth. —JOHN 1:14

When they saw the star, they rejoiced with exceedingly great joy. And when they had come into the house, they saw the young Child with Mary His mother, and fell down and worshiped Him. —MATTHEW 2:10–11 NKJV

A Light from on high will dawn upon [us] . . . To shine upon and give light to those who sit in darkness and in the shadow of death, to direct and guide our feet . . . into the way of peace. —LUKE 1:78–79 AMP

December 23

I AM KING OF KINGS and Lord of lords, dwelling in dazzlingly bright Light! I am also your Shepherd, Companion, and Friend—the One who never lets go of your hand. Worship Me in My holy Majesty; come close to Me, and rest in My Presence. You need Me both as God and as Man. Only My Incarnation on that first, long-ago Christmas could fulfill your neediness. Since I went to such extreme measures to save you from your sins, you can be assured that I will *graciously give you all you need.*

Nurture well your trust in Me as Savior, Lord, and Friend. I have held back nothing in My provision for you. I have even deigned to live within you! Rejoice in all that I have done for you, and My Light will shine through you into the world.

Which God will bring about in his own time—God, the blessed and only Ruler, the King of kings and Lord of lords, who alone is immortal and who lives in unapproachable light, whom no one has seen or can see. To him be honor and might forever. Amen. —1 TIMOTHY 6:15–16

Come, let us bow down in worship, let us kneel before the LORD *our Maker; for he is our God and we are the people of his pasture, the flock under his care.* —PSALM 95:6–7

He who did not spare his own Son, but gave him up for us all—how will he not also, along with him, graciously give us all things? —ROMANS 8:32

And we have the word of the prophets made more certain, and you will do well to pay attention to it, as to a light shining in a dark place, until the day dawns and the morning star rises in your hearts. —2 PETER 1:19

December 24

I SPEAK TO YOU from the depths of eternity. *Before the world was formed, I AM!* You hear Me in the depths of your being, where I have taken up residence. *I am Christ in you, the hope of Glory.* I, your Lord and Savior, am alive within you. Learn to tune in to My living Presence by seeking Me in silence.

As you celebrate the wonder of My birth in Bethlehem, celebrate also your rebirth into eternal life. This everlasting gift was the sole purpose of My entering your sin-stained world. Receive My gift with awe and humility. Take time to explore the vast dimensions of My Love. Allow thankfulness to flow freely from your heart in response to My glorious gift. *Let My Peace rule in your heart, and be thankful.*

Before the mountains were brought forth or ever You had formed and given birth to the earth and the world, even from everlasting to everlasting You are God. —PSALM 90:2 AMP

To them God has chosen to make known among the Gentiles the glorious riches of this mystery, which is Christ in you, the hope of glory. —COLOSSIANS 1:27

Let the peace of Christ rule in your hearts, since as members of one body you were called to peace. And be thankful. —COLOSSIANS 3:15

December 25

As you wait attentively in My Presence, *the Light of the knowledge of My Glory shines upon you.* This radiant knowledge transcends all understanding. It transforms every fiber of your being: renewing your mind, cleansing your heart, invigorating your body. Open yourself fully to My Presence; be awed by My glorious Being.

Try to imagine what I gave up when I came into your world as a baby. I set aside My Glory, so that I could identify with mankind. I accepted the limitations of infancy under the most appalling conditions—a filthy stable. There was nothing glorious about that setting, though angels lit up the sky proclaiming "Glory!" to awestruck shepherds.

When you sit quietly with Me, the process I went through is reversed in your experience. As you identify with Me, heaven's vistas open up before you—granting you glimpses of My Glory. *I became poor so that you might become rich.* Sing hallelujahs to My holy Name!

For God, who said, "Let light shine out of darkness," made his light shine in our hearts to give us the light of the knowledge of the glory of God in the face of Christ. —2 Corinthians 4:6

Who, being in very nature God, did not consider equality with God something to be grasped, but made himself nothing, taking the very nature of a servant, being made in human likeness. —Philippians 2:6–7

Suddenly a great company of the heavenly host appeared with the angel, praising God and saying, "Glory to God in the highest." —Luke 2:13–14

For you know the grace of our Lord Jesus Christ, that though he was rich, yet for your sakes he became poor, so that you through his poverty might become rich. —2 Corinthians 8:9

I AM THE GIFT that continuously gives—bounteously, with no strings attached. Unconditional Love is such a radical concept that even My most devoted followers fail to grasp it fully. Absolutely nothing in heaven or on earth can cause Me to stop loving you. You may *feel* more loved when you are performing according to your expectations. But My Love for you is perfect; therefore it is not subject to variation. What *does* vary is your awareness of My loving Presence.

When you are dissatisfied with your behavior, you tend to feel unworthy of My Love. You may unconsciously punish yourself by withdrawing from Me and attributing the distance between us to My displeasure. Instead of returning to Me and receiving My Love, you attempt to earn My approval by trying harder. All the while, I am aching to hold you in *My everlasting arms*, to enfold you in My Love. When you are feeling unworthy or unloved, come to Me. Then ask for receptivity to *My unfailing Love.*

If anyone acknowledges that Jesus is the Son of God, God lives in him and he in God. And so we know and rely on the love God has for us. God is love. Whoever lives in love lives in God, and God in him. . . . There is no fear in love. But perfect love drives out fear, because fear has to do with punishment. The one who fears is not made perfect in love. —1 JOHN 4:15–16, 18

The eternal God is your refuge, and underneath are the everlasting arms. —DEUTERONOMY 33:27

But I trust in your unfailing love; my heart rejoices in your salvation. —PSALM 13:5

December 27

I AM PREPARING YOU for what is on the road ahead, just around the bend. Take time to be still in My Presence so that I can strengthen you. The busier you become, the more you need this time apart with Me. So many people think that time spent with Me is a luxury they cannot afford. As a result, they live and work in their own strength—until that becomes depleted. Then they either cry out to Me for help or turn away in bitterness.

How much better it is to walk close to Me, depending on My strength and trusting Me in every situation. If you live in this way, you will *do* less but *accomplish* far more. Your unhurried pace of living will stand out in this rush-crazed age. Some people may deem you lazy, but many more will be blessed by your peacefulness. Walk in the Light with Me, and you will reflect Me to the watching world.

Since ancient times no one has heard, no ear has perceived,
no eye has seen any God besides you, who acts on behalf
of those who wait for him. —ISAIAH 64:4

"I am the vine; you are the branches. If a man remains in me and I in him,
he will bear much fruit; apart from me you can do nothing." —JOHN 15:5

For with you is the fountain of life; in your light we see light. —PSALM 36:9

I AM YOUR REFUGE AND STRENGTH, an ever-present Help in trouble. Therefore, you don't need to be afraid of anything—not even cataclysmic circumstances. The media are increasingly devoted to fear-inducing subject matter: terrorism, serial killers, environmental catastrophes. If you focus on such dangers and forget that I am your Refuge in all circumstances, you will become increasingly fearful. Every day I manifest My grace in countless places and situations, but the media take no notice. I shower not only blessings but also outright miracles on your planet.

As you grow closer to Me, I open your eyes to see more and more of My Presence all around you. Things that most people hardly notice, like shifting shades of sunlight, fill you with heart-bursting Joy. You have eyes that see and ears that hear, so proclaim My abiding Presence in the world.

God is our refuge and strength, an ever-present help in trouble. Therefore we will not fear, though the earth give way and the mountains fall into the heart of the sea, though its waters roar and foam and the mountains quake with their surging. —PSALM 46:1–3

Blessed are those who have learned to acclaim you, who walk in the light of your presence, O LORD. —PSALM 89:15

December 29

Trust Me with every fiber of your being! What I can accomplish in and through you is proportional to how much you depend on Me. One aspect of this is the degree to which you trust Me in a crisis or major decision. Some people fail miserably here, while others are at their best in tough times. Another aspect is even more telling: the constancy of your trust in Me. People who rely on Me in the midst of adversity may forget about Me when life is flowing smoothly. Difficult times can jolt you into awareness of your need for Me, whereas *smooth sailing* can lull you into the stupor of self-sufficiency.

I care as much about your tiny trust-steps through daily life as about your dramatic leaps of faith. You may think that no one notices, but the One who is always beside you sees everything—and rejoices. Consistently trusting in Me is vital to flourishing in My Presence.

Blessed is the man who makes the Lord his trust, who does not look to the proud, to those who turn aside to false gods. —Psalm 40:4

When I am afraid, I will trust in you. In God, whose word I praise, in God I trust; I will not be afraid. What can mortal man do to me? —Psalm 56:3–4

Trust in him at all times, O people; pour out your hearts to him, for God is our refuge. —Psalm 62:8

You will keep in perfect peace him whose mind is steadfast, because he trusts in you. Trust in the Lord forever, for the Lord, the Lord, is the Rock eternal. —Isaiah 26:3–4

December 30

I AM LEADING YOU along a way that is uniquely right for you. The closer to Me you grow, the more fully you become your true self—the one I designed you to be. Because you are one of a kind, the path you are traveling with Me diverges increasingly from that of other people. However, in My mysterious wisdom and ways, I enable you to follow this solitary path while staying in close contact with others. In fact, the more completely you devote yourself to Me, the more freely you can love people.

Marvel at the beauty of a life intertwined with My Presence. Rejoice as we journey together in intimate communion. Enjoy the adventure of finding yourself through losing yourself in Me.

Therefore, if anyone is in Christ, he is a new creation; the old has gone, the new has come! —2 CORINTHIANS 5:17

For we are God's workmanship, created in Christ Jesus to do good works, which God prepared in advance for us to do. —EPHESIANS 2:10

Dear friends, let us love one another, for love comes from God. Everyone who loves has been born of God and knows God. Whoever does not love does not know God, because God is love. —1 JOHN 4:7–8

"Remain in me, and I will remain in you. No branch can bear fruit by itself; it must remain in the vine. Neither can you bear fruit unless you remain in me." —JOHN 15:4

December 31

As this year draws to a close, receive My Peace. This is still your deepest need, and I, your *Prince of Peace*, long to pour Myself into your neediness. My abundance and your emptiness are a perfect match. I designed you to have no sufficiency of your own. I created you as a *jar of clay*, set apart for sacred use. I want you to be filled with My very Being, permeated through and through with Peace.

Thank Me for My peaceful Presence, regardless of your feelings. Whisper My Name in loving tenderness. *My Peace*, which lives continually in your spirit, will gradually work its way through your entire being.

For to us a child is born, to us a son is given, and the government will be on his shoulders. And he will be called Wonderful Counselor, Mighty God, Everlasting Father, Prince of Peace. —Isaiah 9:6

But we have this treasure in jars of clay to show that this all-surpassing power is from God and not from us. —2 Corinthians 4:7

"But the Counselor, the Holy Spirit, whom the Father will send in my name, will teach you all things and will remind you of everything I have said to you. Peace I leave with you; my peace I give you. I do not give to you as the world gives. Do not let your hearts be troubled and do not be afraid." —John 14:26–27

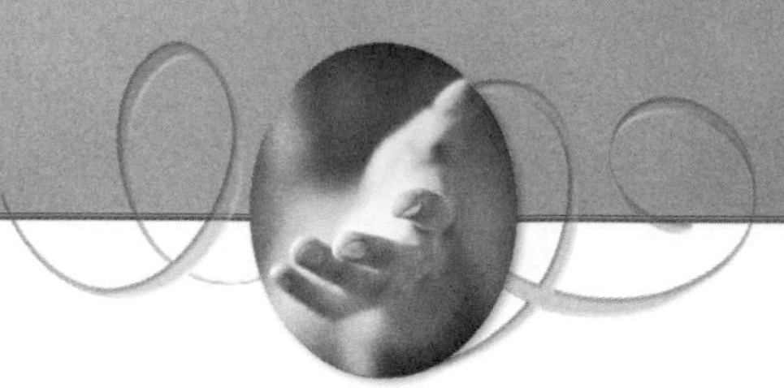

SARAH YOUNG's devotional writings are personal reflections from her daily quiet time of Bible reading, praying, and writing in prayer journals. With sales of more than 14 million books worldwide, *Jesus Calling®* has appeared on all major bestseller lists. Sarah's writings include *Jesus Calling®*, *Jesus Today®*, *Jesus Lives™*, *Dear Jesus*, *Jesus Calling® for Little Ones*, *Jesus Calling® Bible Storybook*, *Jesus Calling®: 365 Devotions for Kids*, and *Peace in His Presence*—each encouraging readers in their journey toward intimacy with Christ. Sarah and her husband were missionaries in Japan and Australia for many years. They currently live in the United States.

Jesus Calling® was written to help people connect not only with Jesus, the living Word, but also with the Bible—the only infallible, inerrant Word of God. Sarah endeavors to keep her devotional writing consistent with that unchanging standard. Many readers have shared that Sarah's books have helped them grow to love God's Word. As Sarah states in the introduction to *Jesus Calling®*, "The devotions . . . are meant to be read slowly, preferably in a quiet place—with your Bible open."

Sarah is biblically conservative in her faith and reformed in her doctrine. She earned a master's degree in biblical studies and counseling from Covenant Theological Seminary in St. Louis. She is a member of the Presbyterian Church in America (PCA), where her husband,

Stephen, is an ordained minister. Stephen and Sarah continue to be missionaries with Mission to the World, the PCA mission board.

Sarah spends a great deal of time in prayer, reading the Bible, and memorizing Scripture. She especially enjoys praying daily for readers of all her books.